AVANT  GUIDE

£ondon

EMPIRE PRESS

Empire ~ New York

EMPIRE PRESS
Empire State Building
350 Fifth Ave., Suite 7814
New York, NY 10118

E-mail: editor@avantguide.com
Web: http://www.avantguide.com

Editor-in-Chief: Dan Levine
Photo Editor: Kim Furrokh

deSign: deMo^wshe {1i6®~mig^25} www.mowshe.cz

Writer/Researchers: Magenta Green, Stewart Klug, Van Johnston-Lewis, Michael Sweden, H. Victor Thomas, Grant Young.

Copy Editors: Jeannette Vota, Jenny Smith
Additional Research: Annica Svensson, Lucy Maggs, Honza Žamboch, Ivana Nosková

Photography: Kim Furrokh, except p205 Chris Gascoigne & Lifschutz Davidson; p218 Hans Gerritsen; p235 Steve Double; p244 Richard Learoyd; p245 Donald Cooper.
Cover: LTB, Kristof Halversham
Digital Imaging by Li6orek

Back Cover Photo: Michael Benabib

Digital Cartography: Copyright © Empire Press
Cover Films: Mousehouse [Ho.Ho. & B0bo]

Web Design: [ ] Lundegaard –> http://www. lundegaard.cz

Very Special Thanks
Petra Lustigová, Pluto, Michael Benabib, Dr. Shedivka, Jonathan Pontell, Chronic, Marilyn Wood and George Ištvánek

ACCLAiM fOR AVANt=GUidE!

"if it's cutting edge you want in a city that teeters between conservative and revolutionary, this is the book to buy."
—Toronto Sun

"Slangy and wired, yet so explicit and well-written that it makes a good read."
—Prague Post

"No other guide captures so completely and viscerally what it feels like to be inside the city."
—San Francisco Bay Guardian

"Sharp writing and a thrilling layout make it a guidebook you can read from cover to cover without a yawn, a fascinating introduction to all that makes the city exciting and extreme."
—San Francisco Examiner

"For travelers who've outgrown the shoestring budget of their college days, there's Avant- Guide, a new series from itinerant genius Dan Levine."
—Elle

"IT'S HIP TO BE THERE... All the usual topics from history to hotels to shopping but with a welcome cutting-edge spin."
—Chicago Sun-Times

"This book understands..."
—Chicago Tribune

"Brutally honest insiders give you the straight scoop on where to be seen so you don't feel or look like a tourist."
—Fitness Magazine

"The brash, Euro-cover girl speaks visual volumes about the hipster tone of this guide."
—The Oregonian

fiercely independent!

Each Avant•Guide is created by independent experts who never accept discounts or payments in exchange for positive coverage.

:∘:

Our visits to restaurants, clubs and other establishments are anonymous, and expenses are paid by Avant•Guide.

∘:∘

FEW OTHER GUIDEBOOKS
CAN MAKE THIS CLAIM.

CONT

ENtS

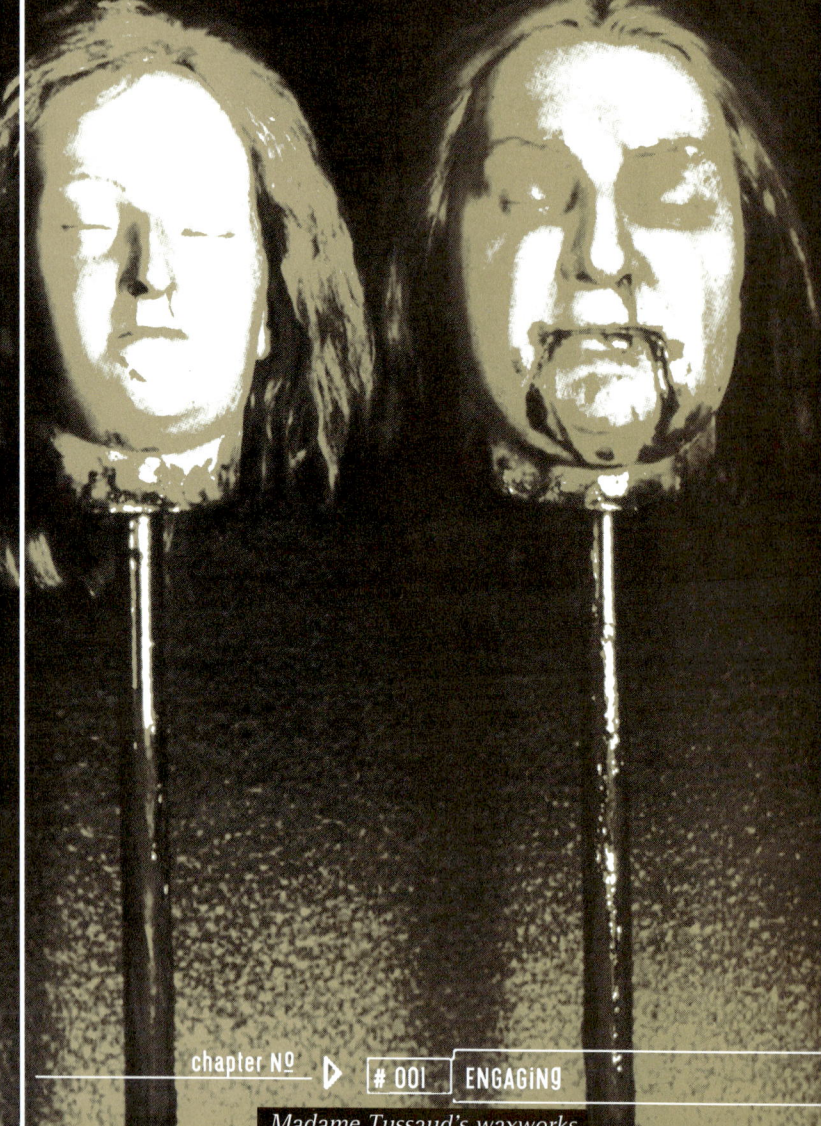

Believe the hype: London hasn't been this great since the 1960s. That's when all the major glossies went ga-ga about "Swingin' London." But now, after a long downward spiral into social dissatisfaction and conservative politics, the British capital is a phoenix rising. Populated by people from almost every country in the world—New York style—London is at last a true pan-national city, attracting residents from far beyond the former Empire. The extreme mix of cultures imparts London with a depth and character that has propelled it to the forefront of the world's art, music and fashion scenes.

And we're happy to report that the antiquated caste system is growing steadily weaker. Meritocracy is overtaking aristocracy, and even the House of Lords is feeling the winds of obsolescence.

There is a greater sense of optimism on the streets as the city blossoms with more ethnic diversity, personal freedom, and raw cash than it has ever known. The election of Tony Blair inaugurated a kinder, gentler London in which pubs are brighter, footballers are mellower, the air seems cleaner and even the food is great. London has become a city of superlatives: the top museums, the best shopping, the coolest hotels and un-paralleled theater. And it's getting better all the time. Tourism is booming, the arts are flourishing, and cars are being banned from Trafalgar Square and Parliament Square—two of city's busiest transport hubs. The obsession with the new this and the new that dominates conversation among Media types over long lunches in Soho. Minimalist chic is so in you could open a vacuum, call it a restaurant and watch it fill up with gullible patrons.

The city is in the process of recreating itself for the 21st century.

In the midst of a massive public building boom, the capitol has been the biggest beneficiary of New Labour's determination to construct a "New Britain." A mindboggling number of massive public works projects are the most obvious manifestations of the city's resolve to reinvent itself. These include the new Millennium Bridge across the Thames, the opening of the Tate Gallery of Modern Art, the extension of the Jubilee Underground line, the construction of the new British Library, the rebuilding of the Royal Opera House, and massive additions to the British Museum, the National Portrait Gallery, the Wallace Collection, the Science Museum, the Tate Gallery/Millbank, and the Victoria & Albert Museum. There is a new high-speed rail link between Heathrow and London, Wembley Stadium is being reconstructed, and, of course, there's that ginormous £760 million Millennium Dome.

To most Londoners the Thames is either a traffic problem to be crossed or a social division. And the banks of the river offer substantial ammunition to those who claim that London is the ugliest capital in

Europe. Between the Great Fire of 1666 and the German bombing Blitz in the 1940s, London has sprawled across across 600-plus square miles to become the largest, most "photogenic" city on the Continent. But there are many terrific elements to the city—neighborhoods, markets, buildings—that London's beauty-challenged skyline appears to be a rare example of the parts being greater than the whole.

It's ironic that a city so steeped in history seems so determined to excape the past and launch itself into the 21st century. Some visitors, hoping to see something historical, are disappointed when they arrive in this contemporary city where all too often the only things marking the past are the little blue plaques commemorating former residences. It's hard to find much "history" on the streets of London because most of the old buildings and monuments have either been demolished or stashed away in a museum. But the past is alive and well; you just have to know how to look for it.

Don't think for a moment that the scandal-ridden royal family is just a harmelss tourist attraction. The Queen heads a very real aristocracy that continues to wield much of the nation's wealth and power. Royal London's pomp and pageantry are increasingly less relevant to today's world, but daily ceremonies, like the Changing of the Guard at Buckingham Palace and the Ceremony of the Keys at the Tower of London, are striking reminders of an influential cultural heritage. Some traditions die harder than others. The official language used when passing bills between the Parliament and the Queen is still Norman French. To this day, when the Queen gives her royal assent to a bill, she writes "*La reine le veult*" ("the Queen wills it"). Now, if they would only do something about those antiquated drinking hours.

CiTY STATiSTiCS/ STUPid fActs

Population: 7,100,000

Licensed Taxis: 18,600

Bars and Pubs: 3,221

Cinemas: 125

Swimming Pools: 116

London Boroughs: 33

Percent of Londoners born elsewhere: 32

AD 43 Romans invade Britain; bridge built over Thames; Londinium founded.

200 City built; Londinium designated capital of Britannia Superior; Population 50,000.

410 Roman troops evacuate Britain.

c600 Saxon London built west of Roman city.

604 First St. Paul's built.

836 Vikings raid London.

c871 Danes occupy London; Office of alderman created.

886 King Alfred of Wessex takes London.

1013 Danes, under Olaf, take London back.

1042 Edward the Confessor constructs palace and Westminster Abbey.

1066 Norman Conquest; William 1 crowned in Westminster Abbey; Population 16,000.

1067 Tower of London breaks ground.

1123 St. Bartholomew's hospital founded.

1170 Weekly horse market established at Smithfield.

1176 Foundation stone laid for London Bridge.

1189 Jews banned from coronation of Richard Coeur de Lion; Population 23,000.

1191 Henry FitzAilwyn named London's first Lord Mayor.

1215 Magna Carta signed by King John and Lord Mayor of London; Independence of the City is strengthened.

1217 London Bridge rebuilt in stone.

1240 First Parliament meets at Westminster.

1280 Old St. Paul's Cathedral completed.

1290 Jews expelled from England.

1301 Temple Bar constructed to prevent King from entering the City without permission.

1348/49 Black Death ravages London, population halves to 30,000.

1381 Peasants' Revolt in effort to end feudalism.

1399 Parliament and City depose Richard II.

1411 First Guildhall built.

1461 House of York wins War of the Roses and takes power.

1476 England's first printing press built by William Caxton at Westminster.

1485 Tudor period begins with the crowning of Henry VII.

1508 Henry VIII crowned.

1534 Henry VIII breaks with the Catholic Church; church lands confiscated.

1566 Royal Exchange is opened by Thomas Gresham.

1577 London's first theater built in Shoreditch.

1599 Shakespeare's Globe Theater built in Southwark.

1605 Guy Fawkes attempts to blow up King James I and Parliament.

1608 First frost fair on frozen Thames.

1613 Globe Theatre burns.

1635 London's first square, Covent Garden Piazza, is created.

1637 Hyde Park opened to the public.

1642 English Civil War.

1649 Charles I beheaded; Oliver Cromwell leads new Commonwealth.

1650 Population 375,000.

1652 First coffee house opens and becomes financial center.

1656 Jews return to London.

1663 Theater opens in Drury Lane.

1664/6 Great Plague strikes London; up to 100,000 killed.

1666 Great Fire destroys the City; Plague ends.

1675 Christopher Wren lays foundation for new St. Paul's Cathedral; Royal Observatory built at Greenwich.

1692 Insurance market opens at Lloyd's; Wren-designed Chelsea Hospital completed.

1694 Bank of England established to pay for war with France.

1717 Development begins in West End.

1732 10 Downing Street becomes official residence of Prime Minister; Covent Garden Theatre opens.

1733 Fleet River is covered over, creating Fleet Street.

1750 London's second bridge completed at Westminster; Population 650,000.

1759 Kew Gardens founded; British Museum opens.

1766 City Wall demolished.

1772 Battersea Bridge built.

1780 Gordon Riots against Catholics and Irish; 850 killed in protest against the repeal of anti-Catholic legislation.

1785 The Times newspaper begins publication.

1802 Stock Exchange founded.

1803 Horsedrawn public railway established.

1807 Gas lighting installed on Pall Mall.

1811 Southwark and Waterloo bridges built.

1812 Prime Minister Spencer Perceval assassinated in the House of Commons.

1824 National Gallery founded.

1828 Regent's Park Zoo opens.

1829 Metropolitan Police established; Horse-drawn buses begin service.

1833 London Fire Brigade established.

1834 Palace of Westminster destroyed by fire.

1835 Madame Tussaud's waxworks opens.

1836 First Railway opens; University of London established.

1837 Queen Victoria takes throne; Buckingham Palace becomes monarch's official residence; New Houses of Parliament breaks ground.

1841 Last Thames frost fair.

1843 Trafalgar Square is created; First tunnel built under the Thames.

1848 Cholera epidemic devastates London, killing 14,000; women admitted to University of London.
1851 Great Exhibition in Hyde Park.
1852 Victoria and Albert Museum breaks ground.
1853 Harrod's opens.
1863 First underground railway opens (Metropolitan line).
1870 Victoria Embankment completed.
1866 Speaker's Corner established in Hyde Park.
1868 Last public execution at Newgate Prison.

1873 Albert Bridge built; Natural History Museum opens.
1877 First Wimbledon tennis tournament.
1880 First cricket test match (England vs. Australia at The Oval)
1884 Greenwich Mean Time established.
1886 Tower Bridge opens.
1888 Jack the Ripper terrorizes East End.
1889 London County Council created.
1893 Tate Gallery breaks ground on the site of old Millbank Prison.

1894	Lyons Tea Shop opens in Piccadilly.
1900	Population of Greater London 6,500,000.
1910	George V brings House of Windsor to the throne.
1915/18	German Zeppelins bomb London.
1928	Science Museum opens.
1936	Edward VIII abdicates throne; British Broadcasting Corporation established.
1939	Population of Greater London 8,600,000.
1940/44	London bombed by Germans. Much of the City is destroyed.
1948	Olympic Games held in London.
1951	Royal Festival Hall opens.
1953	Elizabeth II is crowned.
1958	Race riots in Notting Hill.
1963	National Theater founded.
1966	England wins World Cup at Wembley.
1967	Old London Bridge is sold and rebuilt in Arizona, USA.
1971	New London Bridge opens.
1974	The Covent Garden's market is moved; buildings redeveloped for shopping and entertainment.
1976	Museum of London opens; National Theatre moves to South Bank complex.
1981	Race riots in Brixton; IRA bombs Chelsea Barracks.
1982	Barbican Centre opens; Thames Flood Barrier built; IRA bombs Harrod's.
1986	Margaret Thatcher dissolves Greater London Council.
1987	Docklands Light Railway opens; Heathrow Terminal 4 completed; Dropped cigarette starts fire at King's Cross Station.
1989	Gates erected at Downing Street in response to IRA terror.

1990 Courtauld Galleries open in Somerset House.
1992 Windsor Castle burns.
1993 Buckingham Palace opens to the public.
1995 National Lottery launched, providing billions of pounds to the arts.
1997 Tony Blair elected in Labour landslide.
1998 New British Library opens.
1999 Jubilee Underground line extended to Greenwich.
2000 Millennium Dome built; Millennium Bridge constructed across the Thames; Tate Gallery of Modern Art opens.

ARRIVING

ARRIVING BY PLANE
London is served by two major and three minor airports, all of which have good public transport links to central London.

HEATHROW (LHR)
General info tel. 0181/759-4321; Flight info tel. 0181/759-4321

Miles from Trafalgar Square:	About 15
Metered Taxi (approx.):	£30–35 + tip
Heathrow Express Rail:	£10
Underground:	£3.40
Airbus Express:	£6

BY TRAIN – Brand new **Heathrow Express** (tel. 0845/600-1515) trains shuttle between the airport's four terminals and London's Paddington Station. Trains leave every 15 minutes daily, from 510am to 1140pm. Journey times are 15 minutes from Heathrow Central (Terminals 1,2,3) and 20 minutes from Terminal 4. The one-way fare is £10 (First Class £20). The service is great, but unless you're staying near Paddington you'll have to continue your trip by taxi or tube.

BY TAXI – Metered cabs line up outside each terminal. The journey takes about 50 to 60 minutes and costs £35-£45 plus tip. Taxis accept a maximum of 5 passengers, if there's not a ton of luggage.

BY UNDERGROUND – Heathrow airport has two Underground stations—one shared by Terminals 1,2 and 3, the other at Terminal 4—and both are on the Piccadilly Line. Trains run every 5-9 minutes daily, between 5am and 1130pm. The average time to Leicester Square is 45 minutes. One-way fare into the center is £3.40. If you arrive after 930am, think about buying a One Day Travelcard which costs £4.50 and is valid for unlimited tube and bus travel for the rest of the day. The Underground can get insanely crowded; and you may not find a seat if you're traveling back to Heathrow during peak hours.

BY BUS – Express in name only, **Airbus Express** (tel. 0181/400-6655) lumbers between the airport and city dropping off passengers at fixed points in Central London. Buses depart every 20-30 minutes from about 645am to 830pm and take up to 75 minutes to reach their destinations. Airbus A1 serves Victoria rail station via several London hotels. Airbus A2 serves Russell Square via Euston rail station and also makes drops at some West End hotels. We avoid both like the plague.

GATWICK (LGW)

General info tel. 01293/507140;
Flight info tel. 0990/111666
Miles from Trafalgar Square: About 30

Metered Taxi (approx.):	£35-£40 + tip
Gatwick Express Rail:	£9.50
Flightline Coach:	£7.50

BY TRAIN – The fastest way into the city center is on the **Gatwick Express**, a non-stop shuttle to London's Victoria station. Trains depart daily every 15 minutes from 520am-1am, and hourly throughout the night. The trip takes 30 minutes and costs £9.50 each way.

BY TAXI – Metered cabs line up outside each terminal. The journey takes about 60 to 70 minutes and costs £35-£40 plus tip. Taxis accept a maximum of 5 passengers, if there's not a ton of luggage.

BY BUS – "Coach" sounds a lot nicer than "bus" but believe us, they're the exact same thing. **Flightline Coaches** (tel. 0181/668-7261) operate daily, once an hour between 945am and 745pm and take 70 to 90 minutes. The cost is £7.50 each way.

LONDON CITY AIRPORT

Tel. 0171/646-0000

Miles from Trafalgar Square:	About 9
Metered Taxi (approx.):	£20 + tip
Shuttle Bus/Underground:	£5.40

BY TAXI – Metered cabs line up at the terminal forecourt. The journey to the West End takes about 30 minutes and costs approximately £20. You can get to the North Greenwich Underground Station for about £5.

BY SHUTTLE BUS/UNDERGROUND – Shuttle buses dash between the airport and Liverpool Street Station every 10 minutes throughout the day. The trip takes 20 minutes and costs £4.

STANSTED AIRPORT
Tel. 01279/680500

Miles from Trafalgar Square:	About 35
Skyline Rail Service:	£10
Metered Taxi (approx.):	£45 + tip
Shuttle Bus/Underground:	£5.40

 **BY TRAIN** – The fastest and most frequent link from Stansted to Central London is by **Skyline Rail** (tel. 0345/484950) to Liverpool Street Station. Enroute the train stops at Tottenham Hale, which connects with London Underground's Victoria line. Trains run daily, every 30 minutes, from about 5am to midnight. It takes about 45 minutes and costs £10 each way.

 **BY TAXI** – There is no taxi stand at Stansted, but cabs may be booked at the desk in the International Arrivals area. Travel time to central London is 70 minutes and the average fare is £45.

Arriving By Train
Trains from Paris arrive at **Victoria Station**; visitors from Amsterdam are deposited at **Liverpool Street Station**; and arrivals from Edinburgh pull into **King's Cross Station**. All three stations are major Underground hubs as well.

–"– Arriving By Bus
London-bound buses almost always terminate at **Victoria Coach Station** on Buckingham Palace Road (tel. 0171/730-0202), which is one block from Victoria Railway Station.

–"–Arriving By Car
Major roads in Britain are designated by the letters "M," "A," or "B." M-roads are expressways or "motorways," connecting London with cities to the north, east, south and west. "A" and "B" are smaller, slower and usually more scenic.

The M25 "ring road" circles Greater London and connects to the M1 to Birmingham, the M40 to Oxford, M4 to Bristol, M3 to Southampton, M20 to Dover and the M11 to Cambridge.

London's antique Underground and famous red double-decker buses are operated by **London Transport** (tel. 0171/222-1234) which maintains fares based on a 6-zone system—you pay for each zone you cross. Most visitors usually travel within Zone 1, for which a single-trip ticket costs £1.40; but there are several money-saving options:

A booklet (**carnet**) of 10 tickets costs just £10. Valid for Zone 1 only, these tickets can be purchased in advance at any central London Underground station and are valid for 12 months.

A **1-Day Travelcard** is good for unlimited transportation on the bus and tube Monday through Friday after 930am and anytime during weekends and public holidays. The central London card costs £3.80. There's another one that's valid for all six zones (including Heathrow Airport) and costs £4.50.

Weekend Travelcards, valid for two consecutive weekend days or public holidays, are 25% cheaper than two separate 1-Day Travelcards and have no time restrictions.

Weekly Travelcards cost £14.30 for unlimited travel within Zone 1 and are good for seven consecutive days (cards for other zones are also available). Before you can buy the Travelcard, you'll need to get a Photocard (a passport-size photo is required), which is free and available at most central Underground stations. It makes a great memento.

You can also get Photocards, Travelcards and all your questions answered at any **London Transport Travel Information Centre** located in all the major underground stations, including Heathrow Central, King's Cross, Oxford Circus, Piccadilly Circus, and Victoria Station. Most are open daily from 9am to 5pm.

By Underground

Trains run every few minutes daily, from about 630am to midnight. Exact closing times vary at each station and "last-train" times are posted at Underground entrances. Tickets can be purchased from the station ticket window or from nearby coin-operated machines. Hold on to your ticket throughout the ride; you'll need it to exit. The tube is closed Christmas day. There is a handy Underground map on the inside back cover of this book.

By Taxi

The city's once distinctive black cabs now come in a rainbow of colors (primarily maroon), but the ride remains as luxuriously roomy as ever. In order to get licensed, London's taxi wallas are required to pass an extraordinarily rigorous geography exam called The Knowledge. As a result, they are something of an elite bunch who pride themselves on knowing every mews, court and crescent in the city. Taxis can be booked by telephone, procured at a stand or hailed in the street. A cab is available for hire when its yellow roof light is illuminated. If you know you will be needing a cab in advance, order one by phone from Dial a Cab (tel. 0171/253-5000) or Radio Taxis (tel. 0171/272-0272). The tariff begins at £2 and climbs at a fast clip. There are additional charges for luggage, nights and weekends, but the thrill of viewing the city's famous squares and monuments from the spacious back seat of a London taxi will almost keep your eyes off the meter.

Minicabs are meterless cars driven by any entrepreneur with a license. They usually operate from sidewalk offices, many of which are centered around Leicester Square. They are cheaper than black cabs and are especially handy after the tube shuts down for the night. Always negotiate the fare beforehand. You can order a Minicab from Addison Lee (tel. 0171/387-8888).

By Bus

The classic red open-ended platform buses will one day be a thing of the past, replaced by the more economical driver-only type. But for now, you can still make a flying leap into the back of the departing vehicle. Take a seat, either upstairs or down, and wait for the conductor to collect your fare. On the newer types, pay the driver as you enter and exit through the center door. Bus fare within central London Zone 1 is £1.

Bus routes can be confusing. Get a free bus map from the tourist office or just ask the conductor about the route. When you're not in a hurry to get anywhere, buses are a "top deck" sightseeing adventure. Two of the most scenic routes are no. 53 which passes by Regent's Park Zoo, Oxford Circus, Regent Street, Piccadilly Circus, the National Gallery, Trafalgar Square, Horse Guards, Whitehall and Westminster Square; and no. 11, passing through King's Road, Victoria Station, Westminster Abbey, Whitehall, Horse Guards, Trafalgar Square, the National Gallery, The Strand, Law Courts, Fleet Street and St. Paul's Cathedral.

Like the tube, regular bus service stops around midnight, after which night bus service kicks-in. Night buses have different routes and numbers from their daytime counterparts and most depart only once an hour. One-day Travelcards are not valid on night buses. The central London night-bus terminus is Trafalgar Square.

By Bicycle

Bike lanes are unheard of and cars are unyielding, so very few daredevils pedal around the city for the purpose of transportation. Things get less hectic in the outer boroughs, where wheeling through quaint lanes and massive parks is a thoroughly pleasant day's outing. Rent bikes from Bikefix, 48 Lamb's Conduit St., WC1 (tel. 0171/405-1218);

By Foot

London is not for windshield tourists; walking is the best way to discover each of the city's many villages. Personal experience has proven that it takes 60 to 90 minutes to walk from Chelsea to the West End, depending on how many slow-moving "Meanderthals" are in your way. Beware of cars that do not give right-of-way to pedestrians; the London Tourist Board refuses to divulge statistics on deaths and injuries resulting from visitors looking in the wrong direction as they cross the streets.

MONEY

Dollars & Don'ts

The pound is the coin of the realm, and is divided into 100 pence. Bills come in £5, £10, £20, and £50 denominations. Coins are minted in 1p, 2p, 5p, 10p, 20p, 50p, £1 and £2 denominations. A £1 note is still in circulation in both Scotland and the Isle of Man. They are legal tender in England, but most shopkeepers are loathe to accept them.

Exchange places in the city center are almost as common as pubs, but exchange rates and commissions can be as shocking as the contents of a street-stand sausage. Don't be fooled by an attractive exchange rate; always ask what the commission is first and refuse to pay more than two percent. Banks generally offer the best rates, but American Express and some private exchange offices are not far behind. Beware of Chequepoint and other commercial agencies that sometimes charge nearly ten-percent commissions.

Credit Cards and ATMs

There is absolutely no need to carry a bundle of cash when traveling to London, or any other major European city for that matter. In fact, you can travel to this city without a penny in your pocket and obtain all the dough you need from hundreds of ATMs that work seamlessly with banks around the globe. Connected to the Cirrus and Plus networks, London's cash machines allow 24-hour access to your accounts and offer excellent midpoint exchange rates. Your bank will charge between $1 and $3 for each withdrawal. Almost half of the city's ATMs also accept Visa or MasterCard (make sure you have a PIN).

Credit cards are widely accepted in the city's restaurants, hotels and shops, and usage will usually result in an exchange rate far superior to what you'd get from banks when trading cash. Cash advances on your Visa and MasterCard can be obtained from most banks.

Traveler's Checks

Traveler's Checks are obsolete. You don't use them at home, why embarrass yourself with these clumsy dinosaurs when you're away? Any company claiming their travelers checks are as good as cash is lying. Even the tellers at American Express may refuse to exchange their own checks without your passport in tow. Stick to ATMs and credit cards. If you still insist on giving interest-free loans to multinational concerns in exchange for their private-issue money, you'll find the best exchange rates at **American Express**, 6 Haymarket, SW1 (tel. 0171/930-4411), where checks from all issuers are exchanged commission-free. Some restaurants and many hotels will exchange traveler's checks, but their rates are always much worse than what banks give.

What's a British pound worth? For today's exchange rates, check-out the AvantGuide CyberSupplement™ at www.avantguide.com.

The www.avantguide.com CyberSupplement is the best source for happenings in London during your stay.

Once in the city, head to the nearest newsstand, stock-up on the city's listings magazines and check out the metropolis' mediascape. **Time Out** magazine is indispensable for weekly listings as it offers a comprehensive inventory of current cultural events. Published on Wednesdays, it's available at news-stands throughout the city. **Hot Tickets**, a free listings magazine inserted into Thursday's **Evening Standard** newspaper is another good source for happenings.

Of all the city's newsagents, none tops **A. Moroni & Son**, 68 Old Compton St., W1 (tel. 0171/437-2847) for its huge selection of national and interna-tional newspapers and magazines. They're open Mon-Sat 630am-7pm, Sun 730am-330pm. Tube: Piccadilly Circus.

The London Tourist Board (LTB) maintains several Information Centres throughout the capital. They distribute city maps, answer questions and, in a pinch, can help you find accommodations.

When entering England via Heathrow, visit the LTB in the arrival terminal before making your journey into the city; it's open daily from 9am to 6pm. Those arriving via Gatwick, or by train from Paris, can visit the well-staffed office in Victoria Station's forecourt. The office is open Easter to October daily, from 9am to 8pm; the rest of the year it's open Monday through Saturday from 9am to 7pm and Sunday from 9am to 5pm. Other LTB Information Centres are located in Harrods and Selfridges department stores, both open year-round during store hours; and at the Tower of London, open from 10am to 6pm daily, Easter to October only. For information by phone, call the **British Tourist Authority** (tel. 0171/730-3488) weekdays between 9am and 6pm.

The Britain Visitor Centre, 1 Regent St., just steps from Piccadilly Circus, offers comprehensive travel and accommodation services for England, Wales, Scotland and Ireland. It's open Mon-Fri 9am-630pm, Sat 9am-5pm, Sun 10am-4pm.

ESSENTIAL SERVICES

COMPUTERS/INTERNET – If you have trouble jacking-in, visit **Cyberia**, 39 Whitfield St., W1 (tel. 0171/681-4200), Britain's first internet cafe, with 13 terminals. **Café Internet**, 22-24 Buckingham Palace Rd., SW1 (tel. 0171/233-5786) is the city's largest web zone, boasting 22 terminals. **Webshack**, 15 Dean St., W1 (tel. 0171/439-8000) is another cyber spot with Web access that's the choice of London's digerati.

CREDIT CARDS – American Express/Optima (tel. 01273/696933); MasterCard (tel. 0800/964767); Visa (tel. 0800/895082).

EMERGENCIES – Police/Fire/Ambulance (tel. 999).

EYEWEAR/CONTACT LENSES – **Auerbach & Steele**, 129 King's Rd., SW3 (tel. 0171/349-0001) is one of the coolest places in the city for Yohji Yamamoto, Boz and Theo and other dandy frames. Replacement contacts/glasses in a hurry? Go to **Bromptons**, 306 Old Brompton Rd., SW5 (tel. 0171/373-5753) for fast, inexpensive service. Tube: Earl's Court.

FILM PROCESSING/PHOTOGRAPHY – **Snappy Snaps** is the city's largest chain of 30-minute developing spots with several locations on Oxford Street and throughout the city center. For professional developing head to **Ceta West One**, 1 Poland St., W1. Tel. 0171/434-1235. See Chapter 7/Shopping for info on buying camera equipment.

LAUNDRY/DRY CLEANING – In some neighborhoods you'll find launderettes and dry cleaners on nearly every block. Ask at your hotel or check the yellow pages under "Cleaners." Some of the best are **Buckingham Dry Cleaners**, 83 Duke St., W1 (tel. 0171/499-1253); **Danish Express**, 16 Hinde St., W1 (tel. 0171/935-6306); **Duds 'n' Suds**, in the Brunswick Shopping Centre, Russell Sq., WC1 (tel. 0171/837-1122); and **Shirt Stream**, 484 Fulham Rd., SW6 (tel. 0171/386-8445).

LIQUOR LAWS – Britain's archaic licensing laws make it almost impossible to get a drink after 11pm (1030pm on Sundays) unless you are in a late-licensed restaurant or private club. Liquor stores and pubs are bound by the same hours. Beer and wine is sold in supermarkets, liquor stores ("bottle shops") and food shops advertising "off-license" sales.

LOST PROPERTY – If you lost it in London, it's probably gone forever. If you lose something on the bus or tube, allow two days before contacting **London Regional Transport**, 200 Baker Street., NW1 (tel. 0171/486-2496), open Monday through Friday from 930am to 2pm. The **Taxi Lost Property Office**, 15 Penton Street, N1 (tel. 0171/833-0996), is open Monday to Friday from 9am to 4pm. Lost property offices are also located in all the major British Rail stations. To report a loss or theft, call the local police by dialing 100 and ask the operator to connect you.

PHARMACIES – **Bliss Chemist** fills prescriptions daily incl. bank holidays from 9am-midnight at the following locations: 5-6 Marble Arch, W1 (tel. 0171/723-6116); 33 Sloane Sq., SW1 (tel. 0171/730-1023); 149 Edgeware Rd., W2 (tel. 0171/723-2336).

POLICE – In an emergency, dial 999 from any phone; no money is needed. For non-emergencies, dial the operator (100) and ask to be connected with the police.

POSTAL SERVICES/EXPRESS MAIL – The main post office, 24 William IV St., Trafalgar Square, WC2 (tel. 0171/930-9580), is open Mon-Sat 8am-8pm. DHL, 181 Strand, WC2 (tel. 0345/100300); Federal Express, 9 Elms Lane, SW8 (tel. 0800/123800) and UPS, Forest Rd., Middlesex (tel. 0345/877877).

TELECOMMUNICATIONS – London has two area codes: 0171 (for central London) and 0181 (for outer London). *On Easter Saturday of the year 2000, the area code for all of London will change to 020. Local phone numbers will gain an extra digit in the front: either 7 for 0171 numbers, or 8 for 0181 numbers.*

There are two kinds of pay phones in normal use. The first accepts coins, while the other operates exclusively with credit cards and phonecards; the latter are available from newsagents in denominations ranging from £2 to £20. British Telecom owns the greatest number of sidewalk payphones, but there are many others owned by competing companies that require different cards. Cardphones are especially handy if you want to call abroad, as you don't have to continuously pop in the pounds.

To reach the local operator, dial 100. The international operator is 155. London phone information (a.k.a. "directory inquiries") can be reached by dialing 192 and is free of charge from public phones.

For international calls, dial 00 followed by the country code (US/Canada, 1; Australia, 61; Republic of Ireland, 353; New Zealand, 64; South Africa, 27), the city code, and the telephone number of the person you wish to call.

Be forewarned that hotel surcharges on both long-distance and local calls can be astronomical. Think about using a public pay phone in the lobby.

TIPPING – Here are the rules of thumb: Restaurants, bars, nightclubs, taxis, hairdressers: 10%-15%; bartenders in pubs get nothing.

TUXEDO RENTAL – Lipman & Son, 22 Charing Cross Rd., WC2 (tel. 0171/240-2310) charges about £35 to rent a basic tux. They're open Mon-Fri 9am-8pm, Sat 9am-6pm, Sun 10am-5pm. Tube: Leicester Square.

VIDEO – PAL is the video standard. Tapes and multi-format machines can be rented from Radio Rentals, 87 Baker St., W1 (tel. 0171/486-8338).

The Ritz

London's hotels are some of the very best and very worst in the civilized world.

At the top end, the city boasts some of the most famous names in the business: Brown's Claridges, Ritz, and Savoy, along with super-stylish newcomers like The Hempel and The Metropolitan. Über-hotelier Ian Schrager and architect Philippe Starck are moving their act here from New York, and local restaurateur Terence Conran has thrown his hat into the ring in the form of the trendy Myhotel.

At the other end of the spectrum are hundreds of aging bed-and-breakfasts that haven't been introduced to a can of paint or a vacuum cleaner in aeons. Nowhere in the world have we seen so many poorly-maintained hotels, at prices that soar through the roof. We have gone to great lengths in this guide to flush out the very best of the city's budget hotels.

All the hotels listed below share one thing in common: an enviable location; all are within walking distance to major sights. Hotels far from the action, or difficult to reach by public transportation, are not listed below, as we wouldn't want to stay in them. Every establishment listed below meets our strict criteria for service, facilities and value.

The hotels in this guide represent the very best in each price category that London has to offer. The rates quoted below include all service charges and 7.5% VAT.

The Truth About Pricing

The "rack" is the highest rate that a hotel charges for its rooms. These are the prices printed on the hotels' rate cards, and is the price usually quoted when you simply phone and ask "how much do you charge?" Because of travel agent commissions, discount reservations services (see below), and corporate and club discounts, most hotel rooms are sold for substantially less than rack. The best way to reserve a hotel room is to phone, fax or email and ask for their "best corporate rate." To compare prices and save time, contact several hotels and then immediately cancel the ones that don't work for you.

Apartment Rentals

Several companies rent apartments to short-term visitors when their owners are away. These range from corporate-owned flats to highly-personalized places belonging to vacationing locals. Amenities vary, but every apartment is carefully pre-screened and priced far below a comparable hotel room. The following specialize in holiday lettings:

The Apartment Service, 5-6 Francis Grove, SW19. Tel. 0181/944-1444. Fax 0181/944-6744. Open Mon-Fri 9am-530pm. From £90 double.

Aston's, 39 Rosary Gardens, SW7. Tel. 0171/370-0737. Fax 0171/835-1419. Open daily 9am-6pm, phone inquiries daily 9am-1030pm. From £45 single, £65 double.

Holiday Serviced Apartments, 140 Cromwell Road, SW7. Tel. 0171/373-4477. Fax 0171/373-4282. Open Mon-Fri 930am-530pm. From £80 single/double.

Palace Court Holiday Apartments, 1 Palace Court, Bayswater Road, SW7. Tel. 0171/727-3467. Fax 0171/221-7824. Open Mon-Fri 830am-11pm. £50 single, £65 double.

HOTELS bY AREA

The cost (£) reflects the average price of a double room.

£	= Under £65
££	= £65-£100
£££	= £100-£180
££££	= £180-£260
£££££	= Over £260

Brown's

30 Albemarle St., W1. Tel. 0171/ 493-6020. Fax 0171/493-9381. www.brownshotel.com £239–£279 single, £295–£325 double; suites from £405. AE, MC, V. Tube: Green Park.

There are several major Old Worldish luxury hotels in Mayfair, most of which are household names: Claridges, Connaught, Dorchester, Ritz and Savoy. To be honest, all these starchy places are basically similar, but we like Brown's for its thoroughly English country-house styling that includes oak paneling, crystal chandeliers, four-poster beds and real log fires. Begun in 1837 by James Brown, valet to Lord Byron, the hotel hosted many of the world's biggest fish, before hipper places opened in the late 20th century. Brown's enjoys the best location in London, and makes you feel special each time you walk in. "Superior" rooms, furnished with king-sized beds, are far larger than "Standard" ones, and for not much more money. Even if you don't stay here, you should come for high tea; perhaps the best in the city (see Chapter 8/Afternoon Teas).

161 Rooms: Air conditioning, cable TV, telephone, dataports, hairdryer, minibar, radio, room service (24 hours), concierge, restaurant, bar, business center, fitness center, wheelchair access.

The Hempel

31 Craven Hill Gardens, W2. Tel. 0171/298-9000. Fax 0171/402-4666. thehempel@ easynet.co.uk £260–£300 single/double; suites from £435. AE, MC, V. Tube: Lancaster Gate/Queensway/ Paddington.

Few hotels anywhere have attracted as much attention as the ultra-fashionable Hempel, the latest offering from Anouska Hempel—a.k.a. Weinberg (her married name)—a former actress turned hotelier-to-the-stars. There is no name on the hotel's inconspicuous Georgian facade, but you can locate the entrance by the stylishly-dressed actor/model/doorman standing on the sidewalk. Inside is all about minimalist decor and maximalist prices. In the lofty lobby there are white walls, white furnishings, white orchids... everything seems to be white except the staff, who are dressed in black. There are no numbers on the guest room doors—they are projected from above onto the floor. And it's all very clean, since there's nowhere for dirt to hide. Accommodations are like chic-simple film sets with lots of natural light, streamlined Asianesque furnishings, and fireplaces that appear to be suspended in mid-air. Materials are natural; bleached oak, Portland stone and white fabrics are minimalist fittings that seem to literally bleach out the space. There's even oxygen in the minibar. The Hempel's

celebrated Zen garden, a bucolic space that was the site of the wedding scene in the movie Notting Hill, is really much ado about nothingness. The hotel's ridiculously expensive restaurant, 1-Thai, offers a fashionable pan-Asian menu that kicks off with a £10 martini in the adjacent drinking room that's not called the Shadow Bar for nothing.

47 Rooms: Air conditioning, cable TV, telephone, dataports, hairdryer, minibar, radio, room service, concierge, restaurant, bar, wheelchair access.

The Leonard Hotel

15 Seymour St., London W1. Tel. 0171/935-2010. Fax 0171/935-6700. the.leonard@dial.pipex.com £210-£280 single, £250-£500 double. AE, MC, V. Tube: Marble Arch.

This is the place to tuck yourself into a suite, as that's what most of the accommodations are. There's two great reasons to check into The Leonard: First, compared to bigger, more famous places, you get value for money here. Second, this is a great hotel. The Leonard is an elegantly restored row of 18th-century town houses in which guest rooms are huge and luxurious; furnished with antiques, paintings and flowers, as well as a VCR, decent stereo and other necessities. Some have four poster beds and real log fires. And we love the 24/seven room service, a rarity for such a small hotel. It's close to Hyde Park and Oxford Street, and only about one minute from Marble Arch Underground Station.

28 Rooms: Air conditioning, cable TV, telephone, dataports, hairdryer, minibar, radio, room service, concierge, restaurant, bar, fitness center, wheelchair access.

The Metropolitan

Old Park Lane, W1. Tel. 00171/447-1000. Fax 00171/447-1100. sales@metropolitan.co.uk £195 single, £245-£400 double; suites from £595. AE, MC, V. Tube: Green Park/Hyde Park Corner.

Owner Christina Ong, the proprietor of The Halkin in Knightsbridge and woman of impeccable taste, has scored another hit with her latest hotel venture: a super-stylish magnet for all manner of jet-lagged waifs, advertising urchins, design brats and other hip folk. Welcomed by a friendly staff of 30-somethings dressed in Donna Karan, guests are ushered into a hotel filled with natural light, rich fabrics, deep woods and rich marbles. Except for the necessary furnishings and the occasional Asian antique, there is precious little extra decoration. Situated beside the august Hilton and Dorchester hotels, the Metropolitan's minimalism verges on iconoclastic. Great facilities include dual-line telephones, voice mail, personal fax machines, Kiehl's bath products, and even ISDN lines. There's also a good gym. No doubt some people have checked in here just to book a table at the hotel's ferociously popular restaurant, Nobu (see Chapter 8/Top Food). It's worth it. The same can't be said for the Met Bar, a boring, PR-created space that's open only to members and hotel guests.

155 Rooms: Air conditioning, cable TV, telephone, dataports, hairdryer, minibar, radio, room service, concierge, restaurant, bar, fitness center, wheelchair access.

Number One Aldwych

One Aldwych, WC2. Tel. 0171/300-1000. Fax 0171/300-0501. £245 single; £265 double; suites from £395. AE, MC, V. Tube: Aldwych/Temple.

A great theaterland location, handsome Beaux Arts-inspired architecture, and thoroughly contemporary style make this a great inner-city luxury hotel. Opened by Gordon Campbell Gray, who restored a hotel in East Hampton, NY, One Aldwych is a five-star hotel that rejects dripping deluxeness in favor of a more casual atmosphere which appeals to younger globobosses and entertainment-industry arrivistes. The cavernous, polished-limestone lobby is an energetic urban space with dark oak paneling, oversized modernist art, and cool lounge that's popular with local hedonists. Guestrooms are just as contemporary, created by designers whose slogan is "not an inch of chintz." Sleek bathrooms contain chunky Philippe Starck-designed sinks and tubs, along with conveniently positioned TVs. The hotel is packed with amenities, including a private in-house cinema, a swimming pool, and one thousand telephone lines for just over 100 rooms, the best of which overlook Waterloo Bridge.

105 Rooms: Air conditioning, cable TV, telephone, dataports, hairdryer, minibar, radio, room service, concierge, restaurant, bar, wheelchair access.

The Savoy

Strand, WC2. Tel. 0171/8336-4343. Fax 0171/240-6040.
www.savoy-group.co.uk £285-£315 single, £335-£395 double;
suites from £400. AE, MC, V. Tube: Charing Cross.

A great address for impressing your American friends, the Savoy
is one of London's most classic places to lodge. Unlike London's
other Old World luxury hotels that are stashed away in Mayfair, the
Savoy is located close to Covent Garden and Leicester Square, so you
can conveniently stumble home after an irreverent night in Soho. It's

also closer to the City, which gives the hotel a business edge.
Bedrooms are luxurious and bathrooms are terrific. The best rooms
face south on the River Thames rather than the busy Strand.
Americans love the well-stocked fitness center, the rooftop indoor
swimming pool, and the fact that the hotel's driveway is the
only street in London where cars drive on the right.
207 Rooms: Air conditioning, cable TV, telephone, dataports,
hairdryer, minibar, radio, room service, concierge, restaurant,
bar, fitness center, wheelchair access.

EXPENSIVE

The Beaufort

33 Beaufort Gardens, SW3. Tel. 0171/584-5252. Fax 0171/589-2834. thebeaufort@aol.co.uk £195-£275 single/double; suites from £295. AE, MC, V. Tube: Knightsbridge.

The Beaufort departs from the usual hotel experience in its attempt to recreate the warm atmosphere of a private home. The private home of fabulously wealthy aristocrats, that is; perhaps not too dissimilar from owners Sir Michael and Lady Wilmot. There are no check-in formalities. Guests are greeted at the front door and shown to upscale, richly furnished rooms that won't win any edgy style awards. Then they're handed a key to the front door. The staff is not intrusive, but they don't disappear either. There's room service and a concierge, and the sitting room bar serves gratis brandy, chocolates, shortbread and champagne throughout the night (and day). The Beaufort is on a quiet, tree-lined cul de sac about 100 yards from Harrods.

28 Rooms: Air conditioning, cable TV, telephone, dataports, hairdryer, minibar, radio, room service, concierge, restaurant, bar, wheelchair access.

The Gore

189 Queen's Gate, SW7. Tel 0171/584-6601. Fax 0171/589-8127.
reservations@gorehotel.co.uk £120–£135 single, £180–£250
double. AE, MC, V. Tube: Gloucester Road.

Few other London hotels have a more fanatically loyal clientele
than this slightly eccentric Knightsbridger. Well located, near the
Victoria & Albert Museum and five minutes from Harrods, the
Gore is an extremely detailed charmer, featuring a clutter of
Victoriana that includes Oriental rugs over every available
surface, lots of greenery, and literally thousands of oil
paintings. It's a fairy-tale romantic place that appeals to few
tour groups or business types, except those who appear to
be on holiday. A carved gilt bed, once owned by Judy
Garland, is the centerpiece of The Venus Room. And the
Dame Nellie Room, a boudoir-themed homage to 1950s
Hollywood starlets, is particularly sumptuous.

54 Rooms: Air conditioning, cable TV, telephone,
dataports, hairdryer, minibar, radio, room service,
concierge, restaurant, bar, wheelchair access.

041

Myhotel Bloomsbury

11 Bayley St., Bedford
Square. Tel. 0171/667-6000.
Fax 0171/667-6044. guest@
myhotel.co.uk £155–£175
single; £195–£225 double;
Suites from £395. AE, MC, V.
Tube: Tottenham Court Road.
Terence Conran, who brought fine
dining to the local masses, has
designed this modern, five-story
hotel for the same audience: rank-
and-file New Rich. Unabashedly
promoting itself as a "designer hotel,"
Myhotel is a contemporary townhouse
with a deluxe location on a sophisticated
Regency-era square. The hotel is designed
according to the principles of feng shui,
an ancient Chinese practice of spiritual
design that's currently all the rage in London.
Plenty of cynics say phooey to feng shui and
its gimmicky room-arranging rules that rely
on a compass, and include claims like eight
red fish in a tank can make you rich, while
two black ones will absorb negative energy.
However, we have to admit that there is
a peaceful atmosphere here, created in
part by the great attention given to
color and space. Minimal and airy, the
hotel embraces the ubiquitous
East-meets-West theme that seems to
be slowly taking over the world. If you
do stay here, remember wealth and
prosperity in the southeast, romance
and relationships in the southwest;
north for career, south for fame,
and east for family and health.
76 Rooms: Air conditioning,
cable TV, telephone, dataports,
hairdryer, minibar, radio, room
service, concierge, restaurant,
bar, fitness center, wheelchair
access.

Portobello Hotel

22 Stanley Gardens, W11.
Tel. 0171/727-2777. Fax 0171/792-9641. £175-£260 single/double. AE, MC, V. Tube: Holland Park/Notting Hill Gate. Long known as London's rock star hotel, this luxurious Notting Hill winner frequently hosts A-list celebs, including Van Morrison, Mick Jagger, George Michael, Suede, Iggy Pop, and the members of U2. Blur's Damon Albarn once worked here as a barman, and Room 16, which is said to be a favorite of Tina Turner's, contains a round bed and an enormous bathtub in the same room. Hype notwithstanding (the hotel's PR firm had a field day with the revelation that Kate Moss and Johnny Depp filled their bathtub with champagne), the Portobello is a great place to stay. The hotel's elegant Victorian styling and period guest rooms radiate debauchery. Dressed with intricately carved four-poster beds, potted palms, and some of the most comfortable bedding we've tucked into, the accommodations cater to Edenistic senses.

22 Rooms: Air conditioning, cable TV, telephone, dataports, hairdryer, minibar, radio, room service, concierge, restaurant, bar, fitness center, wheelchair access.

MODERATE ▽

Abbey Court Hotel

20 Pembridge Gardens, W2. Tel. 0171/221-7518.
Fax 0171/792-0858. £100-£135 single, £140-£190
double; suites from £200. AE, MC, V. Tube: Notting
Hill Gate.

Old-fashioned in spirit, up-to-date in substance, Abbey
Court is an elegant 5-story Victorian townhouse hotel
featuring individually designed rooms and an enviable
Notting Hill location. Antique furnishings and Designers
Guild fabrics, combined with Jacuzzi baths, 24-hour
room service, and a heated outdoor swimming pool, make
this hotel a thoroughly enjoyable place to stay. Rates
include breakfast, served in the conservatory.

22 Rooms: Cable TV, telephone, hairdryer, minibar,
radio, bar, fitness center, wheelchair access.

Academy Hotel

17 Gower St., WC1. Tel. 0171/631-4115.
Fax 0171/636-3442. £100-£115 single; £125-£185 double; suites from £190. AE, MC, V. Tube: Goodge Street/Russell Square.
The Academy is the nicest hotel on hotel-packed Gower Street. It's a charming group of five Georgian townhouses in the heart of Bloomsbury, stocked with smart, clean rooms and plenty of facilities, including a library, bar, restaurant, and twin garden patios.
50 Rooms: Cable TV, telephone, radio, restaurant, bar, wheelchair access.

Cranley Gardens Hotel

8 Cranley Gardens, SW7. Tel. 0171/373-3232. Fax 0171/373-7944. £75-£85 single, £105-£115 double. AE, MC, V. Tube: Gloucester Road.
Family-run Cranley Gardens Hotel, in the heart of South Kensington, isn't the nicest place in the world, but it's surprisingly good for the price in this tab-happy city. They will never be featured in Wallpaper Magazine, but every bedroom has the requisite features: private bath, TV with in-house movies, radio, and the like. And although wear is definitely in evidence, regulars shrug it off as "charm."
85 Rooms: Cable TV, telephone, radio, hairdryer, bar, wheelchair access.

Five Sumner Place

5 Sumner Place, SW7. Tel. 0171/584-7586. Fax 0171/823-9962. £90-£140 single, £120-£140 double. AE, MC, V. Tube: South Kensington.
Even if this hotel were in a lesser neighborhood, we'd still recommend its clean and functional rooms. As it happens, Five Sumner Place is on a beautiful tree-lined street in the heart of South Kensington and, for London, the price is light.
13 Rooms: Cable TV, telephone, radio, hairdryer, wheelchair access.

Hallam

12 Hallam St., W1. Tel. 0171/580-1166. Fax 0171/323-4527. £75-£85 single; £95-£100 double. AE, MC, V. Tube: Oxford Circus.
Boasting a great location, close to Oxford and Regent streets, the Hallam is a simple, low-key hotel that's quiet, clean and thoroughly recommendable. No-smoking rooms are available.
25 Rooms: Cable TV, telephone, radio, hairdryer, bar, wheelchair access.

iNEXPENSiVE

Crescent Hotel

49 Cartwright Gardens, WC1. Tel. 0171/387-1515. Fax 0171/383-2054. £40-£65 single, £75-£85 double/twin. MC. Tube: Russell Square/Euston.

The beautiful crescent called Cartwright Gardens contains several Georgian townhouses that have been transformed into the nicest little hotels in Bloomsbury. Aptly named Crescent Hotel is the best-priced of the bunch. Rooms are almost as good as its neighbors, and facilities are on par. In summer, guests can lounge in the florabundant gardens and swing on the hotels' shared private tennis courts. Lower prices are for rooms without private bath.

27 Rooms: Cable TV, telephone, radio, hairdryer, wheelchair access.

Elizabeth Hotel

37 Eccleston Square, SW1. Tel. 0171/828-6812. Fax 0171/828-6814. £40-£55 single, £60-£80 double. No cards. Tube: Victoria.

Announced by a small awning in the middle of a block of rowhouses, this quiet B&B offers small rooms overlooking a noble residential square within five minutes of Victoria Station. The good-value accommodations won't make you oohh and ahh, but are fine for zzzz's.

38 Rooms: Cable TV, telephone, radio, hairdryer, wheelchair access.

Melbourne Hotel

79 Belgrave Rd., SW1. Tel. 0171/828-3516. Fax 0171/828-7120. £30-£50 single, £60-£70 double. MC, V. Tube: Victoria/ Pimlico.

Although it's situated on a busy thoroughfare, Melbourne House keeps its sanity with double glazed windows and unusually spacious rooms equipped with TVs and tea/coffee-making facilities. A relatively simple and spartan place, it's one of the best values in the neighborhood.

14 Rooms: Cable TV, telephone, radio, hairdryer.

Parkwood

4 Stanhope Place, W2. Tel 0171/402-2241. Fax 0171/402-1574. £50-£70 single, £65-£90 double. MC, V. Tube: Marble Arch.

This attractive townhouse bed-and-breakfast is situated on a quiet, residential street close to Oxford Street, Marble Arch and Hyde Park. Rooms are decently furnished, clean and airy.

14 Rooms: Cable TV, telephone, radio, hairdryer.

Kensington Gardens Hotel
9 Kensington Gardens Square, W2. Tel 0171/221-7790. Fax 0171/792-8612. kengarhotel@compuserve.com £55-£60 single, £75-£80 double. AE, MC, V. Tube: Bayswater/ Queensway.

This traditional Bayswater B&B boasts clean, nicely-decorated rooms and a friendly atmosphere that has vaulted this place to the budget hotel pinnacle.

17 Rooms: Cable TV, telephone, radio, hairdryer, bar, wheelchair access.

Rushmore
11 Trebovir Road, SW5. Tel. 0171/370-3839. Fax 0171/370-0274. £60-£75 single, £80-£95 double. AE, MC, V. Tube: Earl's Court.

Unusual for a budget hotel, the Rushmore actually has its own unique style. Unlike most of its neighbors, rooms here are good-sized and individually-themed, draped with an Italian fabric here, and splashed with a trompe-l'oeil mural there. The hotel is in Earl's Court, close to the local underground station.

22 Rooms: Cable TV, telephone, radio, hairdryer.

ChEAP

Albro House Hotel

155 Sussex Gardens. Tel. 0171/724-2931. Fax 0171/262-2278. £40-£60 single, £55-£80 double. MC, V. Tube: Paddington/Lancaster Gate.

Despite its quiet-sounding name, Sussex Gardens is one of Bayswater's busiest thoroughfares. There's hardly a house on either side of the street that doesn't announce itself as a hotel. Although accommodations here are uniformly nondescript, rates are good; and Albro is one of the best. The hotel is located on the south side of Sussex Gardens at the London Street intersection.

18 Rooms: Cable TV, telephone, radio, hairdryer, wheelchair access.

Arran House Hotel

77 Gower St., WC1. Tel. 0171/636-2186. Fax 0171/436-5328. arran@dircon.co.uk £40-£50 single, £50-£70 double. MC, V. Tube: Goodge Street.

Decent prices and an enviable Bloomsbury location make Gower Street's budget hotels some of the city's most popular. Most of the three-story B&Bs lining this street are so similar to one another, with their steep stairs, basic rooms (many without private bath), and fairly uniform prices, that only their addresses distinguish them. But the Arran House stands out because of the wonderful Richards family who run it. Rates include English Breakfast, but no one we know has ever eaten it because it's only served until 9am!

28 Rooms: Cable TV, telephone, radio, hairdryer, wheelchair access.

Elizabeth House Hotel

118 Warwick Way, London SW1. Tel. 0171/630-0741. Fax 0171/630-0740. £20-£35 single, £40-£60 double. AE, MC. Tube: Victoria.

This former YWCA guesthouse offers clean, secure and basic accommodations in the city center. Like most budget hotels in London, this is not much more than a simple place to lay your head. The sparsely furnished rooms will please ascetics and minimalists.

27 Rooms.

Garth Hotel

69 Gower St., WC1. Tel. 0171/636-5761. Fax 0171/637-4854. £30-£45 single, £45-£65 double. AE, MC, V. Tube: Euston/St. Pancras

If you can put up with steep stairs, smallish rooms (only two have private baths), and a modicum of street noise, you will benefit from the clean rooms and terrific location of this well-situated budget find.

17 Rooms: Cable TV, telephone, radio.

The Generator

Macnaghten House, Compton Place, WC1. Tel. 0171/388-7666. Fax 0171/388-7644. generator@lhdr.demon.co.uk £36-£40 single, £46-£55 double; £18 per bed in multishare. AE, MC. Tube: Russell Square.

The Generator is a welcome oasis in a city full of cookie-cutter budget accommodations. Built with an unusual futuristic design theme, this large, six-story hotel features smallish rooms, fitted with good lighting, unique furniture, and lots of "art" on the walls. There are about three dozen multishare rooms, none of which come with private bath. Public spaces include a restaurant and a bar and games room, complete with pool tables. The hotel is located near the new British Library.

217 Rooms: Restaurant, bar, wheelchair access.

Lords Hotel

20 Leinster Sq., W2. Tel. 0171/229-8877.
Fax 0171/229-8377. £35-£50 single, £50-
£65 double. AE, MC, V. Tube: Bayswater/
Queensway.

Located on a quiet square in Bayswater,
Lords features clean budget rooms, decent
prices, and precious little else. Most accommodations have private baths, and a few
have balconies. If Lords is full, don't hesitate
to accept a room in their nearby annex.
68 rooms: Cable TV, telephone.

Melita House Hotel

35 Charlwood St., SW1. Tel. 0171/828-
0471. Fax 0171/932-0988. £35-£45 single,
£50-£65 double. AE, MC, V. Tube: Victoria.

Much of the area around Victoria Station was
destroyed during World War II, when
houses took the near misses directed at
London's transport hub. But most of the
rebuilding remained faithful to the original
Greco-Roman style. And although many of
the local B&Bs aren't even fit for the French,
Melita House does stand out with its
spotless rooms, decent rates, and quiet
location on a small side street.
22 Rooms: Cable TV, telephone, radio,
hairdryer.

Oakley Hotel

73 Oakley St., SW3. Tel. 0171/352-5599.
Fax 0171/727-1190. £35 single, £45
double; £15 per bed in multishare. No
cards. Tube: Sloane Square.

A fun and friendly Chelsea B&B, Oakley
Hotel is far and away London's best
bargain for younger budget travelers. This
international-travelers hotel is packed with
joy-seeking visitors who quickly make friends
in the basement TV lounge, on the rear patio,
or in the common kitchen. There are no
en suite baths, and shared guest rooms sleep
four to six. The location can't be beat. From
the Sloane Square Underground you can
either take a long walk, or hop on the no. 11
or 22 bus, down King's Road to Oakley Street.

hOSTELS / MULTiShARES

In addition to the above-listed Generator and Oakley Hotel, both of which offer budget-price beds in multishare rooms, London has lots of dormitory space in youth hostels. The places listed below are all members of the **International Youth Hostel Federation** (IYHF). Non-members will have to pay an extra £1.75 per night to bed down. However, you can join the IYHF for about £10 at any member hostel. There are no age restrictions.

City of London Youth Hostel

36-38 Carter Lane, EC4. Tel. 0171/236-4965. Fax 0171/236-7681. Reception open daily 7am-11pm, 24-hour access. £20-£25. MC, V. Tube: St. Paul's. 190 Beds.

Set in a wonderfully-restored building that was once a school for choir boys, this hostel boasts a good number of single rooms, as well as multishares with no more than four beds each. The hostel is near St. Paul's Cathedral, in the heart of the City of London. Exit St. Paul's Underground Station, turn right and make your way toward the front steps of the cathedral; follow Dean's Court, a small street, to the corner of Carter Lane.

Earl's Court Youth Hostel

38 Bolton Gardens, SW5. Tel. 0171/373-7083. Fax 0171/835-2034. Reception open daily 7am-11pm, 24-hour access. £20. MC, V. Tube: Earl's Court. 155 Beds.

Earl's Court hostel is in a lively neighborhood where stores tend to stay open late. Most accommodations are 10-bed dorms. Exit Earl's Court Underground Station and turn right. Bolton Gardens is the fifth street on your left.

Holland House Youth Hostel

Holland House, Holland Walk, W8. Tel. 0171/937-0748. Fax 0171/376-0667. Reception open daily 7am-11pm, 24-hour access. £20. MC, V. Tube: High St. Kensington, Holland Park. 201 Beds.

Holland House enjoys the most beautiful setting of all London's IYHF hostels; located right in the middle of Kensington's Holland Park.

Oxford Street Youth Hostel

14 Noel St., W1. Tel. 0171/734-1618. Fax 0171/734-1657. Reception open daily 7am-11pm, 24-hour access. £18.70, £15.25 under-18s. MC, V. Tube: Oxford Circus. 75 Beds.

Small and centrally located, this hostel is the most basic in town. Because it's also one of the best-located, reservations can be tough to get.

04 LONDON'S GREATEST HITS

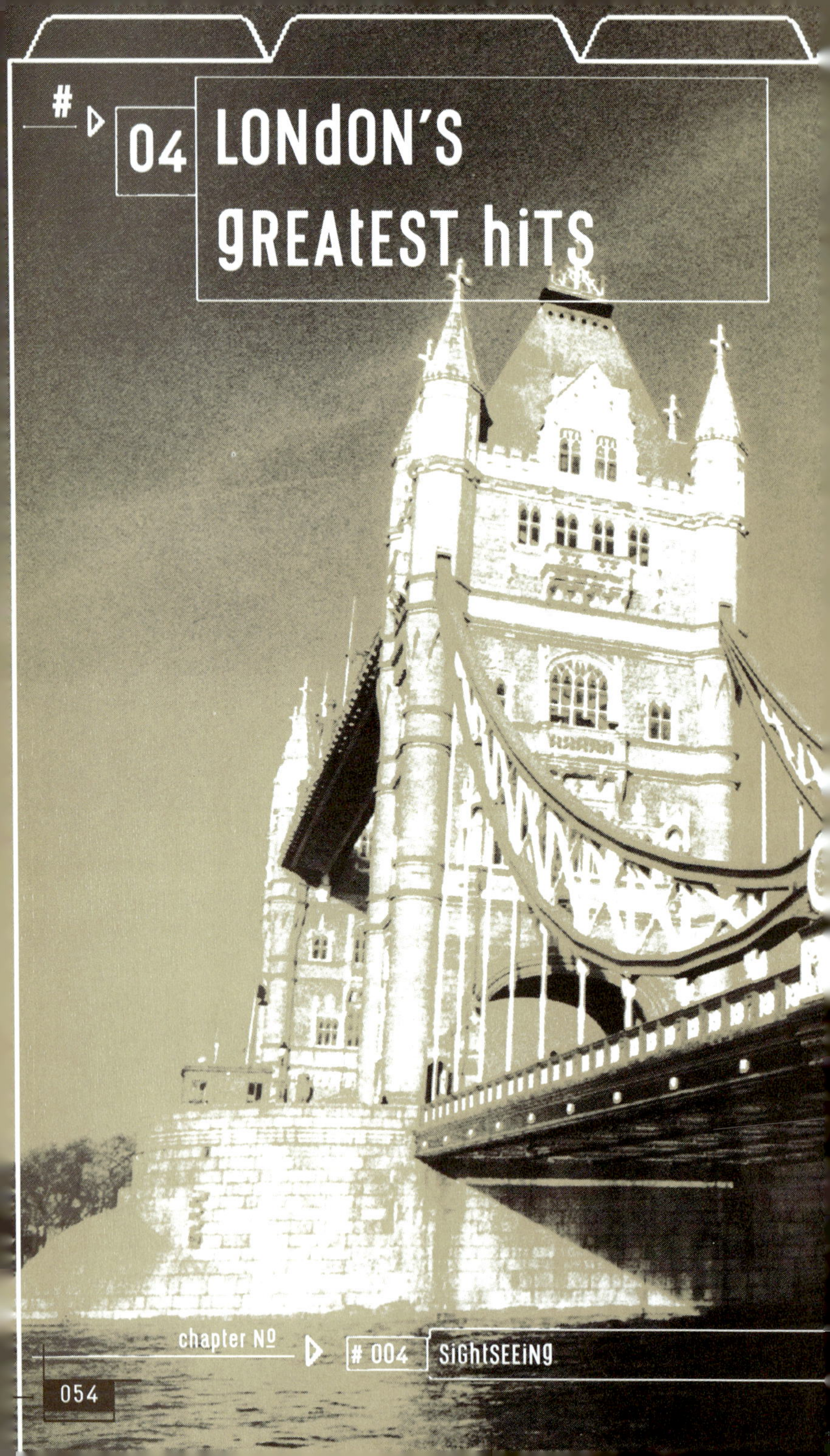

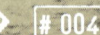

Buckingham Palace

Buckingham Palace Rd., SW1. Tel. 0171/839-1377. Open Aug-Sept only, daily 930am-430pm (last admission). Ticket office in Green Park opens 9am. Advance credit card bookings accepted beginning April 1st (tel. 0171/321-2233). Closed Nov-July. Admission £9.50 adults, £5 children under 16. Tube: St. James's Park/Green Park.

Built for the Duke of Buckingham, the palace was converted into a royal residence in 1837 when Queen Victoria decided to live here. It remains the sovereign's official London residence; when she is at home, the Royal Standard is flown from the flagstaff on the building's roof.

The 1990s brought the royal family down to Earth, not least of which was due to new legislation that, for the first time, required the Royals to pay income taxes just like the rest of us. This slap on

the pocketbook was instrumental in convincing the Queen to open her home to paying visitors—for a limited number of hours, two months of the year. Those lucky enough to snag tickets are escorted through just eighteen of the palace's 300 rooms. But that's enough to grasp the grandeur of the palace as a whole, and get a good idea of the quality of its contents. The entire pad is decked out with enormous crystal chandeliers, complex rugs, fine oil paintings and antique furnishings; and not a stitch of IKEA in sight. But for all its finery, the palace's over-the-top opulence feels devoid of personality—as staid and cold as the Windsors themselves. Most of the art is relatively new, part of the royal collection that was formed in the 300 years since the restoration of the monarchy in 1660. The 90-minute tour leads visitors past the impressive Grand Staircase—all cream, gold and red, not unlike the Ritz Hotel—through several picture galleries, and into the State Dining Room, the Throne Room and several drawing rooms, all of which are used for ceremonies and official entertaining. The Queen's bedroom is off-limits, and it's unlikely you'll see the Duke of Edinburgh running around in his underwear. Peek out the windows, however, and you'll get a good view of the couple's private Palace Gardens.

The Changing of the Guard in the Palace Forecourt remains one of the city's most popular tourist attractions. The Queen's Guard, accompanied by a band, leaves Wellington Barracks at 1127am and marches via Birdcage Walk to the Palace. The 30-minute ceremony takes place daily mid-April through July, and on alternate days the rest of the year. It's canceled during bad weather and for some major state events. Phone for details.

Houses Of Parliament

Parliament Square. Tel. 0171/219-4272. House of Commons usually sits Mon-Tues 230-1030pm, Wed 930am-1030pm, Thurs 1130am-730pm and some Fri 11am-3pm; House of Lords usually sits Mon-Wed from about 230pm, Thurs from about 3pm, and on some Fri 11am-4pm. All times subject to change; phone for the latest. Admission free. Tube: Westminster.

Officially known as the Palace of St. Stephen at Westminster, the spectacular 19th-century Gothic Revival Houses of Parliament, along with its trademark clocktower, is one of the most recognizable buildings in the world. Home to Britain's federal legislature (the chambers of Commons and Lords), the site was originally the home of eleventh-century King Edward the Confessor, who constructed Westminster Abbey, the royal church, next door. Subsequent monarchs improved and enlarged the palace which functioned as the official home of the regent until 1512, when it was gutted by fire.

Today's flamboyant building, designed by Charles Barry and Augustus Pugin, was completed in 1860. Its most famous element is the clocktower at the eastern end. Contrary to popular belief, "Big Ben" doesn't refer to either the tower or the clock; it is the name of the largest bell in the chime. Hung in 1856, the 13.5-ton bell is believed to have been named for either Sir Benjamin Hall, who was Commissioner of Works when the bell was hung, or for Ben Caunt, a popular Victorian prize fighter who, at age 42, fought a boxing match lasting sixty rounds. Each of the tower's four huge clocks includes a minute hand the length of a double-decker bus. At night, when Parliament is in session, a light shines in the tower.

The House of Commons was destroyed by German bombs on May 10, 1941 and rebuilt by Giles Gilbert Scott, the man responsible for the design of London's red telephone booths. The House of Commons remains small and only 437 of its 651 members can sit at any one time; the rest crowd around the door and the Speaker's Chair. The ruling party and opposition sit facing each other, two sword lengths apart.

The Palace is most spectacular from Westminster Bridge, from which you have a clear view of the building's ornate back side. The balcony with the green canopy is the river terrace of the House of Commons; the one with the red canopy is the river terrace of the House of Lords. If you're lucky you can catch an MP stepping out to show his mistress the view.

The Palace of Westminster is usually not open to public tours, though you may be able to arrange one in advance by writing to the **Public Information Office**, 1 Derby Gate, SW1A 2DG. Alternatively, mere mortals may watch debates from the Stranger's Galleries of the two houses of Parliament (see times, above). The visitors' entrance is at St. Stephen's Gate, at the end of the Palace opposite Big Ben. Debates often run late into the night and queues, which often last an hour or more, shrink after 6pm.

The liveliest session is the Prime Minister's Question Time, held most Tuesdays and Thursdays at 230pm. To see this debate you'll have to arrange for tickets in advance from your embassy (see Chapter 11/Foreign Essentials).

Hyde Park

W2. Tel. 0171/298-2100. Open daily 5am-midnight.
It's hard to imagine London without Hyde Park. Its
spacious greenery is an important counterpoint to the
urban madness. The huge green rectangle ingeniously
blends vast meadows, beautiful lakes and formal dress
grounds, making it a wonderful place to explore.
Owned by the monks of Westminster Abbey until it
was seized by Henry VIII and converted into a royal
hunting ground, the park is London's pressure valve;
the place where urbanites come to stroll, catch some
rare sun and just release some pent-up urban steam.

The best way to get to know the park is on foot.
About 1.5 miles long and one mile wide, the park
is a great place for both leisure and exercise. It's
flat, with few flowers and fewer trees, so getting
lost is all but impossible. Wood-and-cloth
chaise lounges are scattered about so you too can
sit in an English garden waiting for the sun. Fee
collectors then appear from nowhere and demand
a small rental fee from seated sunbathers.

The Westbourne river was dammed in the
1930s to form the **Serpentine,** a beautiful lake
that's great for rowboating. You can also trot
a horse down Rotten Row (*see* Chapter
6/Recreation & Exercise).

On Sundays, artists hang their wares along
the Bayswater Road fence. And the northe-
ast corner, near Marble Arch, becomes
Speaker's Corner, where anyone can stand
on a soapbox and lecture on any subject.
Only sometimes is it interesting or funny,
as these days most of the loudmouths are
run-of-the-mill fire-and-brimstone
preachers. This Sunday tradition is often
touted as an example of Britain's tolerance
of free speech, but few people realize
that the ritual began several hundred
years ago when condemned prisoners
were allowed some final words before
they were hanged on Tyburn gallows,
which stood on the same spot. And,
contrary to popular belief, the law has
full jurisdiction of speakers here; only
the free right of assembly applies.

The park is open till midnight, but
it's best to avoid it after dark.

St. Paul's Cathedral

St. Paul's Churchyard, EC4.
Tel. 0171/236 4128. Cathedral open:
Mon-Sat 830am-4pm; Crypt and
Ambulatory open Mon-Sat 845am-
415pm; Galleries open Mon-Sat
930am-415pm. Special services or
events may close all or part of the cathedral. Closed 28 Dec. Open for wors-
hip Mon-Sat 715am-6pm, Sun 745am-
5pm. Crypt and Ambulatory Admission:
£4 adults, £3.50 students/seniors, £2
children under 16, £9 family ticket
(2 adults + 2 children); free after 430pm
and Sun. Gallery Admission: £7.50. Tube:
St. Paul's. Wheelchair access.

Dedicated to the patron saint of The City of
London, and capped by one of the largest
domes in Christendom, St. Paul's Cathedral is
Christopher Wren's masterpiece. Surprisingly,
this great Renaissance edifice is one of the
world's few cathedrals to be designed by a
single architect, and completed during his lifetime.
The Cathedral was commissioned just after the
previous one was toasted in the Great Fire of
1666; and construction lasted only 35 years. It
has been the setting for many important ceremonies,
including the funerals of Admiral Lord Nelson
(1806) and Sir Winston Churchill (1965), and the
wedding of Charles and Diana (1981).

While many churches stun with their splendor,
St. Paul's wows with vastness. It's a grand space,
built with a spectacular sense of Godlike proportion.
There's not a bad angle in sight. Look up at the dome,
frescoed with stories of the life of St. Paul. Back by
the Choir are fantastically colorful mosaics of the
Creation.

It's worth climbing the 259 steps to the Whispering
Gallery. Acoustics here are such that even soft sounds
can be heard on the other side of the dome. Another
steep 271-step climb brings you to the Golden Gallery,
from which there is an unrivaled view of London.

Down below, in the whitewashed Crypt, are grandiose
monuments to Admiral Nelson, the Duke of Wellington,
and other local heroes. Nearby is Wren's own simple tomb
whose epitaph appropriately reads "*Lector, si
monumentum requiris, circumspice*" ("Reader, if you seek
his monument, look around you").

Tower Bridge

SE1. Tel. 0171/ 403-3761. Open Apr-Oct, daily 10am-630pm; Nov-Mar, daily 930am-6pm. Last tickets 75 minutes before closing. Closed 24-26 Dec, 1 and 27 Jan. Admission: £6.15 adults, £4.15 students/ seniors/children 5-15. £14.95 family ticket (2 adults + 2 children). Tube: Tower Hill. Wheelchair access.

The toylike Tower Bridge, built just over one hundred years ago, is a whimsical feat of Victorian engineering that has made it one of the best-known sites in the city. The trademark elevated twin walkways, originally intended for public use, were closed almost immediately after the bridge's opening due to their popularity with prostitutes, thieves and jumpers. Today access is restricted to paying customers, who are also shuttled through a museum of the bridge's history, and offered a glimpse into the engine rooms where the drawbridge's hydraulic lifts are located. But better views can be had elsewhere, and the museum is a snooze, so unless you're particularly fond of Victorian engineering keep your pounds in your pocket and enjoy this fantastical bridge from the outside.

Tower of London

Tower Hill, EC3. Tel. 0171/709-0765. Open Mar-Oct, Mon-Sat 9am-5pm, Sun 10am-5pm; Nov-Feb, Tue-Sat 9am-4pm, Sun-Mon 10am-4pm (last admission 1 hour before closing). Closed 24-26 Dec, 1 Jan. Admission: £9.50 adults, £7.15 students/seniors, £6.25 children 5-15, £28.40 family ticket (2 adults + 3 children or 1 adult + 4 children). Tube: Tower Hill. Wheelchair access.

The Tower of London is the world's best-loved fortress-turned-tourist-attraction. Guarded by the famous Beefeaters (yes, the ones on the gin bottle), the tower is one of the most heavily fortified buildings in the world. It was an excellent place to imprison high-profile criminals like the two young sons of King Edward IV (who, in 1483, were murdered in Bloody Tower), and Henry VIII's second wife, Anne Boleyn (whose head was chopped off here in 1536). The tower is still the repository for the Crown Jewels, displayed in a fortified bunker that's built with moving walkways to help the crowds along. Valuables include the exquisite Koh-i-noor diamond, set in the crown of the Queen Mother; and the Star of Africa, the largest cut diamond in the world, set within the cross of the Queen Mother's Orb and Scepter. The Imperial State Crown, worn by the monarch at major state occasions, is encrusted with more than 2,800 diamonds and must be the world's priciest hat.

Begun in 1078 by William the Conqueror, the Tower has a long history as palace, prison, treasury, arsenal and even zoo. Giant black ravens notwithstanding, the only animals left are tourists; they come in such great numbers on weekends you'd swear the Tower is still a place of torture.

The Martin Tower contains some of London's cruelest exhibits, instruments of torture used to extract confessions from prisoners. Even the smallest disagreement with your monarch about politics or religion was enough to get you stretched on the rack or crushed in the "scavenger's daughter." There's even a special torture device for henpecking wives.

Other towers house extensive arms and armory collections. Be sure to check out Henry VIII's anatomically exaggerated armor in the White Tower (you'll know it when you see it).

The best way to see the Tower of London is on a guided tour led by a Yeoman Warder (included with admission). Tours depart at regular intervals throughout the day from the entrance gate. A visit to the Tower is not cheap, but it's worth every pound.

Westminster Abbey

Parliament Square, SW1. Tel. 0171/222-5152. Nave and Cloisters open daily 8am-6pm; Royal Chapels open Mon-Fri 920am-445pm (last admission 345pm), Sat 920am-245pm (last admission 145pm) and 4-6pm (last admission 5pm). Royal Chapels closed Good Fri, 9 Mar, 25-27 Dec. Admission £5 adults, £3 students/seniors, £2 children 11-16, £10 family ticket (2 adults + 2 children). Tube: Westminster/St. James's Park. Wheelchair access.

It's hard to overestimate the significance of Westminster Abbey as a symbol of Englishness. The Abbey has been part of the cultural landscape since Day One, and is inextricably related to the monarchy and the class system it fronts. It is far from a lump of dead history. To be buried here, or have an honorary plaque erected, remains the highest honor the state can bestow upon a citizen.

Formally a Benedictine abbey, which housed a community of monks as early as AD 750, it was called Westminster, or West Monastery, after its location west of The City of London. In 1050, Edward the Confessor improved the site and moved his palace next door (now the Houses of Parliament), beginning a tradition of church and state that continues to this day. Since William the Conqueror's coronation on Christmas Day, 1066, all but two of England's monarchs have been crowned in the Abbey; and it has been the site of almost every royal funeral for the past seven hundred years, from King Henry III to Princess Diana. Many royals are also buried here, amongst a clutter of tombs of politicians, poets, scientists, artistes and generic rich people.

The north aisle of the soaring nave is so jammed with floor slabs and memorials to public servants and prime ministers (including George, Chamberlain, Disraeli and Gladstone), it has earned the nickname Statesman's Aisle. Charles Darwin is also buried here.

More than 100 writers and other creatives are honored in the south transept, which has come to be known as Poets' Corner. Geoffrey Chaucer and Edmund Spenser are buried here, alongside busts of John Dryden, William Blake, and American poet Henry Longfellow. Here too lie the ashes of actor Sir Laurence Olivier, and memorials to T.S. Eliot, D.H. Lawrence and Noel Coward. And there's a stained glass window honoring Oscar Wilde, among others.

St. Edward's Chapel, at the center of the church just behind the High Altar, is the most sacred part of the Abbey. In it stands a 13th-century shrine to Edward the Confessor, lots of memorials to medieval kings, and the surprisingly modest Coronation Chair. This oak throne has only been removed from the Abbey three times since its construction in 1300: when Oliver Cromwell was installed as Lord Protector in Westminster Hall, and for safety during the two World Wars.

The abbey's Henry VII Chapel is one of the most beautiful places you may ever see. Completed in 1519, the Chapel's exuberant architectural extravagances and exquisite intricate carvings will take your breath away.

You can confidently skip a visit to the adjacent Abbey Museum, with its ancient military gear and wax effigies that were once used in funeral processions.

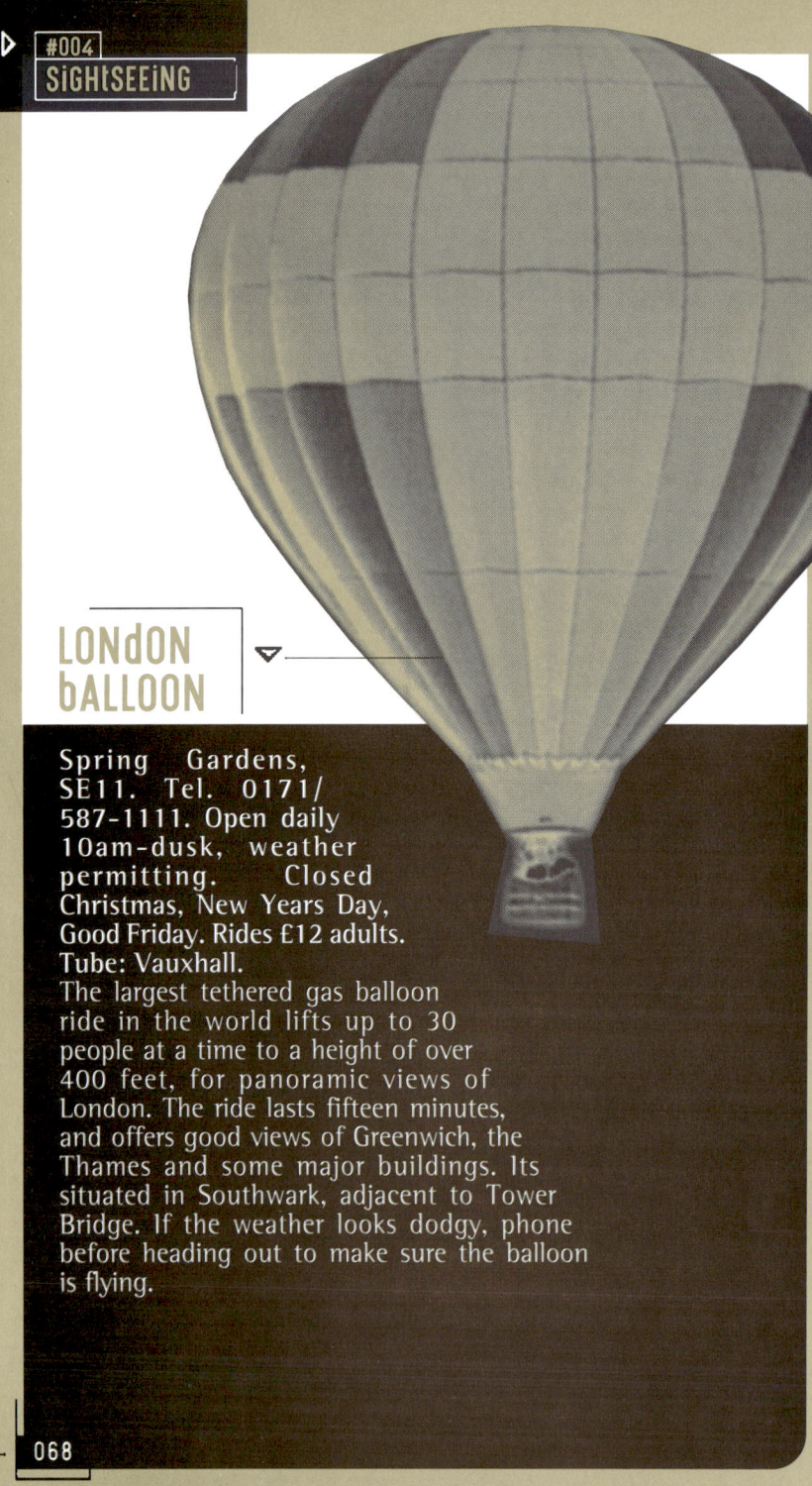

LONdON bALLOON

Spring Gardens, SE11. Tel. 0171/ 587-1111. Open daily 10am-dusk, weather permitting. Closed Christmas, New Years Day, Good Friday. Rides £12 adults. Tube: Vauxhall.

The largest tethered gas balloon ride in the world lifts up to 30 people at a time to a height of over 400 feet, for panoramic views of London. The ride lasts fifteen minutes, and offers good views of Greenwich, the Thames and some major buildings. Its situated in Southwark, adjacent to Tower Bridge. If the weather looks dodgy, phone before heading out to make sure the balloon is flying.

Marketing triumph, or white elephant? Either way, the £758 million Millennium Dome seems to embarrass most locals more than it excites them. But whether you view this giant-white-breast-implant-skewered-by-plastic-surgeon's-needles as a harmless tourist attraction, or an overblown extension of Tony Blair's ego, there's no doubt that it is big, adventurous and somewhat engaging. From January 1, 2000 there are two operating sessions per day during peak times, with a capacity of 35,000 people per session. Boosters anticipate that more than ten million visitors from all over the world will visit the exhibition site. Reservations are required.

The Dome's 14 attractions are arranged in a circle around a central performance area that features a huge stage show created by Mark Fisher and Peter Gabriel. Like a high-tech Cirque du Soliel, the show combines high wire acts and gymnasts with virtual reality and other special effects that attempt to do nothing less than tell the story of humanity.

The themed zones are no less adventurous in scope, celebrating British ideas and technology, and examining the future of the human race. Hand-held audio guides (included with admission) steer visitors around the Dome.

Alongside The Dome is Skyscape, housing an entertainment venue with twin 2,500 seat cinemas that slide aside to reveal the largest performance stage in the UK.

Tel. 0870/606-2000. www. millennium.gov.uk;www.mx2000. co.uk. Reservations required. Open daily from 10am. Admission £20 adults, £16.50 students and children 5-15, £18 Senior Citizens, £57.00 family of five. Tube: North Greenwich. River: City Cruise from Waterloo and Blackfriars to Millennium Pier at the Dome.

The top MUSEUMS

British Museum

Great Russell St., WC1.
Tel. 0171/636-1555.
Open Mon-Sat 10am-
5pm, Sun noon-6pm.
Closed 24-26 Dec, 1
Jan and Good Fri.
Admission free. Tube:
Tottenham Court
Road/Russell Square.
Wheelchair access.

This tremendous warehouse of history is one of the very best museums in the world. It contains encyclopedic collections spanning the entire history of humanity, from flint tools and Swatch watches, to teacups and temples. The museum's vast collections are some of the world's most complete; a one-stop shop for Egyptian tombs, ancient Roman coins, meditating marble Buddhas, pre-Columbian pottery, African ceremonial masks, Renaissance jewelry, muscular Greek torsos, Asian ceramics, Tiffany windows, European arms and armor... the list seems endless as collections move from strength to strength.

The British Museum is something of a misnomer, considering that most everything in it is from someplace else. The museum contains the spoils of Empire; the most significant art and objects pillaged and plundered from all over the globe during England's more than 200 years of expansionism. The collections seem to include one of everything in the world that wasn't nailed down, along with plenty that was.

Most visitors head straight for Room 8 to see the sculptural reliefs that once adorned the Parthenon in Athens (5thC BC). Ironically, they are known as the Elgin Marbles, named for the Englishman who removed these treasures from Greece and sold them to the British government.

The Rosetta Stone (196 BC), yet another treasure now hotly contested by a foreign government, provided the key to hieroglyphics, which were unread for 1,400 years. The sarcophagus of Nectanebo (the last Egyptian pharaoh, 530 BC), a great collection of mummies, and many of the world's most important papyri are other draws that help make this the most comprehensive collection of Egyptian antiquities outside Cairo.

The museum also contains the remains of two

of the Seven Wonders of the Ancient World: the Mausoleum at Halicarnassus (350 BC), and the Temple of Artemis at Ephesus (4thC BC).

The Oriental Antiquities department is best-known for its tremendous trove of Islamic pottery and its collections of 7th-10th-century Buddhist paintings from western China. And the museum has the best collection of Near Eastern and Islamic art in the world, including a board game from the royal cemetery at Ur from 2,600 BC, and the black obelisk of Shalmaneser III (825 BC), emblazoned with the image of Jehu, the King of Israel.

Housing over six million objects, the museum has become something of a catch-all for everything that doesn't have its own special museum in the city. And it's getting bigger all the time. With the 1998 departure of the huge British Library, the museum inherited the Round Reading Room (where Karl Marx wrote *Das Kapital*) and other important areas now being transformed into additional exhibition space for ethnographic collections, including a nine-foot-high Easter Island statue brought back by Captain Cook.

Needless to say, the British Museum is way too big to see it all in one go. The best strategy is to pick-up a floor plan and target specific collections. Better yet, latch on to one of the frequent docent tours, which are led by some of the most erudite and articulate volunteers anywhere. Phone or stop at the information desk for details.

National Gallery

Trafalgar Square, WC2. Tel. 0171/747-2885. Open Mon-Sat 10am-6pm, Wed 10am-9pm, Sun 10am-6pm. Closed 24-26 Dec, 1 Jan, Good Fri. Admission free; occasional charge for major exhibitions. Tube: Leicester Square/Embankment/Charing Cross/Piccadilly Circus. Wheelchair access.

Encyclopedic in scope, the National Gallery owns top examples from nearly all the major schools of Western European painting from the 12th to the 19th centuries. In short, it's one of the very best fine art museums in the world. All the stars are here, including some of the best works by Botticelli, da Vinci, Cézanne, Renoir, Van Gogh and others. And with 22 Rembrandts and 23 Rubenses, the museum's holdings are often as deep as they are vast. Unusually for a place of this size, almost all of the museum's holdings are always on display. Each year, over five million visitors climb the museum's palatial steps in an attempt to negotiate the maze of art-filled rooms. The collection is divided chronologically into four wings. Hits from later years include Monet's *Gare St. Lazare* (1877), Manet's *Music in the Tuileries Gardens* (1862), and Van Gogh's *Sunflowers* (1888). There's usually a terrific loan exhibition on display too. The best way to see the museum is with a volunteer docent. Tours are free, and scheduled regularly throught the day. Phone for times. The museum has a particularly great gift shop.

Natural History Museum

Cromwell Rd., SW7. Tel. 0171/938-9123. Open Mon–Sat and Bank Hols 10am–550pm, Sun 11am-450pm. Closed 23–26 Dec. Admission: £6 adults, £3.20 students/seniors, £16 family ticket (2 adults + 4 children). Free Mon–Sat and Bank Hols after 430pm. Tube: South Kensington. Wheelchair access.

London's warehouse of history is one of the world's largest institutions dedicated to the natural sciences. An astounding 20 million artifacts are stashed inside this landmark building, including over one million species of bugs, and a sparklingly rich gems and minerals department glows with thousands of colorful geodes in glass cases. There's an excellent Human Biology exhibition, Charles Babbage's calculating machine, an Apollo-era command module, and a new interacive Earthquake Experience exhibit that simulates several major shakers. The Challenge of Materials Gallery shows how a dress can be made out of metal, shoes out of chocolate and a coffin out of Bakelite. But, no matter how big this continuously expanding museum grows, dinosaurs will forever remain the star attractions. One of the world's largest collections of dino bones is augmented with ginormous animatronic models. The museum is ridiculously crowded on weekends. It's best during the week after 3pm, when school groups are not clogging the building's arteries.

Science Museum

Exhibition Rd., SW7. Tel. 0171/ 938-8000. Open daily 10am– 6pm. Closed 24–26 Dec. Admission £6.50 adults, £3.50 students/children 5-17. Tube: South Kensington. Wheelchair access.

The Science Museum is the funky and eccentric granddaddy of all science museums. Long before the word "interactive" ever preceded "museum," this engaging place invited people to experience and discover science on a very personal level. The collections highlight the major scientific advances of the last 300 years with spectacularly thorough exhibitions on science, technology and medicine. Highlights include the Space Gallery and the Wellcome Museum of Medical History, a major new wing debuting in the summer of 2000, devoted entirely to contemporary science, medicine and technology.

The Science Museum is situated next to the Natural History Museum (above), near South Kensington underground station.

Tate Gallery/Millbank

Millbank, SW1. Tel. 0171/887-8000. Open daily 10am-550pm. Closed 24-26 Dec. Admission free, except for major loan exhibitions. Tube: Pimlico. Wheelchair access.

Since its inception, the Tate has worn two hats, as both London's museum of modern art and the country's primary gallery for British painting. Beginning in the Spring of 2000, the modern art collection is moving across the river to Bankside (see below), and this Millbank building will be rechristened in 2001 as the Tate Gallery of British Art. The museum has been awarded £18.75 million to help relaunch the building, which will include six new galleries for exhibitions and nine new or refurbished galleries for the permanent collection, showing British art from 1500 to the present day. All of the country's best-loved artists are represented here, including William Hogarth, Sir Joshua Reynolds, Thomas Gainsborough, George Stubbs and John Constable, who painted quintessentially British landscapes. Turner, probably Britain's favorite home-grown artist, is honored with an entire gallery specifically designed to showcase his work. Born at 21 Maiden Lane, a narrow street in the heart of Covent Garden, Turner was obsessed with the subject of London throughout his working life. Hogarth's satirical painting, *Gates of Calais*, established roast beef as the British national dish. After being arrested in Calais under suspicion of spying, the painter drew a canvas depicting starving French soldiers and a fat Catholic friar salivating over a succulent side of English beef. There are also some works by famous foreigners, including Canaletto, who arrived in London in 1746 and produced a variety of scenes typifying 18th-century London.

Tate Gallery of Modern Art

Bankside Power Station, Sumner St., SE1. Tel. 0171/887-8000. Open daily 10am-550pm. Closed 24-26 Dec. Admission free, except for major loan exhibitions. Tube: Southwark. Wheelchair access.

London's newest major museum, scheduled to open May 2000, features 20th Century art ranging from Andy Warhol and Rachel Whiteread to Henri Matisse and Henry Moore. Situated on the south bank of the Thames, opposite St. Paul's Cathedral, the museum displays a world-famous permanent exhibition in luminous new galleries. The collection includes an especially good selection of cubist works, as well as several major pieces by Salvador Dali, David Hockney, and Joan Miro. Look for top temporary shows too.

Victoria and Albert Museum

Cromwell Rd., SW7. Tel. 0171/938-8500. Open daily 10am-545pm. Closed 24-26 Dec. Admission: £5 adults, £3 seniors, free for students 5-18; free for everybody daily after 430pm. Tube: South Kensington. Wheelchair access.

The V&A is an embarrasment of riches; a study in excess containing the world's largest and most diverse collection of decorative arts. If it's pretty and useful, and created within the last fifteen centuries, it's likely you'll find it here. Comprehensive collections from around the world are stashed into 146 galleries, strung along seven miles of corridors. Delve into room upon room filled with porcelain figurines, art glass, costume jewelry, hunting tapestries, enamel washing bowls, books, carved end tables, silver tableware, musical instruments, gilded mirrors, ceramic bowls and plates, ivory letter openers, wax molds, stained glass lamps, lace doilies—the list is endless. The museum's magnificent Victorian and Edwardian buildings also contain a particularly exquisite glass gallery, with a stunning glass staircase; an amazing silver gallery full of superbly made artifacts in precious metal; the Canon Photography Gallery displaying the museum's wonderful collection of photographs from the 19th and 20th centuries; and the famous dress collection that even includes mod suits and Naomi Campbell's platform shoes. The docent tours are great; phone for departure times.

LONdON'S SPECiAL-iNtEREST MUSEUMS

A–C

- **Alexander Fleming Laboratory Museum**

St. Mary's Hospital, Praed St., W2. Tel. 0171/886-6528.

The laboratory in which penicillin was discovered.

- **Architecture Centre**

66 Portland Place, W1. Tel. 0171/307 3699.

A half-million drawings from 1520 to the present day.

- **Bank of England Museum**

Bartholomew Lane, EC2. Tel. 0171/601-5545.

History from its foundation in 1694 to its role today as the nation's central bank.

- **BBC Experience**

Broadcasting House Portland Place, W1. Tel. 0870/603-0304.

Studios, archives and plenty of hands-on displays about radio and television.

- **Bethnal Green Museum of Childhood**

Cambridge Heath Rd., E2. Tel. 0181/980-2415.

Branch of the V&A with toys, costumes and nursery antiques.

- **Bramah Tea and Coffee Museum**

The Clove Building, Maguire St., SE1. Tel. 0171/378-0222.

Charting 350 years of history in teapots, traditions and associated paraphernalia.

- **Building Centre**

26 Store St., WC1. Tel. 0171/692 1022 ext. 4000.

Largest display of building products in Europe.

- **Cabaret Mechanical Theatre**

33/34 The Market, Covent Garden, WC2. Tel. 0171/379-7961.

The most important collection of contemporary automata in England.

- **Canada House Gallery**

Trafalgar Square, SW1. Tel. 0171/258 6600.

Cultural centre promoting Canadian music, films and visual arts, eh.

- **Centre for the Magic Arts**

12 Stephenson Way, NW1. Tel. 0171/ 387-2222.

Museum of magic and meetinghouse for magicians.

- **Chelsea Physic Garden**

66 Royal Hospital Rd., SW3. Tel. 0171/ 352-5646.

Old botanical garden with rare collection of exotic plants, shrubs and trees.

- **Clink Prison Museum**

1 Clink St. Bankside, SE1. Tel. 0171/ 403-6515.

Gloomy former prison with exhibits on medieval punsihments and torture.

- **Clock Museum**

Guildhall Library, Aldermanbury, EC2. Tel. 0171/ 332-1865.

Single room with 600 old watches, 30 clocks and 15 marine timekeepers.

National Portrait Gallery

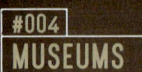
• **Darwin Museum** (Down House) Luxted Road Downe, Orpington, Kent. Tel. 01689/859119. Original manuscripts and belongings of the famous naturalist and author of *On the Origin of the Species*.

• **Estorick Collection of Modern Italian Art** Canonbury Square, N1. Tel. 0171/704-9522. 20th-century paintings and sculpture by Italian artists.

• **Fan Museum** 12 Crooms Hill, SE10. Tel. 0181/305-1441. One of the world's finest collections of hand-held fans.

• **Freud Museum** 20 Maresfield Gardens, NW3. Tel. 0171/435-2002. The psychoanalyst's London filled with his papers, collection of antiquities and furniture.

• **Fuller Smith & Turner plc** Griffin Brewery, Chiswick Lane South, W4. Tel. 0181/996-2175. London's only public brewery tour.

• **Geffrye Museum** Kingsland Rd., E2. Tel. 0171/739-9893. English domestic interiors from 1600 to the present day in a series of period rooms.

• **Golden Hinde Museum** St. Mary Overie Dock, Cathedral St., SE1. Tel. 0171/403-0123. Full-scale reconstruction of Sir Francis Drake's world-famous sailing galleon.

• **Golders Green Crematorium** Hoop Lane, NW11. Tel. 0181/455-2374. The city's first crematorium with the remains of many famous Londoners.

• **Guards Museum** Wellington Barracks Birdcage Walk, SW1. Tel. 0171/414-3428 Uniforms and artifacts from 300 years of the Queen's Foot Guards.

• **Highgate Cemetery** Swain's Lane, N6. Tel. 0181/340-1834. Strange, overgrown cemetery includes the tomb of Karl Marx.

• **HMS Belfast** Morgan's Lane, Tooley St., SE1. Tel. 0171/940-6300. World War II cruiser, now a floating naval museum.

• **House of Detention** Clerkenwell Close, Clerkenwell Green, EC1. Tel. 0171/ 253-9494. Stupid tour on the site of one of London's earliest prisons.

• **Linley Sambourne House** 18 Stafford Terrace, W8. Tel. 0181/994 -019. asdf. Home of chief political cartoonist of Punch, filled with cartoons, pictures and photographs.

• **London Canal Museum** 12/13 New Wharf Rd., N1. Tel. 0171/ 713-0836. Commercial and social history of the canals and waterways of southeast England.

• **London Fire Brigade Museum** Southwark Bridge Rd., SE1. Tel. 0171/ 587-2894. Fire service appliances, equipment, and memorabilia dating back to the 16th century.

• **London Planetarium** Marylebone Rd., NW1. Tel. 0171/935 6861. Star shows and a virtual reality trip through space.

- **London's Museum of Jewish Life**
80 East End Rd., N3. Tel. 0181/ 349-1143.
Traces Jewish immigration and settlement in London.
- **London Toy and Model Museum**
21-23 Craven Hill, W2. Tel. 0171/ 706-8000.
Over 20 themed galleries of trains, dolls, working models and a miniature steam railway.
- **London Transport Museum**
Covent Garden Piazza, WC2. Tel. 0171/379-6344.
Buses, trams and trains of old.
- **Marx Memorial Library**
37A Clerkenwell Green, EC1. Tel. 0171/ 253-1485.
Over 100,000 books, pamphlets and periodicals connected with Marxism and labor movements.
- **Museum of Instruments**
Royal College of Music, Prince Consort Rd., SW7. Tel. 0171/589-3643.
Keyboard, string and wind instruments from the 16th to 19th centuries.
- **Museum of Rugby**
Rugby Rd., Twickenham, TW1, Middlesex. Tel. 0181/892 8877.
The history of rugby includes tours of the dressing rooms, player's tunnel and stadium.
- **National Army Museum**
Royal Hospital Rd. Chelsea, SW3. Tel. 0171/730 0717.
The British Army's own propaganda through five centuries.
- **National Maritime Museum**
Romney Rd., SE10. Tel. 0181/858 4422.
Tracing Britain's worldwide influence through its explorers, traders, migrants and naval power.
- **Old Operating Theatre**
Museum and Herb Garret, 9A St. Thomas' St., SE1. Tel. 0171/955-4791.
The only 19thC operating room in England, with exhibits on surgery and herbal medicine.

- **Percival David Foundation of Chinese Art**
53 Gordon Square, WC1. Tel. 0171/ 387-3909.
1,700 Chinese ceramics from the Song, Yuan, Ming and Qing dynasties.
- **Peter Pan Gallery**
Great Ormond Street Hospital, WC1. Tel. 0171/405-9200. ext. 5920.
Small collection relating to Peter Pan and his creator, J.M. Barrie.
- **Petrie Museum of Egyptian Archaeology**
University College, Malet Place, WC1. Tel. 0171/504-2884.
Huge collection of ancient Egyptian artifacts showing the development of culture and technology.
- **Photographers' Gallery**
5-8 Great Newport St., WC2. Tel. 0171/ 831 1772.
Britain's leading center for contemporary photography.
- **Pollock's Toy Museum**
1 Scala St., W1.
Tel. 0171/636-3452.
Dolls, dolls' houses, toy theaters, teddy bears, tintoys and folk toys from around the world.
- **Royal Air Force Museum**
Grahame Park Way, NW9. Tel. 0181/205-2266.
Over 70 full-sized aircraft, a Flight Simulator, and related high-tech toys.

- **Royal College of Surgeons**
  35-43 Lincoln's Inn Fields, WC2. Tel. 0171/973-2190.
  Historical medical instruments and specimens.
- **Royal London Hospital Archives and Museum**
  Whitechapel, E1. Tel. 0171/377-7608.
  The history of the Royal London Hospital and the development of medicine in the East End.
- **Royal Mint Sovereign Gallery**
  7 Grosvenor Gardens, SW1. Tel. 0171/592 8601.
  Everything you ever wanted to know about the famous gold coin.
- **Shakespeare's Globe Theatre**
  New Globe Walk, Bankside, SE1. Tel. 0171/902-1400.
  Dioramas, graphics, videos and models tell the story of Shakespeare's workplace.
- **Sherlock Holmes Museum**
  221B Baker St., NW1. Tel.0171/935-8866.
  The fictious Holmes' apartment is on first floor; Doctor Watson's room is on second floor.
- **Soseki Museum in London**
  80b The Chase, SW4. Tel. 0171/720-8718.
  Everything you every wanted to know about the celebrated Japanese novelist Soseki Natsume.
- **Theatre Museum**
  Russell St., WC2. Tel. 0171/836-7891.
  The history of performance in the UK including theater, ballet, dance, puppetry, rock and pop.
- **Wesley's Chapel, House and Museum of Methodism**
  49 City Rd., EC1. Tel. 0171/253-2262.
  John Wesley's House traces the history of Methodism from the 18th century to the present day.
- **William Morris Gallery**
  Lloyd Park, Forest Rd., E17. Tel. 0181/527-3782.
  Boyhood home of artist William Morris with a permanent exhibition on his life and work.
- **Wimbledon Lawn Tennis Museum**
  Church Rd., Wimbledon, SW19. Tel. 0181/946-6131.
  Tour of the All England Tennis Club's grounds and trophies.
- **Winston Churchill's Britain at War Experience**
  64-66 Tooley St., SE1. Tel. 0171/403-3171.
  Theme museum about Britain's home front during World War II.

OTHER MAJOR COLLECTIONS & EXHIBITION SPACES

The British Library

96 Euston Rd., NW1. Tel. 0171/412-7000. Open Mon & Thurs 930am-6pm, Tues-Wed 930am-8pm, Fri-Sat 930am-5pm. Tube: Kings Cross/St. Pancras. Opened in 1998, the British Library houses the National Library of the United Kingdom and is the world's foremost warehouse of works on paper housing over 18 million bound books and periodicals, 2.1 million cartographic items, 1.6 million music scores, 39.4 million patent specifications, and 8.1 milllion philatelic items. Three exhibition galleries feature rotatating displays of the Library's immense holdings. Many of the written world's most valuable works are here, including a 4th Century vellum manuscript of the Bible, the *Harley Gold Gospels*, written entirely in gold at the court of Charlemagne around 800, and the *Lindisfarne Gospels*, written and illuminated around 698 in a Northumbrian Island monastery. Other treasures include a Gutenberg Bible (c1455), the first Western printed book using movable type; Shakespeare's First Folio of 1623; Columbus's letter to Queen Isabela of Spain announcing his discovery of America; and the *Magna Carta*, King John's 1215 guarantee of human rights, displayed alongside the royal stamp with which he sealed it. And there are lots of examples of ancient scrolls and manuscripts from around the world on paper, papyrus, vellum and palm leaves. Many of the documents are scanned into computers, so visitors can "turn the pages." The map collection includes over 50,000 charts and plans of North America from King George IIIs personal library.

Courtauld Gallery

Courtauld Institute of Art, Somerset House, Strand, WC2. Tel. 0171/873-2526. Open Mon-Sat 10am-6pm (last admission 515pm), Sun and some Bank Hols 2-6pm. Closed Easter Weekend, 24-27 Dec, 1 Jan. Admission: £4 adults, £2 students/seniors/children under 18. Tube: Embankment/Charing Cross/Temple (not Sun). Where do you go to see the finest collection of Impressionist paintings in Britain? To the Courtauld, that's where. Here, masterpieces by Botticelli, Cézanne, Tiepolo, Rubens and Goya are housed in one of the most beautiful 18th-century buildings in London. The emphasis on quality rather than quantity makes this collection of impressionists and post-impressionists the best in Europe. Masterpieces include Manet's *Bar at the Folies-Bergeres*, Van Gogh's *Self Portrait with a Bandaged Ear* and Renoir's *La Loge*. The newly restored building, which includes a new Early Renaissance Gallery and a gallery for exhibitions of the Courtauld's collection of old master prints and drawings, makes quite an impression too. The Gilbert Collection of silver, gold and mosaics, one of the most important art collections ever to have been given to Britain, opened in Somerset House at the end of 1999. Assembled in California over the past 35 years by English-born real estate developer Arthur Gilbert, the collection is installed in a new £75 million gallery.

Design Museum

Shad Thames, SE1. Tel. 0171-401-2636. Open daily 1130-6pm (last admission 530pm). Closed 25 and 26 Dec. Admission: £5.25 adults, £4 students/seniors/children 5-18. Tube: Tower Hill. Wheelchair access.

Art and commerce collide in this terrific museum, in which contemporary icons from a Coke bottle to an Austin Mini car are raised to high art. The international collection includes cars, furniture, domestic appliances and cameras. There's also a great graphic design gallery, displaying some of the world's best new works on paper. Temporary shows have focused on everything from vacuum cleaners to Porsche cars. The museum is situated on the South Bank, east of Tower Bridge, and includes Terence Conran's **Blue Print Cafe** (tel. 0171/378-7031), a good restaurant with a great view and outdoor waterfront dining in summer.

Institute of Contemporary Arts

Nash House, The Mall, SW1. Tel. 0171/930-3647. Open daily noon-7pm. Closed 23 Dec-1 Jan. Admission: £1.50 adults, £1 students/seniors, free to children under 14. Tube: Piccadilly Circus/Charing Cross. Wheelchair access.

ICA has been a vanguard of contemporary art since its inception in 1948. Its mandate is to show the best new art and, happily, it often does. The Institute was the first major London gallery to give space to Pablo Picasso, Max Ernst, and even local badboy Damien Hirst. There is no permanent collection. ICA's trio of galleries present frequently changing exhibitions that often invite controversy. But as any follower of the contemporary scene knows, you have to wade through a lot of crap to find the artistic gems. The fine arts are complimented by a wide range of performance events, and avant films screened in two cinemas. It's all housed in an elegant Regency building, between Buckingham Palace and Trafalgar Square. There's a good cafe serving light Italian meals throughout the day, and a bar that stays open most weekends until 1am.

Museum of London

150 London Wall, EC2. Tel. 0171/600-3699. Open Mon-Sat 10am-550pm, Sun noon-550pm. Closed 24-26 Dec and 1 Jan. Admission: £5 adults, £3 students/seniors/children 5-17, £9.50 family ticket (2 adults + 3 children); Free to all daily after 430pm. Tube: St. Paul's/Barbican. Wheelchair access.

History buffs, and those who love them, stroll these galleries following two millennia of local lore, from prehistoric times to the present day. Built on the site of a two-thousand-year-old Roman fort, the museum encompasses fine and decorative arts, as well as items of social and civic significance. Galleries are in chronological order, but each is self-contained so that you can start at any period and understand the whole story. Exhibits include a marble head of Mithras (discovered in a nearby Roman

temple), a model of old London Bridge (the real one is now in Lake Havasu, Arizona, U.S.A.), a glittering hoard of Elizabethan jewellery, reconstructed Victorian shops, a grizzly cell from Newgate Prison, and the Lord Mayor's ornate 1756 coach, which is still used each November in the Lord Mayor's Show (*see* Chapter 11/When to Go). The Great Fire Experience depicts the enormous blaze in 1666 that destroyed more than three quarters of the city , including many of its churches and St. Paul's Cathedral.

Museum of the Moving Image

South Bank, SE1. Tel. 0171/928-3535. Open daily 10am-6pm, (last admission 5pm). Closed 24-26 Dec. Admission: £6.25 adults, £5.25 students/seniors, £4.50 children 5-16, £17 family ticket (2 adults + 2 children). Tube: Waterloo/Embankment (cross Hungerford footbridge). Wheelchair access.

MoMI is an unusually fun place devoted to the magic of cinema and television. Lots of the exhibits are interactive experiences related to motion picture sound and editing. And there are lots of hands-on displays detailing the technical wizardry of a modern TV studio. Chronologically arranged exhibits are staffed by costumed actors who never step out of c haracter. The museum itself is as entertaining as a top movie. Displays strike the perfect balance between technology and the culture it produced. You can watch Russian movies on a agitprop train, create your own animated strips for a zoetrope, read the news from a teleprompter, then watch yourself on a monitor, and "fly" over London using chromakey technology. There are also regular demonstrations of digital imaging and morphing. Famous costumes, ancient cameras, cool props, studio stills, and a new IMAX cinema round out the offerings. The emphasis here is on things British, but MOMI's extraordinarily popular slant is right out of Hollywood.

National Portrait Gallery

St. Martin's Place, WC2. Tel. 0171/306-0055. Open Mon-Sat 10am-6pm, Sun noon-6pm. Closed 24-26 Dec, 1 Jan, May Day. Admission free (except for some special exhibitions). Tube: Charing Cross/Leicester Square. Wheelchair access.

Nobody likes a portrait as much as the British, and this large museum proves it. Likenesses of famous and infamous British men and women, from the Tudors to the present day, are depicted in oil, watercolor, sculpture and drawings. Founded in 1856, the museum is something of a repository for centuries of British social history. The likenesses of poets and princesses, sportsmen and statesmen are all on display (Margaret Thatcher and Tony Blair included). The galleries are full of fabulous faces: Keats, Jane Austen, Charles Darwin, Stephen Hawking... and—oh yeah—there are plenty of Royals too. Hits include a portrait by Holbein of King Henry VIII, the only known portrait of William Shakespeare, Queen Elizabeth by Andy Warhol, and the best-known painting of Princess Diana, commissioned by the Royal Family.

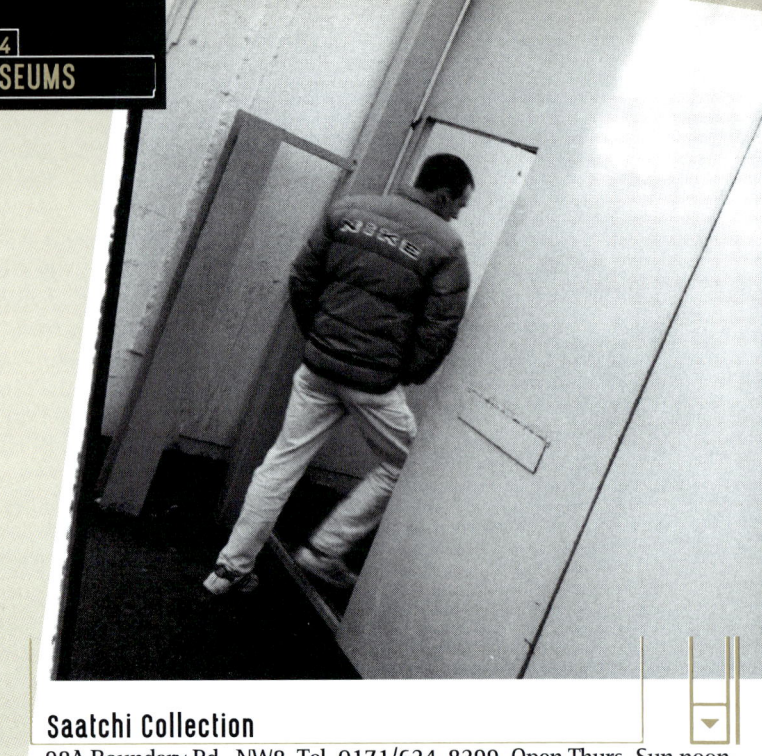

Saatchi Collection

98A Boundary Rd., NW8. Tel. 0171/624-8299. Open Thurs–Sun noon–6pm on exhibition days. Admission £4 adults; £2 students/seniors. Tube: St. John's Wood.

Britain's largest private collector of contemporary art purpose-built this gallery to house rotating displays from his vast and brilliant holdings. Although Saatchi collects international art, the focus here is largely on YbA's (young British artists). Exhibits here have included Damien Hirst's animals in formaldahyde, Marc Quinn's *Frozen Head*, cast from nine pints of his own blood, and Richard Wilson's installation of 2,500 gallons of used sump oil, which flooded an entire gallery. In short, one of the city's best museums.

Sir John Soane's Museum

13 Lincoln's Inn Fields, WC2. Tel. 0171/430-0175. Open Tue-Sat 10am-5pm; also first Tues of every month 6-9pm. Closed Good Fri, Easter Sun and Mon, 24-26 Dec, 1 Jan and Bank Hols. Admission free (except for some special exhibitions). Tube: Holborn.

Sir John Soane was not only one of London's greatest architects, he was a wealthy art collector with a keen eye, an open wallet, and more than a bit of eccentricity. Soane's former residence is now home to over 20,000 architectural drawings, a fantastic array of archeological antiquities (Egyptian sarcophagus included), and hundreds of oils, including works by Hogarth, Turner, Watteau, and Canaletto. It's absolutely jam-packed with goodies. In the small room where Hogarth's *The Rake's Progress* is displayed, ask the guard to show you the room's secret. You'll be convinced that there's a method to the madness.

Wallace Collection

Hertford House, Manchester Square, W1. Tel. 0171/935-0687. Open Mon–Sat 10am–5pm, Sun 2–5pm. Closed Good Fri, May Day, 24–26 Dec and 1 Jan. Admission free. Tube: Bond Street/Baker Street. Wheelchair access.

Bequeathed to the nation in 1897, this fabulous collection and even more marvelous home is a fantastic haven of art and antiques, just steps from Oxford Street. The permanent collection includes European paintings, miniatures and sculpture, as well as 18th-century French furniture, porcelain, goldsmiths' work, and oriental and European arms and armor. There's a small collection of oils by Rembrandt, Rubens, Murillo, and van Dyck too. Four new galleries are due to be completed in the summer of 2000, when the Wallace Collection will be designated a National Museum.

Hayward Gallery

Southbank Centre, Belvedere Rd., SE1. Tel. 0171/928-3144, or 0171/261-0127 for recorded message. Open during exhibitons only, Mon and Thurs–Sun 10am–6pm, Tue–Wed 10am–8pm. Closed 24–26 Dec and 1 Jan. Admission: £6 adults, £4 students/seniors/children under 12. Tube: Embankment/Waterloo. Wheelchair access.

The Hayward Gallery has been the originator or host of many of the world's most influential exhibitions of contemporary and historical art. There's usually something good happening. Cross your fingers and call.

Alexander Fleming Laboratory Museum

St. Mary's Hospital, Praed St., W2. Tel. 0171/886-6528. Open Mon-Thurs 10am-1pm. Closed Bank Hols, 24-26 Dec, New Year's Day, Easter Weekend. Admission: £2 adults, £1 students/seniors/children 5-16. Tube: Paddington/Edgware Road.

Alexander Fleming discovered penicillin in 1928, begining the antibiotic age and revolutionizing medicine. His small laboratory in St. Mary's Hospital has been restored to its original appearance strewn with petri dishes, old microscopes, flasks, beakers, open books and test tubes. Other displays tell the stories of the wonder drug, and the man who pursued it.

Apsley House (Wellington Museum)

149 Piccadilly, Hyde Park Corner, W1. Tel. 0171/499-5676. Open Tue-Sun 11am-5pm (last admission 430pm). Closed Bank Hols, 24-26 Dec, New Year's Day, May Day. Admission: £4.50 adults, £3 students/seniors/children 12-17. Tube: Hyde Park Corner.

Built for Lord Apsley in the 1770s, and sold to the first Duke of Wellington in 1817, this house was known in the 18th century as "Number One London" because it was the first mansion one encountered when entering the city through the old Knightsbridge toll gate. The Duke of Wellington, as we are sure you know, was the victor over Napoleon at Waterloo, and, later, Prime Minister of England. His palatial, grandly restored house overlooks the north side of Hyde Park Corner, and is filled with the Duke's own collection of masters paintings, and priceless porcelain, silver, sculpture, and antique furniture. Gifted to the nation, and administered by the V&A Museum, it's an amazing palace, full of art by Goya, Velasquez, Rubens, Brueghel, and the like. Many of the items on display are spoils of war, or expensive gifts that, if accepted by a politician today, would constitute a serious breach of ethics. One standout is the Sēvres Egyptian tableware originally commissioned by Napoleon for the Empress Josephine.

Association Gallery

81 Leonard St., EC2. Tel. 0171/739-6669. Open Sept-Jun, Mon-Fri 930am-6pm; Sat noon-4pm. Closed July-Aug. Admission free. Tube: Barbican/Old Street.

One of the city's top photography galleries focuses on contemporary professional British photographers. It's in a great new space too.

Architecture Centre—Royal Institute of British Architects

66 Portland Place, W1. Tel. 0171/307-3699. Open
Mon, Wed, Fri and Sat 8am-6pm, Tues and Thurs
8am-9pm. Admission free. Tube: Regent's Park/Great
Portland Street/Oxford Circus. Wheelchair access.
The home of the British Architectural Library displays
rotating exhibitions of architectural design and sculpture
culled from their extensive collections. There are well
over a half-million drawings from 1520 to the present
day, including drawings by Andrea Palladio, Inigo
Jones and Frank Lloyd Wright, encompassing
everything from simple plans to complex elevations.

Bank of England Museum

Bartholomew Lane, EC2. Tel. 0171/601-5545. Open Mon-Fri 10am-5pm. Closed Bank Hols. Admission free. Tube: Bank. Wheelchair access.

Housed within the Bank of England, this museum traces the history of the Bank from its foundation by Royal Charter in 1694 to its role today as the nation's central bank. The exquisite, neo-classical museum itself is reason enough to go. It's a historical landmark, designed in the late 18th century by Sir John Soane, one of London's best-known architects. The exhibition is good too. There's a large collection of coins and banknotes, gold bars dating from Roman times, and documents relating to famous customers including Horatio Nelson and George Washington. Computer-based exhibits tackle contemporary issues, like dealing in foreign exchange.

BBC Experience

Broadcasting House, Portland Place, W1. Tel. 0870/603-0304. Open Mon 1-430pm, Tue-Fri 10am-430pm, Sat-Sun 930am-430pm. Closed 25 Dec. Admission: £7 adults, £6 students/seniors, £5 children under 16. Tube: Oxford Circus/Great Portland Street.

The BBC Experience is London's answer to a Hollywood studio tour. Small groups of visitors are guided through Broadcasting House, and shown how the Beeb operates. Allow about two hours for visit.

Bethnal Green Museum of Childhood

Cambridge Heath Rd., E2. Tel. 0181/980-2415. Open Mon-Thurs and Sat 10am-550pm, Sun 230-550pm. Closed 24-26 Dec and 1 Jan. Admission free. Tube: Bethnal Green.

All of the holdings at the Victoria and Albert Museum relating to childhood have been spun off into this East End museum. The collections are typially extensive, and include games, dolls, puppets, children's clothes, nursery antiques, and one of the largest toy collections in the world. The best displays are the numerous doll's houses; spectacular miniatures that date from the 17th century. There are special children's activities on Saturdays and holidays.

Bramah Tea and Coffee Museum

The Clove Building, Maguire St., SE1. Tel. 0171/378-0222.
Open daily 10am-6pm. Closed 25-26 Dec. Admission:
£4 adults, £2.50 students/seniors/children under 14, £8
family ticket (2 adults + 4 children). Tube: Tower
Hill/London Bridge. Wheelchair access.

A hallowed shrine to England's national drink, the Bramah
Museum charts 350 years of social and commercial history
that is inextricably intertwined with expansionism and
Empire. Coffeehouses were the cultural clubs of
yestercentury, giving rise to such establishments as
Lloyd's Insurance and the London Stock Exchange.
Packed with informative displays on production
and trade, the museum appeals equally to
academics and caffine addicts. There are
records from the era of the Boston Tea
Party, but the best exhibits are the 1,000-
plus tea and coffee pots, and
extensive packaging displays.

Cabaret Mechanical Theatre

33/34 The Market, Covent Garden, WC2. Tel. 0171/379-7961. Open Mon-Sat 10am-630pm, Sun 11am-630pm. Closed 25-26, 31 Dec and 1 Jan. Admission: £1.95 adults, £1.20 students/ seniors/children 5-16, £4.95 family ticket (2 adults + 4 children). Tube: Covent Garden.

Cabaret Mechanical Theatre is a fancy name for a penny arcade; something of a living necropolis for arcade games of yore. The museum's got about a hundred fascinating mechanical contraptions from the beginning of the last century, all modified to account for inflation (bring plenty of 10p coins). Amongst the usual fortune-telling gypsy and dancing chicken machines you'll find lots of early kinescopes, a cast-iron wizard that rates your sexual prowess, and moving miniature scenes of "The Drunkard's Dream," "In the Sultan's Harem," and "The Opium Den." The Museum is located in the cellar of Covent Garden Market.

Canada House Gallery

Canada House Cultural Centre, Trafalgar Square, SW1. Tel. 0171/258-6600. Open Mon-Fri 10am-6pm. Closed Jan-Apr. Admission free. Tube: Charing Cross.

One of the biggest benefits to Canada for being part of the British Empire is that it got this prime piece of Trafalgar Square real estate. While the Canadian Cultural Center is busy promoting its country's hockey players and freezing winds, its full-time gallery is showcasing some of the nation's best painting, sculpture, crafts, technology, music and film.

Clink Prison Museum

1 Clink St., SE1. Tel. 0171/403-6515. Open daily 10am-6pm (winter), 10am-9pm (summer). Closed 25 Dec and 1 Jan. Admission: £4 adults, £3 students/seniors/children 5-16, £9 family ticket (max 4 people). Tube: London Bridge. Wheelchair access.

The prison that gave its name to all others is a dark, dank place that once catered to debtors, hookers, religious dissenters and other enemies of its owner, the Bishop of Winchester—who also controlled the surrounding bear fighting rings, playhouses and brothels. Inside are some original cells and torture instruments, as well as exhibits on local history, medieval punsihments and prostitution. Ironically, the gloomy, rock-walled dungeon also rents itself out for private hire for weddings, birthdays and conferences. It would make a great S&M party.

Clock Museum

Guildhall Library, Aldermanbury, EC2. Tel. 0171/332-1865. Open Mon-Fri 930am-445pm (except 1 hour on Mon mornings (11am-noon) for rewinding). Closed Bank Hols. Admission free. Tube: Bank/St. Paul's.

Show up on the hour and you'll have no trouble

locating the Clock Museum. It's a great one-room museum, displaying the collection of the Worshipful Company of Clockmakers, an old workers guild that owns the oldest horology collection in the world. Displays rotate, but usually include some 600 watches, clocks and marine chronometers, most of which are several hundred years old. Hits include a starshaped watch made in 1625 for King Farouk of Egypt, the first electrical clock, and a mid-19th Century clock designed to rewind itself by manufacturing highly explosive hydrogen gas.

Darwin Museum (Down House)

Luxted Road Downe, Orpington, Kent. Tel. 01689/859119. Open Apr-Oct, Wed-Sun 10am-6pm; Nov-Mar, Wed-Sun 10am-4pm. Closed 24-25 Dec. Admission: £5 adults, £3.80 students/seniors, £2.50 children 5-15. Rail: Bromley South, then bus 146 to Downe or Orpington, then bus R2 to house.

The common image of Charles Darwin is as a wise, bearded old man. But when the naturalist was on the *HMS Beagle*, he was a young man in his twenties, enjoying a once-in-a-lifetime trip to the South Atlantic collecting things. Down House, Darwin's home from 1842 to 1882, displays a collection of original manuscripts and belongings of the famous naturalist and author of *On the Origin of Species by Means of Natural Selection.* The best room is the Old Study, in which Darwin did most of his scientific work. Original furniture is in the usual places. In the back garden is the Worm Stone, on which Darwin would study how long it took for worms to unearth stuff. Phone before heading out for exact diretions and transport times.

Dulwich Picture Gallery

College Rd., SE21. Tel. 0181/693-5254. Open Tues-Fri 10am-5pm, Sat 11am-5pm, Sun 2-5pm. Closed Bank Hol Mon, 10 and 13 Apr, 24-26 Dec. Admission: £3 adults, £1.50 students/seniors/children under 16. Tube: Brixton, then bus 3, 37, P4. Wheelchair access.

One of the country's best collections of Master paintings is stashed in a quiet village, four miles south of Piccadilly Circus. Designed by celebrity architect Sir John Soane in 1811, the neoclassical museum was Britain's first purpose-built gallery, a disparate showcase for some of the best works of Poussin, Claude, Rubens, Rembrandt, Van Dyck, Teniers, Gainsborough, Murillo and Canaletto. An adjacent mausoleum is an eerie showcase for the sarcophagi of the museum's founders. There's usually a good temporary exhibition going on too. Phone before heading out for exact directions and transport times.

Estorick Collection of Modern Italian Art

39A Canonbury Square, N1. Tel. 0171/704-9522. Open Wed-Sat 11am-6pm, Sun noon-5pm. Closed 24 Dec-5 Jan, Good Fri. Admission: £2.50 adults, £1.50 students/seniors. Tube: Highbury and Islington. For all the Modern Italian art aficionados out there, the Estorick Collection delivers with an interesing collection of paintings and sculpture by 20th-century Italians. While the lion's share of space is given over to Futurist works by Balla, Boccioni, Carra, Russolo and Severini, there are also a few figurative pieces by artists such as Modigliani, Marino Marini, Giorgio Morandi and Giorgio de Chirico.

The Collection is housed in a pretty Georgian villa that also includes a summer garden cafe serving alfresco lunches.

Freud Museum

20 Maresfield Gardens, NW3. Tel. 0171/435-2002. Open Wed–Sun noon–5pm. Telephone for Easter and Christmas hours. Admission: £4 adults, £2 students/seniors/ children under 12. Tube: Finchley Road. Wheelchair access.

Sigmund Freud and his family escaped to London from Nazi-occupied Vienna, and lived here for about a year, until he died in 1939. He brought with him his library papers, his collection of Egyptian, Roman, and Oriental antiquities, and his furniture, including his desk and famous couch—most of which still remains as the Shrink would have known it. Freud's daughter, Anna, continued to live in this rather plain house until her death in 1982, after which the house was turned into a museum and shrine for the inventor of psychoanalysis. Videos shown upstairs include some of Freud's home movies.

Golden Hinde

St. Mary Overie Dock, Cathedral St., SE1. Tel. 0171/403-0123. Telephone for opening times. Admission: £2.30 adults, £1.90 students/seniors, £1.50 children 4–14. Tube: London Bridge.

The *Golden Hinde* is a full-scale reconstruction of Sir Francis Drake's world-famous sailing galleon. The explorer sailed around the world in his triple-masted original, and allegedly claimed California for Queen Elizabeth. This beautiful replica also has a circumnavigation under her belt. It's a small wooden warship, carrying cannon typical of Tudor times. As the crew, dressed in period costume, point the way around the ship's five levels, it's easy to imagine you're peeking through a porthole to another age. It's located on the south side of the Thames, between Southwark and London bridges.

Golders Green Crematorium

Hoop Lane, NW11. Tel. 0181/455-2374. Open Mon–Fri 10am–5pm, Sat–Sun 10am–4pm. Admission free. Tube: Golders Green.

London's first crematorium is one of the city's most unusual "tourist" sights. Extensive columbaria contain the remains of many notable Londoners, from Neville Chamberlain and Sigmund Freud to actor Peter Sellers and rocker Marc Bolan. Cool architecture too. The Crematorium is located off Finchley Road, about five minutes' walk from Golders Green Tube station. Announce yourself at the main office.

Geffrye Museum

Kingsland Rd., E2. Tel. 0171/739-9893. Open Tue-Sat
10am-5pm, Sun and Bank Hol Mon 2-5pm. Closed Good
Fri, 24-26 Dec, 1 Jan. Admission free. Tube: Liverpool
Street, then bus 149 or 242 or 15-minutes' walk.

Named for a former Lord Mayor of London who partially
funded it, the Geffrye Museum is a local ethnographic
museum, depicting city life from Elizabethan times to the
present day. Untiring in size, it conveniently threads the
interior design styles of over 400 years into an easily
digestable hour-long tour. A chronological series of
rooms are set with period furnishings, paintings and
decorative art, reflecting tastes and styles of urban middle
classes. A recent infusion of cash has added several new
20th Century rooms, as well as a temporary exhibitions
gallery, a design centre, a new museum shop and a
decent restaurant.

Highgate Cemetery

Swain's Lane, N6. Tel. 0181/340-1834. Guided tours of East Side, Sat–Sun 11am–3pm; West Side, Mon 10am–4pm, Sat–Sun 11am–3pm. Phone for tour times and prices. Tube: Archway, then about 15 minutes' walk. Wheelchair access.

One of the best cemeteries anywhere, Highgate is a macabre architectural wonderland featuring bizarre Victorian buildings, colonnades, chapels and catacombs. Swain's Lane divides London's Highgate Cemetery in two. The overgrown "Egyptian" West Side is the main draw, but it's accessible only by taking a guided one-hour tour. Access is easier on the East Side, which contains a veritable who's who of famous permanent residents, including George Eliot and Karl Marx, whose grave is marked with a granite bust bearing the famous mantra "Workers of all lands unite." The cemetery is closed to thrill-seekers during funerals, and cameras and young kids are forbidden. Phone for opening times to avoid dissappointment.

HMS Belfast

Morgan's Lane, Tooley St., SE1. Tel. 0171/940-6300. Open daily 10am–5pm (last admission 415pm). Closed 24–26 Dec. Admission: £4.70 adults, £3.60 students/seniors, £2.40 children 5–16, £11.80 family ticket (2 adults + 2 children). Tube: London Bridge. Wheelchair access.

HMS Belfast is Europe's only surviving big gun armoured warship from the Second World War. Now a floating naval museum, the ship offers 9 decks to explore, from the captain's bridge to the engine rooms. Commissioned just one month before the outbreak of World War II, the ship began service guarding Russian convoys, then supported the Allied landings on D-Day before moving on to the Korean War.

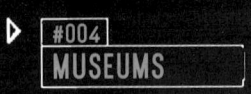

Jewel Tower

Abingdon St., SW1. Tel. 0171/222-2219. Open 22 Mar-Sept, daily 10am-6pm; Oct-Mar, daily 10am-4pm (last admission 1 hour before closing). Closed 24-26 Dec. Admission: £1.50 adults, £1.10 students/seniors, 80p children 5-16. Tube: Westminster.

Built by King Edward III to store his personal jewels and wardrobe, this moated tower now houses an exhibition tracing the history of English parliaments from their origins to the present day. For us, the tower itself is the main draw; it's one of two surviving parts of the original medieval Palace of Westminster, which is today's Houses of Parliament. The Items on display include the Speaker's robes from the collection of Houses of Parliament and an interactive touch screen computer giving a virtual reality tour of both Houses of Parliament.

Jewish Museum-Camden

Raymond Burton House, 129-131 Albert St., NW1. Tel. 0171/284-1997. Open Sun-Thurs 10am-4pm (last entry 315pm). Closed Jewish Hols, Bank Hols, 25-26 Dec and 1 Jan. Admission: £3 adults, £1.50 students/seniors/children under 16, £7.50 family ticket (2 adults + 2 children). Tube: Camden Town, then 3 minutes walk. Wheelchair access.

The elegant premises of the Jewish Museum houses exhibits related to the history of Jews in Britain, and galleries filled with ceremonial art and objects recovered from Eastern Europe. Highlights include a 16th Century Italian synagogue ark, silver Torah bells made in London, and two cups that were presented by the Spanish and Portuguese Synagogue to London's Lord Mayor in the 18th Century.

Kensington Palace State Apartments

Kensington Gardens, W8. Tel. 0181/781-9540. Open Mid-Mar to mid-Oct, daily 10am-5pm, last tour 330pm; mid-Oct to mid-Mar, open Wed-Sun 10am-3pm. Admission £7.50. Tube: High Street Kensington.

The second most important royal residence in London (after Buckingham Palace), Kensington Palace has been home to princes and princesses for over a hundred years. Princess Diana lived here, as did several future queens, from Mary II and her sister, Anne, to Victoria who, on June 20, 1837 was awakened with the news of her accession to the throne following the death of her uncle William IV. As you might expect, the palace was decorated by some of England's finest artisans, and is filled with artwork by some of Europe's best-known painters and sculptors. Most of the rooms in which state functions are held are so ornately embellished that hardly an inch of wall or ceiling remains unadorned. It would be gaudy, except that this is the real McCoy. The tour peeks into the in-house tailor's and dressmaker's workshop, and includes a visit to the Royal Ceremonial Dress Collection, a fashion museum that includes a century's worth of royal dresses right up to the wedding gowns worn by Diana, Fergie and Sophie. There's plenty of precious jewellery too, much of which is from Cartier's Antique Collection.

Leighton House Museum and Art Gallery

12 Holland Park Rd., W14. Tel. 0171/602-3316. Open Mon-Sat 11am-530pm. Closed Bank Hols, 24-26 Dec, 1 Jan. Admission free. Tube: High Street Kensington.

The former home of Lord Leighton, a classical Victorian painter, was built in the late 19th Century in the center of what was then a burgeoning artists' colony adjacent to Holland Park. Unlike many of his fellow artists, however, Leighton was also fabulously wealthy. The centerpeice of his extravagant house is Arab Hall, an Arabian Nights-themed room that's covered from floor-to-ceiling with fantastic Islamic tiles. The artist's studio is filled with lots of works by top pre-Raphaelites, put there to inspire his own work, and the rest of the house is richly decorated with paintings, drawings and sculpture from the Arts and Crafts movement.

London Planetarium

Marylebone Rd., NW1. Tel. 0171/935-6861. Star shows: Mon-Fri at 1220pm then every 40 minutes until 5pm, Sat-Sun and during school hols 1020am-5pm. Admission: £5.85 adults, £4.50 seniors, £3.85 children 5-15. Tube: Baker Street. Wheelchair access.

If you haven't been to a star show since grade school, this is the one to visit. London Planetarium features one of the world's most advanced projectors, and the performance itself is state-of-the-art. Because it's connected to Madame Tussaud's, this is a pop-oriented performance that often plays to full houses. Beware the long lines on weekends.

London Transport Museum

39 Well St., Covent Garden, WC2. Tel. 0171/379-6344. Open Sun-Thurs 10am-6pm, Fri 11am-6pm (last admission 515pm). Closed 24-26 Dec. Admission: £4.95 adults, £2.95 students/seniors/children 5-15, £12.85 family ticket (2 adults + 2 children). Tube: Covent Garden. Wheelchair access.

Trains, trams and buses are the centerpieces of this upbeat and intelligent, kid-friendly museum. Sure, you can learn about the history of London transport, but most people come to explore the vehicles and be awed by the engineering. The museum is housed under a lofty cast-iron and glass Victorian building, in the south-east corner of Covent Garden Piazza.

Old Operating Theatre, Museum and Herb Garret

9A St. Thomas' St., SE1. Tel. 0171/955-4791. Open Daily 10am-4pm. Closed 25 Dec. Admission: £2.90 adults, £2 students/seniors, £1.50 children under 16, £7.25 family ticket (2 adults + 3 children). Tube: London Bridge.

If you ever pined for the old days, this restored 1821 hospital operating room will make you think twice. The operating theater is a fascinating glimpse into the past, set in an historic building that housed St. Thomas' Hospital, from the 13thC to 1862. Exhibits tell the story of surgery and herbal medicine. Take the third left at the end of London Bridge into St. Thomas' Street.

Percival David Foundation of Chinese Art

53 Gordon Square, WC1. Tel. 0171/387-3909. Open Mon-Fri 1030am-5pm. Closed Bank Hols, Easter and Christmas to New Year. Admission free (donation requested). Tube: Russell Square/Goodge Street/Euston Square.

The best way to see this fantastic collection of Chinese ceramics is by guided tour, which you should book as soon as you read this. The Foundation's unique collection encompasses 1,700 pieces of pottery, presented to the University of London in 1950 by the late Sir Percival David. The ceramics are mainly from the Song, Yuan, Ming and Qing dynasties, and many were once owned by Chinese emperors. You will never see a finer Chinese vase.

Petrie Museum of Egyptian Archaeology

University College London, Malet Place, WC1. Tel. 0171/504-2884. Open Mon-Fri 10am-noon and 115-5pm. Closed 3 weeks in summer, Easter Weekend, 24 Dec-2Jan. Admission free. Tube: Warren Street/Euston Square/Goodge Street.

If you didn't get enough of ancient Egypt from the British Museum, head to this specialist spot boasting one of the largest and most fascinting collections of Egyptian archaeology anywhere. Over 80,000 artefacts detail the development of Egyptian culture, technology and daily life, from prehistoric to Roman times, and includes a five thousand year old dress, the world's earliest surviving garment. Enter through the DMS Watson Library, in Malet Place off Torrington Place.

Photographers' Gallery

5 & 8 Great Newport St., WC2. Tel. 0171/831 1772. Open Mon-Sat 11am-6pm, Sun noon-6pm. Closed Bank Hols. Admission free. Tube: Leicester Square. Wheelchair access.

Britain's leading center for contemporary photography runs four exhibition spaces, a print sales room, specialist bookshop, library and cafe.

Prince Henry's Room

17 Fleet St., EC4. Tel. 0181/ 294-1158. Open Mon-Sat 11am-2pm. Admission: Free. Tube: Temple.

A pocket-sized, second-floor museum, Prince Henry's Room is situated in an amazing plaster and wood building that was one of the few to survive the Great Fire of 1666. Inside, surrounded by original oak paneling and ceilings, is a fantastic collection of memorabilia relating to Samuel Pepys, a 17th century naval leader who kept extensive diaries from 1660 to 1669. Thanks to his diaries, we know more about Pepys (pronounced "Peeps") than any other 17th century Englishman. Shockingly candid, the writer concealed the contents of his diary by employing his own personal code; a complex mix of foreign and invented words. And as with most diaries, reading this one often feels voyeuristic. Caught in bed with his maid, Pepys wrote that his wife pulled aside the bed curtain and with red hot tongs "made as if she did design to pinch me with them."

Queen's Gallery Buckingham Palace

Buckingham Palace Rd., SW1. Tel. 0171/839-1377. Open daily 930am-430pm (last admission 4pm). Closed 10 Apr, 25-26 Dec. Admission: £4 adults, £3 seniors, £2 children 5-16, £10 family ticket (2 adults + 2 children). Tube: St. James's Park/Victoria.

The Queen's Gallery displays rotating exhibits of the royal family's extensive holdings, offering the public a glimpse of rarely-seen works of art from the Royal Collection. It's a small place, in a building that was once the palace chapel, and recommended only for those who have already familiarized themselves with all pictures in the humongous National Gallery.

Royal Academy of Arts

Burlington House Piccadilly, W1. Tel. 0171/300-8000. Open Sun-Thurs 10am-6pm (last admission 530pm), Fri-Sat 9am-10pm (last admssion 930pm). Closed Good Fri, 25 Dec. Admission depends on current exhibition. Tube: Piccadilly Circus/Green Park. Wheelchair access.

The oldest fine arts society in Great Britain curates several top-notch exhibitions each year. Their permanent collection includes works by Joshua Reynolds (the Society's first President), Turner, Gainsborough and Constable, and a single marble masterpiece by Michaelangelo depicting the Madonna and Child with the Infant St. John; one of only four sculptures by him outside Italy. The Academy building is the last of a half-dozen aristocratic mansions that lined Piccadilly in the mid-seventeenth century.

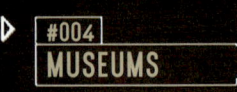
Royal Air Force Museum

Grahame Park Way, Hendon, NW9. Tel. 0181/ 205-2266. Open daily 10am-6pm. Closed 24-26 Dec, 1 Jan. Admission: £6.50 adults, £4.90 seniors, £3.25 students/children 5-16, £16.60 family ticket (2 adults + 2 children). Tube: Colindale. Wheelchair access.

Britain's National Museum of Aviation features over 70 full-sized aircraft, a flight simulator, and a "Touch and Try" Jet Provost Trainer. It's a huge place, with lots of galleries, each of which is dedicated to individual periods of aviation, from the Royal Engineers' balloon experiments in the 1870s to the RAF of today. The endless displays of uniforms, decorations and trophies are strictly for fanatics, but the planes are great and the well-stocked souvenir shop alone is worth the trip to Hendon.

Shakespeare's Globe Theatre Tours and Exhibition

New Globe Walk Bankside, SE1. Tel. 0171/902-1400. Open daily 10am-5pm (hours limited during May-Sept theater season). Closed 24 and 25 Dec. Admission: £6 adults, £5 students/seniors, £3.50 children 5-15, £14 family ticket (2 adults + 3 children). Tube: London Bridge/Mansion House.

Constructed in the 1990s with clay brick, English oak, thatch, and lime plaster, the round Globe Theatre mimics the original 1598 construction of Shakespeare's famous playhouse. The most important theater of the Tudor period, the original Globe was where Shakespeare would spend the majority of his career, staging sixteen of his plays from "As you Like It" to "Pericles." When there is no performance scheduled, specially trained guides detail the colourful history of Elizabethan Bankside and tell the story of the research and determination that allowed the Globe to be rebuilt. Theater performances are held almost daily in summer (see Chapter 9/Stage).

Sherlock Holmes Museum

221B Baker St., NW1. Tel. 0171/935-8866. Open daily 930am-6pm. Closed 25 Dec. Admission: £5 adults, £3 children 8-16. Tube: Baker Street.

Holmes buffs (and they only) will get a kick out of this "museum" dedicated to the fictional sluth. True to the storyline, Holmes' apartment is on first floor, while Mrs. Hudson's room and Doctor Watson's room are on second floor. And what would a place like this be without an extensive souvenir shop on the ground floor?

Thames Flood Barrier

Unity Way, SE18. Tel. 0181/305-4188. Visitor Centre open Mon-Fri 10am-4pm, Sat-Sun 1030am-430pm. Admission £3.40. Closed Christmas week, New Years' Eve. Rail: Charlton.

The Flood Barrier is facinating for engineering geeks, and cool for photographers, but the real reason to visit is because it's a great excuse to take a boat down the Thames. A series of huge, steel, shell-shaped pods are strung across the river to protect London from devastating floods. It's the largest of its kind in the world. There are great views from the Visitors' Centre, in which there are several working scale models and audio-visual displays. Boats to the Barrier depart from Westminster Pier, and take 75 minutes. There are also boats from Greenwich. The nearest rail station is Charlton, followed by a 15-minute walk.

Wimbledon Lawn Tennis Museum

All England Lawn Tennis & Croquet Club, Church Rd., Wimbledon, SW19. Tel. 0181/946-6131. Open Mon-Sat 1030am-5pm, Sun 2-5pm. During Championships only open to those visiting the tournament. Phone for Christmas hours. Admission: £4 adults, £3 students/ seniors/children under 16. Tube: Southfields, then 15 minutes' walk. Wheelchair access.

It makes sense when you think about it: the advent of tennis was inextricably related to the invention of the lawnmower and the rubber ball. Discover this, and more, at the spiritual home of the sport, where you can also see the hallowed turf of the world famous Centre Court, an exhibit on racket-making, and shelves sagging with championship trophies.

Thames Flood Barrier

ThE CitY

The City may be where London began, but these days, only 6,000 people live within the heart of London. Almost from the get-go, the Square Mile, as the City is often called, was the region's main market place and financial center, and it hasn't looked back since. Each morning, a quarter of a million bond traders, stock brokers and insurance marketers roll in to this capitol of capitalism on the Tube. During the day, the district is full of suits with ulcers who battle with tourists for the sidewalks. As five o'clock rolls around, the streets become clogged with chauffeur-driven Town Cars—coveted industry perks—that whisk the money men and women back to suburbia. After dark, The City becomes eerily empty and quiet—except for the odd restaurant or theater performance.

The neighborhood's haphazard tangle of streets harks back to horse-and-carriage days, and several centuries-old structures are still hidden amongst the modern skyscrapers. Chief among these is the ruins of the **Temple of Mithras,** on Queen Victoria Street (Tube: Mansion House) a good place to begin your exploration of The City. Discovered in 1954, when developers were excavating a new building site, the Temple dates from the Third Century, when the Persian cult of Mithraism was at the height of its popularity. In the 4th Century, Rome recognized Christianity as the official religion of the Empire, and pagan temples like this were often destroyed. The temple's sculptures and other artifacts are now on display in the nearby **Museum of London** (*see* Chapter 4/ Other Major Collections & Spaces).

A few blocks away, on Cheapside, is the **Church of St. Mary-Le-Bow** (tel. 0171/248-5139). It's said that an authentic Cockney is one who was born within the sound of Bow Bells. Like most of the buildings surrounding it, the church was scorched in the Great Fire of 1666. Rebuilt by Sir Christopher Wren, the present building was modeled after the Church of the Basilica of Maxentius in Rome. It's 217-foot steeple is widely considered to be Wren's finest. Inside, look up at the capitals atop the support columns. Each features a stone relief of a W.W.II Allied head of state, including Winston Churchill, Charles De Gaulle, and Franklin Roosevelt. Go to the cellar and check out the old Norman Crypt, along with the bowed Norman arches that gave this church its name. It's open Mon-Thurs 730am-6pm, Fri 730am-4pm. Admission is free (Tube: Mansion House, St. Paul's or Bank).

Smithfield Market, on Charterhouse Street (Tube: Farringdon/ St. Paul's) is a spectacular ten-acre, cast-iron Victorian structure housing Europe's largest meat market. Trading in sheep, pigs, cattle, and poultry started here in 1173, but was removed to Islington in the 19th century. Today these saw-dust covered floors cater to the butcher trade exclusively. It's a fascinating place to explore. Trading occurs throughout the night, and wraps up around daybreak.

The Monument, on Monument Street (Tube: Monument), is a tall column built to commemorate the Great Fire of 1666. The fire is believed to have started just one hundred yards away, in Pudding Lane at 2am on September 2, 1666. Four days later, nine-tenths of the city laid in smoke-blackened ruin; 13,200 houses, 87 churches, and 44 livery halls were destroyed. Miraculously, only nine lives were lost. Designed by Sir Christopher Wren, The Monument is a 202-foot-high tower and open to the public. You can climb its 311 stairs for an obstructed view of London's rooftops.

Nearby, a small statue protrudes from a building at the corner of Giltspur Street and Cock Lane. Known as **The Fat Boy**, or Golden Boy, it was erected by the City of London along with a plaque that reads: "This boy is in memory put up of the late Fire of London, occasioned by the sin of gluttony 1666." Popular myth holds that London's Great Fire was God's punishment of overindulgent citizens.

The Central Criminal Courts, better known as **The Old Bailey** for the street on which it's located, is a rather nondescript building on the site of the former Newgate Prison. The Criminal Courts are open to the public. Inside, you can visit any trial in progress, all of which are presided over by those famous bewigged judges. It's open Monday through Friday from 10am to 1pm, and again from 2pm to 4pm.

At the heart of The City lies the ugly, fortress-like **Barbican complex** (Silk St., EC2. Tel. 0171/382-7105), home to the Barbican Arts Centre, the London Symphony Orchestra and the Royal Shakespeare Company. There are also theaters, cinemas and the Barbican Art Gallery, which hosts a wide range of avant exhibitions.

The City contains almost as many churches as it does pubs. But they are not all created equal. **St. Bride's Fleet Street** (Fleet St., EC4; Tel. 0171/353-1301), distinguished by its wedding cake spire, is one of the finest of the Wren churches. Its excellent crypt museum tells the story of the 6 previous churches which stood on the site. Arrive at lunch time and catch a free classical musical concert. The church is open Mon-Fri 8am-430pm, Sat 9am-445pm, Sun services only 11am & 630pm. Admission free. Tube: Blackfriars.

St. Clement Danes Church (Strand, WC2; Tel. 0171/242-8282) is the "Oranges and Lemons" church featured in a popular children's rhyme. Also Rebuilt by Sir Christopher Wren, the church features a pulpit carved by Grinling Gibbons, and a statue of the famous lexicographer Samuel Johnson. It's open Mon-Fri 9am-4pm, Sat-Sun 930am-3pm. Admission is free (Tube: Temple/Embankment/Holborn).

Of all the contemporary buildings in The City, the most awesome must be the Lloyds of London (Lime St., EC3. Tel. 0171/327-6210). Designed by Richard Rogers (co-architect of Paris's Pompidou Center), these headquarters of the world's most famous insurance market opened in 1986 to much critical attention. All the "guts" of the building (elevators, water pipes, electrical conduits) are on the exterior, and cranes are permanently affixed to the roof, ready to help with further expansion should it become necessary. At night, special lighting lends an extraterrestrial quality to the site. The building is usually not open to the public, but small groups can make reservations to visit the Underwriting Room. Tube: Monument or Bank.

The South Bank

To most Londoners the River Thames is either a traffic problem to be crossed or a social division that separates the Royals from their subjects. All this is changing, however, now that the south side of the river is booming. The South Bank Borough of Southwark stretches along the Thames through central London. Centered around London Bridge, which was the only bridge over the Thames until the 18th century, Southwark can lay claim to being one of London's most historic boroughs. In the Middle Ages, travelers en route to Canterbury would stop at the inns around Borough High Street. **The George Inn** (77 Borough High St. Tel. 0171/407-2056), one of the last galleried coaching inns in London, remains one of the very best pubs on the South Bank (see Chapter 9/Pubs).

Southwark has long been associated with entertainment in London. The Elizabethans flocked here to attend theaters, watch brutal bear fights (the ugly British answer to bull-fighting), and visit brothels, which located here after being banned from The City. During the eighteenth and nineteenth centuries, the riverfront was the city's prime port and warehouse district, before falling into disrepair in the 20th century, as commerce moved elsewhere.

The new millennium represents something of a renewal for the South Bank. A recent resurrection has once again put it at the center of London with new attractions, restaurants, the opening up of a river path and in general, a large-scale regeneration of the area. The neighborhood is the site of the new **London Aquarium,** County Hall, Riverside Bld., Westminster Bridge Rd., SE1 (tel. 0171/967-8000); as well as the **Tate Gallery of Modern Art,** located at the former Bankside Power Station (*see* Chapter 4/The Top Museums).

The South Bank Centre, the largest arts center in Europe, is the hub of today's Southwark. The enormous concrete complex encompasses theaters, concert halls, museums and exhibition venues. **Royal Festival Hall** presents live music, opera, and dance. The **Royal National Theatre** is actually three separate stages offering six productions in repertoire, from classical drama and musicals to ground-breaking new plays. The Centre also includes the **National Film Theatre,** the Hayward Gallery and the **Museum of the Moving Image** (*see* Chapter 4/Other Major Collections & Exhibition Spaces).

Nearby is a theater from a much earlier age. Actually it's a full-size replica of William Shakespeare's famous **Globe Playhouse** (New Globe Walk, Bankside. Tel. 0171/902-1400), an oak-and-thatch circular structure that originally opened in 1599. To maximize light, the theater is shaped like a wooden "O", with the center open to the sky.

Of course this also meant that performances could only take place during the day, and in good weather. In Elizabethan times, a flag flying on the turret would advertise to the citizens in The City, across the river, that a play was to be performed. When there is no play scheduled, visitors can tour the theater, which includes extensive exhibits on the world of Shakespeare, from the 16th century to the present day. It's open daily 10am to 5pm and admission is £5. See Chapter 9/Stage for show information.

Southwark Cathedral (Montague Close. Tel. 0171/407-3708), founded in the 7th century, is the oldest Gothic church in London. After the Dissolution of the Monasteries (1537-1539) it became the parish church of St. Saviour at Southwark—the name by which Shakespeare would have known it. It wasn't until 1905 that the diocese of Southwark was created and the church became Southwark Cathedral. By any name, this is a terrific building that's definitely worth exploring. Inside is a 20th-century Shakespeare Memorial, featuring the Bard in what appears to be a rather uncomfortable repose. Behind him is an interesting frieze depicting Southwark in the 16th-century.

A small stone by the altar is inscribed with the name "Edmond Shakespeare," the playwright's younger brother, who died of Bubonic plague in 1607. The Cathedral also contains the Harvard Memorial Chapel, dedicated to the American university

III

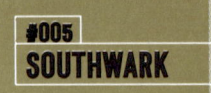
founder, John Harvard, who was baptized here in the same year. The Cathedral is open daily 8am-6pm; admission is free (Tube: London Bridge).

If you're looking for something more pastoral, check out the **Bankside Gallery** (48 Hopton St., SE1. Tel. 0171/928-7521), home to The Royal Watercolour Society and The Royal Society of Painter-Printmakers.

Close to Tower Bridge is the **HMS Belfast**, the last survivor of the Royal Navy's World War II-era big gun ships, now preserved as a floating museum. See Chapter 4/Specialty Museums & Sights.

To the west is the **Battersea Power Station**, the incredible brick building with the famous four chimneys that appears on the cover of Pink Floyd's "Animals" album. During the photo-shoot in 1976, the cover star—a fully inflated 40-foot pink pig—broke free of its moorings and caused some trouble as it floated past planes landing at Heathrow. A developer is currently turning the structure into two hotels, two theaters and a shopping complex with a multi-screen cinema.

hOLbORN & CLERkENWELL

On the northern border of the City of London, the adjacent Holborn and Clerkenwell have long been something of a no-man's land of dreary offices and cheerless shops. That is, until recently, when the area began a major renaissance, becoming a thriving business and residential community. As usual, starving artists were the first to rediscover the neighborhood's potential, and now that the real estate agents have noticed, there has been a huge influx of restaurants and bars and tie-wearing City folk who come here after their veal-fattening pens have closed.

The neighborhood gets its name from the **Clerk's Well** which, in the fourteenth century, supplied water to nearby Charterhouse Monastery. You can still see the remains of the well through the windows of 16 Farrington Lane. In the seventeenth century French Huguenots established the area as a center for jewelry and clock-making.

Today Clerkenwell is best known as the home of **City University**, and the beautifully restored **Sadler's Wells Theatre** (*see* Chapter 9/Nightlife).

During the day, you can visit the Marx Memorial Library, 37A Clerkenwell Green, EC1 (tel. 0171/923-2994), packed with over 100,000 books, pamphlets and periodicals connected with Marxism and the labor movement. You can also chat up some old Leftist docents, and see the room in which Marx worked. It's open Mon 1-6pm, Tues-Thurs 1-8pm, Sat 10am-1pm. Admission is free (Tube: Farringdon).

Charles Dickens' House, 48 Doughty St., WC1 (tel. 0171/405-2127), is another popular stop in the 'hood. Home to one of London's most famous novelists for a short but prolific period from 1837 to 1839. It was here that the writer worked on *The Pickwick Papers*, *Nicholas Nickleby*, and *Oliver Twist*. The author's letters, photographs, furniture, and first editions are all on display. It's open Mon-Fri 945am-530pm, Sat 10am-5pm. Admission is £3.50 (Tube: Russell Square/Chancery Lane). Not coincidentally, some of the most famous scenes in Dickens' *Oliver Twist* are set in nearby Saffron Hill, a notorious 19th-century

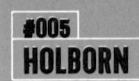

criminal rookery. It was here where Fagin had his lair, training young children in the art of pickpocketing.

At the southern border of Holborn is **Dr. Johnson's House**, 17 Gough Sq., Fleet St., EC4 (tel. 0171/353-3745), a wonderful Georgian townhouse where famous lexicographer Samuel Johnson lived and worked, compiling the world's first English dictionary. There's not much here in the way of furnishings, but the long upstairs room in which Johnson worked is awash in ambience. Johnson's first dictionary, which is on display, includes this definition of dull: "To make dictionaries is dull work." It's open summer, 11am-530pm; winter 11am-5pm. Admission is £3 (Tube: Blackfriars).

bLOOMSbURY

Bloomsbury is a quiet residential neighborhood with an ideal location, just north of Soho and west of The City. Londoners have long coveted the area for its pretty Georgian architecture, tree-lined streets and large public squares. To visitors, the area evokes hazy memories from a college survey course in English lit. Bloomsbury has become mythologized by the Bloomsbury Group in the 1920s, a circle of famous friends who met weekly at each other's homes to discuss art, literature and the issues of the day. Gertrude Stein contemptuously dismissed the soirees as "the Young Men's Christian Association, with Christ left out." Often called "elitist" and "arrogant" by its peers, the dozen or so revolving members included writer Virginia Woolf and her husband, Leonard; her sister, painter Vanessa Bell, and her husband, the art critic Clive Bell; painter Duncan Grant; writer/historian Lytton Strachey; economist John Maynard Keynes; and journalist Desmond McCarthy. The Woolf's Hogarth Press published the works of Gertrude Stein, Sigmund Freud and T.S. Eliot, who gave his first reading of The Waste Land in front of the "Bloomsberries."

The neighborhood's intellectual connections are strengthened by the presence of the **British Museum** (*see* Chapter 4/The Top Museums), and the **University of London**, which opened its doors here in 1836. Bloomsbury has developed into a curious mix of private residences and public institutions, a well-balanced combination that translates into beautifully manicured streets, history-laden buildings and several major tourist sites.

To this day, most of the local real estate is in the hands of a single aristocratic landowner, the Earl of

Bedford, whose 18th-century forefathers laid out the series of squares that fashioned this area into London's newest social center.

Russell Square is the largest in London and the de facto center of Bloomsbury. Here the Underground Station emerges from beneath the **Hotel Russell,** one of the most flamboyant buildings in London, rivaled only by the Victorian-era Houses of Parliament, and nearby St. Pancras train station. The hotel is on the site of the former Pankhurst house, once home to England's most famous suffragettes, sisters Christabel, Sylvia, and Adela Pankhurst. Around the corner, at number 24, novelist T.S. Eliot worked as a book publisher with the firm Faber and Faber. Recently Russell Square has become a night time meeting place for gay men seeking casual sex. In response the local council is erecting gates that will shut the gardens from dusk until dawn for the first time in its 199-year history.

Nearby **Bloomsbury Square,** ringed by elegant Regency-style houses, is one of London's most famous greens. A plethora of blue plaques testify to the square's popularity with famous former residents. Here you can find the former homes of author Isaac Disraeli (the father of Victorian Prime Minister Benjamin Disraeli) and Gertrude Stein, who lived here for one year before moving to Paris.

Gordon Square is most closely associated with the Bloomsbury Group, and there are several blue plaques marking the residences of former members. John Maynard Keynes lived at 46 Gordon Square. The economist had a major hand in creating the International Monetary Fund. A few doors down is the former home of Lytton Strachey, a novelist whose seminal book *Eminent Victorians,* is widely considered to be the first biographical novel.

To the west, Bloomsbury abuts **Fitzrovia,** a former warehouse district that's now home to several trendy production companies. Wandering the streets of Fitzrovia you could be forgiven for thinking nobody lives here. The grimy buildings and faded Georgian houses are still home to fashion wholesalers and a generous number of old-fashioned Greek tavernas and greasy-spoon cafes. But Fitzrovia is experiencing a renaissance. Galleries have sprung up and new restaurants are coming in. This is a neighborhood to watch.

Except for a few good restaurants and a handful of tourist-traps, there's not a whole lot in Marylebone to attract visitors. It's been this way since the 14th century, when the area became best-known to Londoners as the site of Tyburn Gallows. **Madame Tussaud's** is here, as is **London Planetarium** and the **Sherlock Holmes Museum** (*see* Chapter 4/Specialty Museums & Sights).

To the north is **Regent's Park**, a horseshoe-shaped oasis of green that remains central London's best-manicured public space. This city playground is well-known for its rose gardens and boating lake, as well as summer concerts and open-air theater. **London Zoo** (tel. 0171/722-3333), on the north side of the park, gets high marks for being as unexploitative of animals as a place of this kind can be. Some of the enclosures do look uncomfortably small, but newer exhibit spaces are absolutely politically correct. One of these is Web of Life, a major new exhibit that explains biological diversity and the interconnectedness of nature by focusing on insects. Take the Tube to Regent's Park, Baker Street, or Camden Town.

MAYFAIR & St. JAMES'S

The neighborhood of St. James's grew up around **St. James's Palace,** the official residence of the monarch since the days of King Henry VIII. Throughout the seventeenth and eighteenth centuries, aristocrats built their elegant homes around this royal court, and business sprouted up in the area catering to the gentry. Since Queen Victoria vacated St. James's Palace in favor of nearby **Buckingham Palace** (*see* Chapter 4/Crucial London), the Court of St. James's has been occupied by other members of the royal family.

St. James's Park, opposite Buckingham Palace, is the most beautiful park in London. A central location, beautiful lake, and plentiful benches make this park perfect for picnicking. Swans, geese and other waterfowl, including a family of pelicans, make their home here (feedings daily at 3pm).

Adjacent **Green Park,** which is owned by the Royal Family, is named for its absence of flowers. Although no one is sure how this became London's only flowerless park, popular legend recalls that King Charles II was walking here when he announced that he was going to pick a flower and give it to the most beautiful lady present. When he gave it to a milk maid from the local dairy, Queen Katharine become so furious that she ordered all the park's

flowers removed. Around the corner from St. James's Palace is **Spencer House,** 27 St. James's Pl. (tel. 0171/499-8620), a fantastic Palladian-style palace that was home to the ancestors of Princess Diana. Completed in 1766, and restored by Jacob Rothschilds in 1989, the mansion contains some extravagant murals and beautiful function rooms that are now managed by the Spencer Trust. It's open to the public most Sundays from 1145am to 445pm. Admission is £6.

St. James's Street, the main thoroughfare that ends at St. James's Palace, is one of the swankiest strips in the world. Many of the buildings on the street are occupied by London's most famous gentleman's clubs. For centuries, these bastions of aristocracy have been the exclusive haunts of the well-heeled. Membership usually requires a pure pedigree, and can take years to obtain. Women are not allowed into the majority of clubs. And don't look for big signs announcing them either; if you don't know where the clubs are, you probably weren't meant to.

Brook's Club, 60 St. James's St., was built in 1778 for Whip politicians who supported the American revolutionaries, who they regarded as fellow Englishmen who were challenging the rule of King George III. On a pair of lead water containers, located to the left of the club's front door, you can see a depiction of St. George killing the dragon of tyranny along with the date 1776.

The club across the street is **Boodles,** 28 St. James's St., long known for serious drinking, heavy gambling and gourmet eating. Past members have included abolitionist William Wilberforce, socialite "Beau" Brummell, and the Duke of Wellington.

Further up the street is **White's,** 37-38 St. James's St., the oldest and grandest of the St. James's clubs. Founded on the site of White's Chocolate House, the club has a long history of conservatism, and still claims many Tories as members. Prince Charles is a member too.

St. James Church, 197 Piccadilly, straddles the fence between St. James's and Mayfair. Known as "The Visitors Church," this Christopher Wren-designed masterpiece is an elegant structure befitting its noble location. Inside, Corinthian columns rise to support the splendid barrel vaults decorated with ornate plasterwork. The marble font (in which poet William Blake was baptized), the organ case, and the five stone carvings behind the altar were all created by Grinling Gibbons, England's most celebrated Stuart-era carver.

St. James's Street, along with nearby **Savile Row** and **Jermyn Street,** are some of the most expensive shipping streets in the world. Many of the shops that line these swanky strips are famous for their long histories of service to aristocratic and royal clients. Several display Royal Warrants; coats of arms that are given to shops for supplying goods to members of the Royal Family. These include tobacco merchant **Alfred Dunhill** (48 Jermyn St.), Royal shirtmakers **Turnbull and Asser** (71 Jermyn St.), cobblers **John Lobb** (9 St James's St), and haberdasher **James Lock** (6 St. James's St.). See Chapter 7/Shopping for complete details.

Savile Row was also the headquarters of the Beatles' record label, Apple. It was on the roof of the **Beatles Building** (3 Savile Row), one lunchtime in January 1969, that the Fab Four ran through a 42-minute set which would prove to be the last time they ever played before an audience.

Throughout the 1960s, Mayfair and St. James's attracted all manner of pop and avant artists, who worked and played in the area's clubs and art galleries. "Mama" Cass Elliott died in a flat at **3 Curzon Place**, in July, 1974. Four years later the Who's Keith Moon died in the same apartment, following the premiere for the film The Buddy Holly Story. Ironically, the drummer overdosed on the tablets prescribed to help his alcoholism.

SOHO & LEICESTER SQUARE

Soho is London's entertainment district. The British film industry is based here, the major West End playhouses are here, and the country's largest cinemas are here. Needless to say, there are plenty of restaurants, bars, pubs and cafes too.

Traditionally an immigrant center, Soho blossomed with artists and writers in the 1950s and '60s, like Francis Bacon, who famously referred to his "gilded gutter life." Even earlier the neighborhood's little streets were home to music stars, including the composer Handel, who lived on Brook Street. Just a few doors down is the former home of rocker **Jimi Hendrix** (25 Brook St.), which, in 1997, became the first rock 'n' roll location to be commemorated by English Heritage with a blue plaque. It was unveiled by Pete Townshend.

Ringo Starr owned the house at **36 Montague Square** from 1965 to 1969, which he rented out to his friends. John Lennon first lived with Yoko Ono here. And the house was where the couple shot their nude Two Virgins album cover.

Denmark Street too has lots of musical associations. The Rolling Stones, Genesis, and the Kinks all had their first recording sessions in a studio at number 4. The Sex Pistols jammed in a studio at No. 6, and Elton John got his first paying job as a tea boy at Mills Music, formerly at No. 20.

To the south is **Leicester Square**, a busy pedestrian hub that anchors Soho like a large department store anchors a large shopping mall. The Square is ringed by several big-screen cinemas, late-opening eateries, and tourist-awful mega-dance clubs. In the center of the square is a small park dotted with statues of local heroes and entertainment-industry immortals, including William Shakespeare and Charlie Chaplin.

On the east side is the **Half-Price Ticket Booth**, which sells discounted theater tickets for the day of performance only (see Chapter 9/Stage for complete information). And on the north side is one of the last places in the London where you can see a traditional red phone box.

The square was originally the front yard of the mansion of the Earl of Leicester (pronounced "Lester"). After Leicester House was demolished in 1792, the park fell into disrepair. Eighty years later, Member of Parliament Albert Grant purchased it and commissioned public gardens surrounding a memorial to Shakespeare and busts of four famous residents. The plane trees that now tower over the square were soon planted, huge legitimate theaters opened, and Leicester Square was transformed into the entertainment center it is today.

The four short blocks between Leicester Square and Piccadilly Circus are the heart of London. At least, that's what the tourists must think, judging from how many rip-off shops and theme traps there are here catering to them. Rock Circus, Planet Hollywood, Fashion Cafe... this short strip incorporates every insult known to tourism. A chaotic carnival of crass commercialism, the area is jam-packed with shops selling the worst kind of tourist-oriented junk (T-shirts, plush toys, refrigerator magnets), along with several classic tourist-traps masquerading as museums. In between are dozens of mediocre-to-offensive restaurants, few of which care if they ever see a repeat customer. Worst of all, that's what the people want: Leicester Square and Piccadilly Circus have perfected their appeal to the lowest common denominator to become the most visited sections in the city.

Piccadilly Circus itself is far more benign than its flashy reputation would have you believe. Filled with neon, like a mini Times Square, this busy traffic hub is best known for its diminutive **Eros Statue**, not the God of love, but the Angel of Christian Charity erected as a memorial to Lord Shaftesbury.

Nearby **Chinatown** is pint sized compared with the ones in Vancouver, New York and San Francisco. It's a lot newer too; only here since the 1950s. The whole thing centers around the three blocks of Lisle Street where Hong Kong immigrants opened a number of restaurants. British soldiers returning from war in Asia created a demand for Chinese cuisine, not to mention the brothels and bars that located here too. Unlike American Chinatowns, this one no longer attracts new Asian immigrants. Chinese may converge here to pick-up groceries and buy herbal medicines, but few of them actually live here. For visitors, Chinatown is little more than a big cluster of mediocre Cantonese restaurants—which is reason enough to go.

Finally, no place is more identified with London in the 1960s than **Carnaby Street**, the center of street fashion in those supposedly *swingin'* days. A *Time* magazine article brought the street fame, and the Oxford English Dictionary has guaranteed "Carnaby Street" immortality by defining it: "fashionable clothing for young people." The street was in a slump throughout the Thatcher years. But with the advent of 1960s retro chic, this two-block long strip is enjoying a mini revival.

Named for a convent that once stood here, and the wholesale flower market that followed, **Covent Garden Market** is now a hugely touristy crafts emporium that has seen an enormous shopping and restaurant district sprout up around it. The market building itself is a boring, family-oriented place featuring the usual street entertainment: comedic fire-eaters, hyperactive jugglers and Peruvian pipe players. While there's nothing "edgy" about the market or its contents, there's nothing crass about it either. There are no schlock-gift shops, no "My Brother went to London and All I Got..." T-shirts, and, believe it or not, no stupid "museums." That's what Piccadilly Circus and Leicester Square are for. Area restaurants are mostly forgettable. But shopping can be quite good, especially on Long Acre, Neal Street and Shorts Gardens.

St. Paul's Church, on the west side of the square, was designed by Inigo Jones in the 1630s. Long known as the Actors' Church, the interior is lined with memorials to local luminaries like Charlie Chaplin, Vivien Leigh and Boris Karloff. It's open Mon 930am-230pm, Tues-Fri 930am-430pm. Admission is free.

The **London Transport Museum** (tel. 0171/379-6344) is housed under a lofty cast-iron and glass Victorian building, in the southeast corner of Covent Garden Piazza. See Chapter 4/Specialty Museums for complete information.

Westminster and Victoria, adjacent neighborhoods united by their central locations and frenetic daytime pace, are, respectively, London's centers of government and transport.

Aptly named **Parliament Square** is home to both **Westminster Abbey** and the **Houses of Parliament** (*see* Chapter 4/Crucial London). On the square itself are over a dozen statues of military men and statesmen (and they're all men), from Metropolitan Police Force founder Sir Robert Peel and Boar War General Jan Smuts (who appears to be ice skating) to England's first Jewish prime minister, Benjamin Disraeli, and Winston Churchill, who is depicted in his famous "bulldog" stance looking towards the House of Parliament. Note that Churchill's the only statue in the square without pigeon-shit on its head: the bronze figure is wired with a small electrical charge to keep the birds away. The statue of Abraham Lincoln, the lone foreigner in this pantheon of great locals, was a gift from the American people. It's a copy of a statue in Chicago's Lincoln Park.

As long as we're on the subject of sculptures, note the **statue of Oliver Cromwell**, depicted with a Bible in one hand and a sword in the other, in front of the Houses of Parliament. England's 17th-century Lord Protector guided the Parliamentarians in a revolt against the monarchy—a revolution that lead to the hanging of King Charles I. Upon his death, in 1658, Cromwell was buried across the street in Westminster Abbey, the country's most distinguished burial place. But two years later, when the monarchy was restored, King Charles II ordered Cromwell's body exhumed, hung and beheaded. The Lord Protector's head was then skewered on a spike and positioned high above Parliament's Westminster Hall, where it remained for twenty years before blowing down in a gale. The head was recovered by a night watchman who took it home as a family memento. Cromwell's head passed to various owners for the next three hundred years, until 1960, when it was reburied in Cambridge, in a spot that's kept secret to protect it from would-be Royalist thieves.

Whitehall, the street that connects Parliament Square with Trafalgar Square, is the city's primary street of government, home the Home Office, Foreign Ministry, and New Scotland Yard, and other federal offices.

It feels as though time has stood still in the **Cabinet War Rooms,** Clive Steps, King Charles St., SW1 (tel. 0171/930-6961), just off Whitehall, a World War II-era bunker that served as Winston Churchill's underground headquarters during the Blitz. The complex of 21 historic rooms, protected by a reinforced concrete slab, is a unique time capsule, the only concession to modernity being air conditioning. Constructed in 1938, the bunkers included a Map Room, in which all the latest military intelligence was collected and plotted onto a map of the world that takes up an entire wall. In Room 65A, which served as Churchill's office and bedroom, the Prime Minister made some of his most famous BBC broadcasts. It's open 1 Oct-31 Mar, daily 10am-6pm (last admission 515pm); 1 Apr-30 Sep, daily 930am-6pm. Admission is £4.60 (Tube: Westminster/St. James's Park).

The white stone monolith in the center of the Whitehall is the **Cenotaph**, a memorial to the soldiers who died fighting in both World Wars.

The column takes its name from the Greek *kenos*, "empty" and *taehos* "tomb."

Just across the road is **Downing Street**, the official residence of the Prime Minister. Although gates and guards keep you from knocking on Tony Blair's door, you can easily see Number 10, on your left. Number 11, opposite, is the home of the Chancellor of the Exchequer.

Further along Whitehall is **Horse Guards**, home to the Queen's Household Cavalry. Two mounted troopers are posted at the front gates daily, until 4pm. There is a **posting of the guards ceremony** here Monday to Saturday at 11am, and Sunday at 10am.

Directly across the street is **Banqueting House** (tel. 0171/839-8919), the last remaining section of the 17th century palace of Whitehall that once occupied the entire street. Designed by celebrity architect Inigo Jones, this ceremonial hall is best known for its spectacular ceiling, which is decorated with nine large paintings by Flemish artist Peter Paul Rubens. On January 30, 1649 King Charles I declared himself a "martyr of the people" and was beheaded here in front of a large crowd of spectators. The King stepped out of a window onto a scaffold, laid his neck on the block and stretched out his hands as a signal to the executor to strike. The head was severed with a single blow, then held up before the crowd with the words "behold the head of a traitor!" Ironically, Charles I commissioned Rubens to paint this ceiling with images symbolizing the divine right of kings. It's usually open Mon-Sat 10am-5pm, but can close for special occasions on short notice. Admission is £3.50.

Whitehall terminates at **Trafalgar Square**, with its trademark stone lions and **Nelson Column**. The **National Gallery** occupies the north side of the square (*see* Chapter 4/The Top Museums), and **St. Martin-in-the-Fields Church** (tel. 0171/930-0089) is situated on the east. The historic church was designed by James Gibbs in 1726. There are free lunchtime recitals Mondays and Tuesdays. There is also a cafe in the crypt, and a daily crafts market in the courtyard. It's open Mon-Fri 745am-6pm, Sat 845am-6pm, Sun 745am-730pm. Admission is free (Tube: Charing Cross/Leicester Square).

On the other side of Parliament Square, closer to Victoria Station is **Westminster Cathedral**, Victoria St., SW1 (tel. 0171/798-9055), the principal Roman Catholic Church in England. It's a spectacular Byzantine-style building, completed in 1903, that stands in brilliant contrast to the stark office buildings around it. Filled with tall columns and detailed mosaics, the interior is just as fabulous. You can take an elevator to the top of the cathedral's landmark white stone and red brick tower for unobstructed views over Westminster. It's open Sun-Fri 7am-7pm, Sat 8am-7pm. Church admission is free; the tower costs £2 (Tube: Victoria/St. James's Park).

kNiGhTSbRidGE & SOUth KENSiNGTON

ChELSEA

Third-World Nannies and ladies who lunch are the stereotypical images of Knightsbridge, one of the city's most prestigious neighborhoods. In the fashion triangle between Sloane Street, Brompton Road and Beauchamp Place, shoppers dripping with Eurogelt floss in and out of the world's most expensive designer boutiques. Meanwhile, the masses throng to **Harrods** and **Harvey Nichols** (*see* Chapter 7/Department Stores).

Several of the city's best museums—including the **Science Museum** and the **Victoria and Albert**—are located in adjacent South Kensington. (*see* Chapter 4/The Best Museums). **Kensington Palace** is here too (*see* Chapter 4/Specialty Museums & Sights), close to the **Albert Memorial** in Kensington Gardens, which has been completely refurbished and restored. This grandiose monument to Queen Victoria's husband recently emerged from a multi-year restoration. Modest Albert himself would have been embarrassed, but Victoria would be pleased.

Chelsea has long been one of London's most desirable residential neighborhoods. Take a close look; you've probably never seen so many beautiful city buildings that you'd like to own. Needless to say, it's a very expensive part of town, home to executive class couples who work in The City by day, and vie for parking spaces with other Beemer and SUV owners each night. So many accomplished artists have lived in Chelsea, the neighborhood has become awash with blue plaques honoring them. Actor **Sir Laurence Olivier** and novelist **Bram Stoker** both lived on St. Leonard's Terrace. Winnie the Pooh creator **A.A. Milne** lived in Wellington Square, near the house in which American novelist **Thomas Wolfe** wrote *Look Homeward, Angel.* **Mark Twain** lived at 23 Tedworth Square, and the Irish dramatist **Oscar Wilde** lived at 34 Tite Street for over ten years. **George Eliot** lived at No. 4 Cheyne Walk, one of the most beautiful little streets in London. **Mick Jagger** lived on this star-packed street too, at No. 48, and **Keith Richards** lived at No. 3. In 1971, when the Rolling Stones went into self-imposed tax exile in France, it was reported that Keith's assistants picked up all the furniture, clothes, bottles, and half-full ashtrays, transported them across the Channel, and rearranged everything in the same pattern in his new home in St. Jean Cap Ferrat.

If you want to see what an original interior of one of these beautiful homes looks like, visit **Carlyle's House,** 24 Cheyne Row, SW3 (tel. 0171/352-7087), a Queen Anne town house occupied by historian and philosopher Thomas Carlyle from 1834-1881. The house, which contains books, furniture, portraits and personal relics, remains virtually unaltered, to the extent that some of the rooms are without electric light. When the friendly live-in curator is not looking, you can sit in one of the writer's original Victorian chairs, or touch a piano that Chopin played. It's open 1 Apr-1 Nov, Wed-Sun 11am-5pm (last admission 430pm). Admission is £3.40.

King's Road is the commercial center of the enclave, filled with stores aimed at admirers of Terrance Conran, Laura Ashley and Martha Stewart (*see* Chapter 7/Shopping). The King's Road rose to fame in the Sixties as the home of the mini-skirt, and later, Vivienne Westwood's punk shop, Sex. The Road, which remained private until the 1830s, was built in the 17th century for the exclusive use of King Charles II who used it to travel between London and Hampton Court.

Royal Hospital Road, which runs roughly parallel to King's Road, is Chelsea's other major thoroughfare. The main sight here is **Chelsea Royal Hospital,** Royal Hospital Road ◁ —

Chelsea, SW3 (tel. 0171/730-0161), an elaborate 17th-century estate designed by Sir Christopher Wren for men "broken by war and old age." Inspired by the Hôtel des Invalides in Paris, the so-called "hospital" still serves its original function as a home to unwaged and unmarried war vets. About 450 "Chelsea Pensioners" make their homes here, and are allotted food, shelter, clothing and a small weekly allowance, which they happily supplement by showing visitors around the buildings. Enter the Hospital through the main door, beneath the clock. Check out the Wren chapel, to the right, and the Great Hall, probably the most awesome dining room you've ever seen. It's open Mon-Fri 10am-noon and 2-4pm, Sat 10am-noon. Admission is free.

The nearby **National Army Museum,** Royal Hospital Road Chelsea, SW3 (tel. 0171/730-0717), tells the story of over five centuries of British soldiering. The best exhibits are Florence Nightingale's gas lamp, a large section of the Berlin Wall, and "passion killers," the enormous regulation underwear worn by the women's army in the early 20th century. It's open daily 10am-530pm. Admission is free.

Up the street is the **Chelsea Physic Garden,** 66 Royal Hospital Rd., SW3 (tel. 0171/352-5646), London's most exquisite walled garden. Turn into the discreet, unadorned gateway and you enter a secret, shaded fantasyland planted with willows and fruit trees. If you could sneak into the garden at night, it feels like you'd probably see unicorns cavorting with minotaurs and nymphs. The botanical garden was founded in 1673 by the Society of Apothecaries to teach their apprentices how to identify medicinal plants. In the 19th Century, seeds from here were sent to Georgia's cotton plantations. Today, the garden is filled with old and exotic plants, shrubs and trees, some of which are rare species from the New World. It's open Apr-Oct Wed noon-5pm, Sun 2-6pm. Admission is £3.50.

HAMPSTEAD

Like Chelsea, Hampstead has always attracted more than its fair share of writers, artists and thinkers. It's an insular, villagy place, perched atop a hill overlooking London. The Hampstead Underground Station deposits you near the **High Street**, filled with conservative clothes shops and staid bars. Stroll along **Heath Street**, and turn into **Church Row**, the most celebrated residential road in the neighborhood. Most of the 18th century houses here remain intact. Artist and writer George de Maurier (1834-1836) lived at No. 27, and Oscar Wilde's lover, Lord Alfred Douglas, lived at No. 26.

East of Heath Street you'll find **Burgh House**, New End Square, NW3 (tel. 0171/431-0144), a beautiful Queen Anne building with a terraced garden out back and a working buttery in the basement. The house contains the small Hampstead Museum, and always has an art exhibit on show. It's open Wed-Sun noon-5pm. Admission is free (Tube: Hampstead).

Nearby is **Keats' House**, Wentworth Place, Keats Grove, NW3 (tel. 0171/435-2062), the former home of romantic poet John Keats, who penned "Ode to a Nightingale" under a tree in the front garden. Inside is a collection of letters, manuscripts and personal effects belonging to the writer and his contemporaries. It's open Apr-Oct, Mon-Fri 10am-1pm and 2-6pm, Sat 10am-1pm and 2-5pm, Sun and Bank Hols 2-5pm. Nov-Mar, Mon-Fri 1-5pm, Sat 10am-1pm and 2-5pm, Sun 2-5pm. Admission is free. (Tube: Hampstead/Belsize Park).

Finally, Hampstead owes its uniqueness to its wild **Heath**, an untamed wilderness that's eons away from London, despite its being right in the middle of it. A walk across the varied landscapes of Hampstead Heath can breathe life back into even the most jaded Londoner.

WhiTEChAPEL & SPiTALfiELdS

The East End, comprising the adjacent areas of Whitechapel and Spitalfields, has long been one of the city's poorest neighborhoods. Known for cheap housing, the area was the first stop in the city for Irish and French immigrants, followed by Eastern European Jews who dominated the neighborhood from the late-19th to the mid-20th century. Originally, the area was undesirable because both the prevailing winds and the flow of the River Thames move from west to east. In the plague-ridden days before sewers, life on the "wrong" side of The City was dangerous indeed.

Although few Jews remain, at the turn of the century, the East End was one of Europe's largest Jewish ghettos, known as an intellectual hotbed and a creative center. It was at this time too that the neighborhood was terrorized by everyone's favorite serial murderer, Jack the Ripper.

The Yiddish theaters and kosher food shops are history, but some vestiges of the Jewish past can be seen in discount clothing stores and bagel shops on Brick Lane. Today the East End is largely a Bangladeshi stronghold, and ragas have replaced klezmer. It's still home to the capital's famous Cockneys too.

There's a building on the corner of Fournier Street and Brick Lane that has uniquely reflected the changing demographics of the East End since its construction in 1742. Constructed as a Huguenot Chapel, the building was transformed in 1809 into a Christian society house. At the turn of the last century, it was once again converted into a Jewish synagogue. Abandoned in 1965, the structure was revitalized a few years later when it became a mosque, which it remains to this day, serving the area's Bangladeshi immigrants.

Today, most Londoners know the East End at the best section of town for a late-night curry run, as the neighborhood has several good, inexpensive restaurants from the Sub-Continent (*see* Chapter 8/Eating).

Brick Lane is also a popular destination on Sunday mornings, when a ten-block stretch transforms into a street market for all manner of used clothes and cheap household goods.

Whitechapel Art Gallery, 80 Whitechapel High St (tel. 0171/377-0107), established a century ago as a showcase for local artists, now displays some of the world's best contemporary art. Admission is free.

The nearby **Bethnal Green Museum of Childhood**, Cambridge Heath Rd., E2 (tel. 0181/980-2415) contains one of the largest toy and nursery collections in the world. Entry to the museum is free, but a guided tour plus cream tea will set you back about £5 (*see* Chapter 4/Specialty Museums & Sights).

gREENWich

Greenwich, on the south bank of the Thames about five miles east of central London, was the headquarters of the navy when the British ruled the seas. It was also the traditional docking site of ocean sailing ships that, for centuries, traveled upriver to dock here. But Greenwich is best known as the place where Greenwich Mean Time is fixed, and is poised for a renaissance with the opening of the much-hyped **Millennium Dome**. If you just can't do without a picture of yourself straddling the famous meridian, head to the **Old Royal Observatory**, Greenwich Park, SE10 (tel. 0181/858-4422), the base point for world time and the site of Longitude 0. Inside this fantastic Christopher Wren-designed building is an interesting museum of time and space with some ancient timekeeping devices, the largest refracting telescope in Britain, and old apartments that once were home to the Royal Astronomers. It's open daily 10am-5pm (last entry 430pm). Admission is £5, and includes entrance to the nearby **National Maritime Museum**, Romney Rd., SE10 (tel. 0181/858-4422). These galleries detail the nation's fascination and former domination of the high seas through its explorers, traders and naval power. There are literally millions of treasures here, from Viking boats and Admiral Nelson's bloodstained coats to Prince Frederick's gilded royal barge, round-the-world yachts, and Seacat ferries. It's open daily 10am-5pm. Admission is £7.50.

While you're at it, check out the **Royal Naval College** (tel. 0181/858-2154). Designed by Christopher Wren, it's one of the most magnificent classical structures in Britain. It's open Fri-Wed 230-5pm. Admission is free.

The famous Cutty Sark Clipper Ship, King William Walk, SE10 (tel. 0181/858-3445), is now permanently in dry-dock and open as a museum. This most famous of 19th-century clipper ship made regular tea runs to China covering almost 400 miles of ocean per day. The cabins have been reconstructed to show life at sea in the 1870s, and the Lower Hold has a terrific collection of ships' figureheads. It's open Apr-Sep, Mon-Sat 10am-6pm, Sun noon-6pm; Oct-Mar, Mon-Sat 10am-5pm, Sun noon-5pm. Admission is £3.50.

See Chapter 4 for information on the Millennium Dome.

HOW TO GET THERE: Greenwich can be reached in 15 minutes via the Docklands Light Railway from Tower Gateway or Bank Station. Alternatively, you can take a leisurely 45-minute cruise down the river from Westminster or Charing Cross Piers. boats run every 45 minutes from 1030am to 3pm, and cost about £5 each way. For more information call Catamaran Cruisers (tel. 0171/987-1185).

133

KEW

The reason any visitor to London goes to the suburb of Kew is to see the massive **Royal Botanic Gardens** (tel. 0181/940-1171). Popularly known as Kew Gardens, the three hundred acre expanse contains living collections of over 40,000 varieties of plants and includes one of the world's largest collections of orchids. Some of the most exotic are housed in a series of seven spectacular iron-and-glass greenhouses, themselves adjacent to twin art galleries and a Japanese and rock garden. The gardens are open Apr-Sept, daily 930am-7pm; Oct-Mar, daily 930am-5pm. The greenhouses close 330pm mid-winter and 530pm mid-summer. Admission is £5 (Tube: Kew Gardens).

NOttiNG hiLL

Sure, you can still score some crack or heroin near the All Saints Road, or get knifed by Golborne Road, but Notting Hill has also become London's hippest (and most expensive) neighborhoods. It's been going steadily uphill since the 1960s, when Jimi Hendrix died from an overdose at his girlfriend's Notting Hill flat. Today's Notting Hillbillies include media heiress Elisabeth Murdoch, actors Alan Rickman and Miranda Richardson, and loads of millionaire trustafarians who wear dreads, look ethnic, carry a basket, and have holes in their cardigans. They've all got interesting clothes, interesting flats, and interesting creative jobs (if they work at all).

They've cleared out the tramps and beggars who used to live under the Westway (the raised A40 out of London) to make room for trendy new eateries such as Belgo and the Ion bar. Lots of clothes shops have jumped on the Notting Hill bandwagon too, including Joseph, Jigsaw, and Voyage. But they're still far from edging out the beautiful one-off boutiques that are also opening in droves.

Each Saturday the legendary **Portobello Road Market** draws tens of thousands of outsiders into the neighborhood to one of the longest street markets in Europe. The antique market, commonly referred to as "The Lane," is the most popular part, selling everything from jewelry and silverware to home furnishings.

If you're lucky enough to be in London during the last weekend in August you'll certainly head to the world-famous **Notting Hill Carnival**, an enormous street party and parade that has become one of the largest annual events in Europe.

ORGANiZEd tOURS

BY BUS If you're just into seeing as many "sights" as you can in the space of 90 minutes, then an open-top double-decker bus tour is the way to go. Several companies offer what is essentially the same McTourist service, and charge £12 for adults and £6 for children. You don't book in advance, just show up at the most convenient departure point. **The Big Bus Company** (tel. 0181/944-7810) runs all its tours with a live commentary in English. Tours run daily, every 20 minutes from 9am. There are departures from Victoria Station (outside the Royal Westminster Hotel), and Green Park (by the Ritz Hotel). The **Original London Sightseeing Tour** (tel. 0181/877-1722) is available with taped commentary in eight languages. Buses depart from Victoria station, Haymarket (near Piccadilly Circus), Marble Arch, and Baker Street (near Madame Tussaud's). Buses leave every 5 to 6 minutes, from about 9am, with the last bus at around 7pm.

BY BOAT Hour-long cruises depart daily from Westminster Pier, every 40 minutes from 11am to 5pm. Attractions seen from the river include the Houses of Parliament, the South Bank Centre, St. Paul's Cathedral, Shakespeare's Globe Theatre, the Tower of London and Tower Bridge. There's no need to book in advance, simply buy your ticket on the pier. Tickets cost about £5.50. For information call **City Cruises** (tel. 0171/237-5134). There are lots of other boat services too, plying the waters between Westminster Pier and Greenwich, with stops at Tower Bridge, the Millennium Dome, and the Thames Flood Barrier.

ON FOOT There's no better way to learn about London than on a walking tour. Competition between companies is brutal, but the are led by **The Original London Walks** (tel. 0171/624-3978, which offers several group tours daily. There are literally dozens of itineraries to choose from, each priced under £5. The best thing to do is pick up their brochure at Victoria Station's London Tourist Board office, or phone the number above.

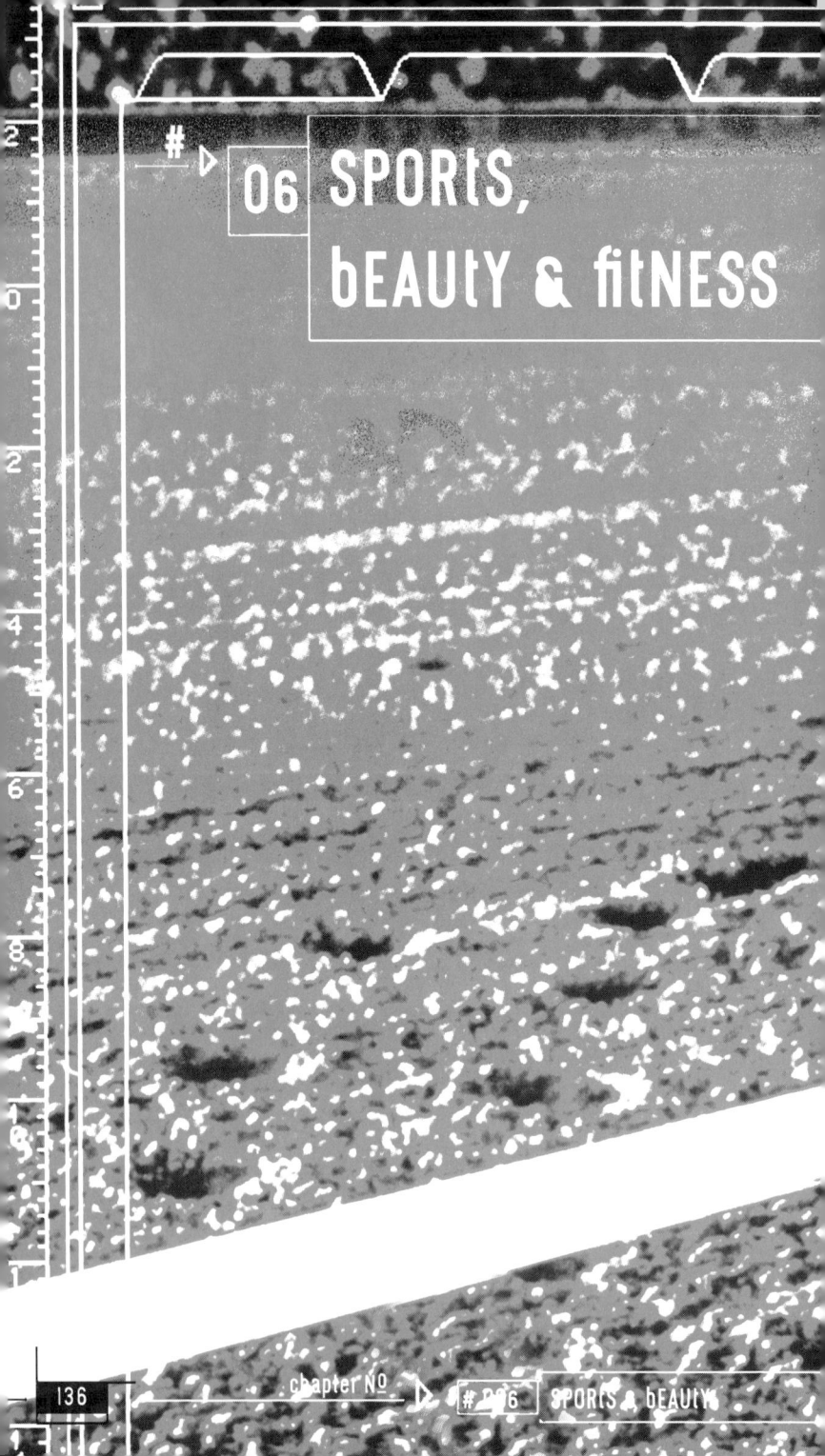

06 SPORTS,
bEAUTY & fitNESS

Bicycling

London street cycling is not for the timid, but with a helmet and *cojones* you can tangle with the taxis and cover a lot of ground. Urban cycling around the small streets of Soho and Covent Garden can be a lot of fun. There's also great biking along the Thames, in either direction. If a pedal in the park is more your speed, then you'll love Hyde Park, with its miles of relatively flat, winding paths.

You can rent bikes from several shops, including **Bikefix** (48 Lamb's Conduit St., WC1; tel. 0171/405-1218), and **Scootabout** (1 Leeke St., WC1; tel. 0171/833-4607). Both places stock the *Thames Cycle Guide*, a great route map of historic houses, parks and museums from Hammersmith to Weybridge.

Billiards/Snooker

An upscale fad in the 1980s, pool has now thankfully returned to its scummy roots. The best halls are divvy places with tens of tables, good lighting, and late closing times, if any at all. Open daily from 11am-6am, **Centerpoint Snooker Club**, New Oxford St., WC1 (tel. 0171/240-6886) is one of the best in the city. It's a membership club, but you can usually get in for £2. Like the name says, it's all snooker, as they have just one pool table. Centerpoint is at the corner of Charing Cross Road (Tube: Tottenham Court Road).

Ritzy's Pool Shack, 16 Semley House, Semley Place, SW1 (tel. 0171/823-5817) is one of those upscale spots, complete with lounge music and a cocktail bar. There are 17 pool tables upstairs, and a dozen for snooker in the cellar. They're open Mon-Sat 11am-11pm, Sun noon-1030pm. Tube: Victoria.

Boating

You can rent a rowboat or paddleboat at the **Hyde Park Serpentine**, for a scenic paddle in the middle of the city. It's a relatively quiet spot, perfect for watching the world glide by. Boats are available from March to October, and cost £7 per hour. They're open daily from daily 9am-5pm.

Horseback Riding

Hyde Park Stables, 63 Bathurst Mews, W2 (tel. 0171/723-2813), rents horses for trotting in Hyde Park. Only guided group rides are offered so jockeys don't need any training. A wad of cash and a signature on the liability waver gets you on a mount. The stables are open in summer, Tues-Sun 715am-7pm; winter, Tues-Sun 715am-5pm. Rides cost £25 and reservations are essential.

Ice Skating
Broadgate Ice Rink
Broadgate Circus, Eldon St., EC2. Tel. 0171/505-4068. Admission £5, £3 students/seniors. Skate hire £2, £1 students/seniors. Tube: Liverpool Street. From October through March you can glide around this rinky-dink rink in the center of The City. Broadgate is London's answer to New York's Rockefeller Center Ice Rink.

Queens Ice Bowl
17 Queensway, W2. Tel. 0171/229-0172. Admission £5. Skate hire £1.50. Tube: Bayswater/Queensway.

A terrific indoor rink for figure skaters and hockey speedsters, Queens is a decent-sized oval, with a convenient Bayswater location, steps from two Underground stations. Ninety-minute sessions run throughout the day, and there's disco nights on weekends.

Swimming
To find your nearest swimming pool, call **Sportsline** (tel. 0171/222-8000). Two of the best central London pools are **Ironmonger Row Baths**, Ironmonger Row, EC1 (tel. 0171/253-4011; Tube: Old Street); and **The Oasis**, 32 Endell St., WC2 (tel. 0171/831-1804; Tube: Covent Garden/Holborn).

Tennis
Many of the city's public parks have tennis courts that are available to non-residents on a first-come, first-served basis. You can take your chances at Battersea Park, Holland Park, Hyde Park or Regent's Park, or book at one of the private clubs, below.

Islington Tennis Centre, Market Road, N7. Tel. 0171/700-1370. Outdoor courts £5.50-£5.50/hour; indoor courts £14/hour. Tube: Caledonian Road.

Market Sports, 65 Brushfield St., Spitalfields, EC1. Tel. 0171/377-1300. Indoor courts £10-£20/hour. Tube: Liverpool Street.

Westway Sports Centre, 1 Crowthorne Rd., W10. Tel. 0181/969-0992. Outdoor courts £6-£8; indoor courts £8-£14. Tube: Latimer Road.

BEAUtY SERViCES

DAY SPAS

Aveda Urban Retreat

Harvey Nichols, 4th floor, 190-125 Knightsbridge, SW1. Tel. 0171/201-8610. Open Mon-Fri 10am-9pm, Sat 8am-7pm, Sun noon-6pm. Tube: Knightsbridge.

The uber-stylish Aveda salon caters to both sexes with facials, manicures, and all manner of aromatic body treatments using their trademark plant and flower essences. Most insiders come for the salon's incredible ninety-minute facials.

Elisabeth Arden Red Door

29 Davies St., W1. Tel. 0171/ 629-4488. Open Mon-Tues and Fri 9am-6pm, Wed-Thurs 9am-8pm, Sat 9am-530pm. Tube: Bond Street.

Behind Elisabeth Arden's trademark red door is a spotless two-level spa offering a huge array of hair-to-toenail beauty treatments, from lip waxing and pedicures, to aromatherapy, reflexology, cellulite reductions and salt glows. Their Visible Difference Day is four hours of indulgence, with lunch thrown in for good measure.

Men on Top

7 Silver Place, W1. Tel. 0171/287-3334. Open Mon-Fri 1030am-8pm, Sat 10am-6pm. Tube: Oxford Circus/Picadilly Circus.

Catering exclusively to the male animal, the all-female staff at this top-of-the line beauty parlor offers specialized groomings that include back waxing, chest tinting and eyebrow plucking. Facials and nail treatments too.

HAIR SALONS

Andrew Jose

1 Charlotte St., W1. Tel. 0171/323-4679. Open Mon-Fri 9am-7pm, Sat 9am-6pm. Tube: Goodge Street/Tottenham Court Road.

When Andrew isn't busy with magazine work, he's directing this hip salon that's become the choice of London's trendiest. Cuts cost between £50 and £80.

L´Oréal Technical Centre

30 Kensington Church St., W8. Tel. 0171/938-5952. Open Mon-Fri 9am-5pm. Tube: High Street Kensington.

This high-style training center is the place to go for a terrific vogueish cut at amazingly pauperish prices. Prices range from £5, and color is just £14. Make an appointment as far in advance as possible.

Truefitt & Hill Gentleman´s Grooming

71 St. James's St., SW1. Tel. 0171/493-2961. Open Mon-Fri 830am-530pm, Sat 830am-1230pm. Tube: Green Park.

This "barber to the aristocracy" is the place to go for a blueblood cut and thorough pampering that even includes having your shoes shined at no extra charge.

TATTOOING

New Wave Tattoo

157 Sydney Rd., N10. Tel. 0171/444-8779. Open Mon-Fri and Sun by appointment only, Sat 930am-530pm. Tube: Bounds Green/East Finchley.
Something of an underground institution, Lal Hardy's New Wave Tattoo is the choice of contemporary rockers, including Oasis's Liam Gallagher. Such renown translates into prices that are at the high end of the spectrum. But hey, you can't put a price on fine art.

SPECtATOR SPORtS

From football and rugby to cricket and snooker, the English are great at inventing games, even if they're not so adept at playing them.

Questions pertaining to any London sport, either spectator or participatory, will be answered free of charge by Sportsline (tel. 0171/222-8000), Monday through Friday from 10am to 6pm.

Note that Wembley Stadium is currently closed and will not reopen until 2002 when it will be the core of England's bid for the 2006 World Cup.

CRICKET

It's astonishing how many people love watching grown men stand around for hours on end, playing a three day game which invariably ends in a draw. And it's ironic that the English cricket team can be so spectacularly bad at playing a game which they themselves taught to their former colonies.

Having said that, it is still tough to score tickets to the summer test matches between England and the lucky international touring team. Tickets to County Matches are far easier to get. The cricket season runs from April to September.

Lord's

St. John's Wood Road, NW8. Tel. 0171/432-1066. Tickets £6-£40. Tube: St. John's.
This spiritual home of cricket is an intimate venue, and really the only place to see a match. Middlesex play here.

Foster's Oval

Kennington Oval, SE11. Tel. 0171/582-6660. Tickets £6-£40. Tube: Oval.
Home to the Surrey team, The Oval is a huge ground, so you should have no problem getting tickets to one of the sparsely-attended County games.

SOCCER/FOOTBALL

The football season runs from mid-August to early May and attracts fiercely loyal crowds. The Premier League, the top of the four league heap, includes twenty clubs, six of which are based in London. Tickets are hardest to snag when Manchester United is in town, or when two London teams are playing each other. The biggest local rivals are Tottenham Hotspur and Arsenal. Thankfully tribal violence seems to be a thing of the past, but stands can still get rowdy. Think about splurging for seats.

Most games kick off at 3pm on Saturday, though midweek games are not unheard of. Following are the London Premiership clubs:

Arsenal, Arsenal Stadium, Avenell Rd., N5. Tel. 0171/704-4000. Tkts. £12-£28. Tube: Arsenal.

Charlton Athletic, The Valley, Floyd Rd., SE7. Tel. 0181/333-4010. Tkts. £14-£16. Rail: Charlton.

Chelsea, Stamford Bridge, Fulham Rd., SW6. Tel. 0171/385-5545. Tkts. £15-£50. Tube: Fulham Broadway.

Tottenham Hotspur, White Hart Ln. Stadium, High Street, N17. Tel. 0181/365-5000. Tkts. £20-£35. Tube: Seven Sisters.

West Ham United, Boleyn Ground, Green St., E13. Tel. 0181/548-2700. Tkts. £18-£30. Tube: Upton Park.

Wimbledon, Selhurst Park, Whitehorse Lane, SE25. Tel. 0181/771-8841. Tkts. £15-£30. Train: Selhurst (from Victoria).

GREYHOUND RACING

There are three big venues in which to see the dogs. Admission to this ultimate working-class pastime rarely, if ever, tops £5. **Walthamstow Stadium** (tel. 0181/531-4255; Tube: Walthamstow Central) schedules races Tuesdays, Thursdays and Saturdays at 730pm. **Wimbledon Stadium** (tel. 0181/946-8000; Tube: Wimbledon Park) races Tuesdays, Fridays and Saturdays at 730pm.

HORSE RACING

Five London–area racecourses ensure there is always something going on. At each course you can either bet with the state-run Tote, in which all the money placed on a race is divided amongst the winners, or with independent trackside bookies. The bookies, or "tic-tac men" as they are known, provide the best show. While they are updating odds and entering bets into ledgers, they carry on a running communication amongst themselves, using strange hand signals.

Ascot

High St., Ascot, Berkshire. Tel. 01344/22211. Admission £6-£20. Rail: Ascot (from Waterloo).

The country's top glamour course hosts many of the biggest flat-races. The Queen and her retinue come to watch Her Majesty's horses during Royal Ascot, held in mid-June. The great unwashed can easily get in too. The season runs from April to September.

Epsom Downs

Epsom, Surrey. Tel. 01372/470047. Admission £5-£16. Rail: Epsom Downs (from Waterloo, Victoria or Charing Cross).

The Epsom Derby, a 1.5-mile race for three–year–olds in early June, is the most prestigious race of the season.

Kempton Park

Sunbury-on-Thames, Surrey. Tel. 01372/470047. Admission £5-£30. Rail: Kempton Park (from Waterloo). Kempton holds races on the flat from April to September, and over jumps the rest of the year.

Sandown Park

Esher, Surrey. Tel. 01372/470047. Admission £5-£26. Rail: Esher (from Waterloo).

The nicest track in London holds the Whitbread Gold Cup in April, and the Coral Eclipse Stakes in July.

Windsor

Maidenhead Rd., Windsor. Tel. 01753/865234. Admission £5-£15. Rail: Windsor (from Waterloo or Paddington).

Adjacent to Windsor Castle, this beautiful Thames-side course is laid out in an unusual figure-8. The best way to get here on warm summer days is by boat (see Chapter 10/Excursions).

RUGBY

The rugby revolution in the mid-1990s brought professional status, extra tournaments, and big bucks to a game previously run on gentleman's agreements. There are two kinds of Rugby:

Rugby League, long a professional sport, is a 13-a-side game that is played almost exclusively in northern England. The **London Broncos**, Stoop Memorial Ground, Twickenham (tel. 0181/410-5000), are the city's lone team. Their season runs from March through August, and games are usually played on Saturday afternoons. Tickets cost £10-£15. Rail: Twickenham (from Waterloo).

Most of the Rugby played in London is part of the **Rugby Union**, a 15-a-side game that only turned professional in the mid-1990s. The two big London teams are the Wasps and the Harlequins. The biggest Union games are played at **Twickenham**, (tel. 0181/892-8161), for which tickets can be hard to get. Regular league games, at each club's own stadium, are held from September through April.

Harlequins, Stoop Memorial Ground, Craneford Way, Twickenham. Tel. 0181/892-0822. Tickets £10-£12. Rail: Twickenham (from Waterloo).

Wasps, Repton Ave., Sudbury. Tel. 0181/902-4220. Tickets £10-£12. Tube: Sudbury Town.

TENNIS

The **Wimbledon Lawn Tennis Championship**, of course, is the nation's premiere tennis event. The two-week-long championships begin the last week of June. It's usually quite easy to buy tickets at the gate for early rounds of play. Needless to say, however, tickets for later rounds and the center court can be hard to come by. But with some perseverance and a little bit of luck, you might be able to snag some.

A limited number of center court tickets are released on each tournament day. Queues usually start to form around dawn; and if you arrive by 630am there's a pretty good chance you'll be happily watching the Big Show later that afternoon.

If you can plan seven months in advance, then, before December 31st, send away for a ticket application to: **All England Lawn Tennis & Croquet Club**, PO Box 98, Church Road, S W 1 9 (tel. 0181/944-1066). Include a self-addressed envelope.

Auerbach & Steele

chapter Nº ▷ # 007 bUYiNG

It's
not news that London is
one of the world's great shopping cities. In
the wake of Vivienne Westwood its designers
have become known the world over. Japanese pour
into Sloane Street for classical English clothes, young
Europeans flock across the Channel for the latest in clubwear
and French fashion houses are falling all over themselves to
sign up the brightest YbD's (young British designers).
Conspicuous consumerism and binge buying are definitely on
the ins, fueled by stock market optimism and tourist
dollars. There are lots of great things here, from art and
antiques to clothes and comestibles that you just can't
get anywhere else. Problem is that everything else,
name brands in particular, costs far more
here than you'd pay Stateside.

ThE MAjOR NEiGHbORhOOds

Bond Street, Sloane Street and **Knightsbridge** are the places to go to find street-smart international names like Donna Karan, Armani, Tommy Hilfiger and Versace, some of the streets, most recent arrivals (*see* High-End Hotlist).

Covent Garden in general, and Neal Street, Longacre and Shorts Gardens in particular, are some of the best hunting grounds for everyday streetwear. Home to Jones, Paul Smith, Jigsaw Menswear, Sports Locker and Burro, nearby Floral Street has become somewhat of a center for men's fashion.

Chelsea's **King's Road** has a similar feel, with dozens of high-end chain stores appealing to moneyed youngsters. Everyone loves a King's Road trawl, especially on warm Saturdays, when it boasts some of the best people-watching in London.

Mile-long **Oxford Street**, terminally congested with locals and tourists, is a place one either loves or hates. Almost every shop is the McDonald's of its genre (Virgin Megastore, John Lewis, Top Shop, Marks & Spencer and the like) catering to the lowest common denominator.

Regent Street, a far more elegant thoroughfare that bisects Oxford Street in midsection, is lined with jewelers, china shops and some interesting boutiques.

A few blocks west are some of the swankiest shopping strips in the world: Savile Row, St. James's Street, Jermyn Street and the Burlington Arcade.

Armani, 37 Sloane St., SW1. Tel. 0171/235-6232. Tube: Knightsbridge.

Cartier, 175 New Bond St., W1. Tel. 0171/493-6962. Tube: Bond Street/Green Park.
Branch: 20 South Molton St., W1. Tel. 0171/235-9023.

Chanel, 31 Sloane St., SW1. Tel. 0171/235-6631. Tube: Knightsbridge.

Christian Dior, 22 Sloane St., SW1. Tel. 0171/235-1357. Tube: Knightsbridge.

Christian Lacroix, 8A Sloane St., SW1. Tel. 0171/235-2400. Tube: Knightsbridge.

Comme des Gar|ons, 59 Brook St., W1. Tel. 0171/493-1258. Tube: Bond Street.

Dolce & Gabbana, 175 Sloane St., SW1. Tel. 0171/235-0335. Tube: Sloane Sq.

Donna Karan, 19 New Bond St., W1. Tel. 0171/ 495-3100. Tube: Bond Street

Etro, 14 Old Bond St., W1. Tel. 0171/495-5767. Tube: Bond Street.

Gianfranco Ferre, 29 Sloane St., SW1. Tel. 0171/838-9576. Tube: Sloane Sq.
Menswear: 84 Brompton Rd. SW1. Tel. 0171/ 581-8736. Tube: South Kensington.

Gianni Versace, 34-36 Old Bond St., W1. Tel. 0171/499-1862. Tube: Bond Street/Green Park.
Womenswear: 183-184 Sloane St., SW1. Tel. 0171/259-5700. Tube: Knightsbridge.

Gucci, 17-18 Sloane St., SW1. Tel. 0171/235-6707. Tube: Knightsbridge.
Branch: 32-33 Old Bond St., W1. Tel. 0171/ 629-2716. Tube: Bond Street.

Hermès, 179 Sloane St., SW1. Tel. 0171/823-1014. Tube: Sloane Square.
Branch: 155 New Bond St., W1. Tel. 0171/499-8856. Tube: Bond Street/Green Park.

Issey Miyake, 270 Brompton Rd., SW3. Tel. 0171/581-3760. Tube: South Kensington.

Jean Paul Gaultier, 171-175 Draycott Ave., SW3. Tel. 0171/584-4648. Tube: South Kensington.

Joseph, 23 Old Bond St., W1. Tel. 0171/629-3731. Tube: Piccadilly Circus.
Branches: 16 and 26 Sloane St., SW1. Tel. 0171/235-1991. Tube: Knightsbridge

Katharine Hamnet, 20 Sloane St., SW1. Tel. 0171/823-1002. Tube: Knightsbridge.

Louis Vuitton, 17-18 New Bond St., W1. Tel. 0171/399-4050. Tube: Bond St.
Branch: 198 Sloane St., SW1. Tel. 0171/235-3356. Tube: Sloane Square.

MaxMara, 32 Sloane St., SW1. Tel. 0171/235-7941. Tube: Knightsbridge.
Branch: 153 New Bond St., W1. Tel. 0171/491-4748. Tube: Bond Street/Green Park.

Nicole Farhi, 58 New Bond St., W1. Tel. 0171/499-8368. Tube: Bond Street/Green Park.
Branch: 193 Sloane St., SW1. Tel. 0171/235-0877. Tube: Sloane Square.
Menswear: 55-56 Long Acre, WC2. Tel. 0171/240-5240. Tube: Covent Garden.

Patrick Cox, 8 Symons St., SW3. Tel. 0171/730-6504. Tube: Sloane Square.
Branch: 129 Sloane St., SW3. Tel. 0171/730-8886. Tube: Sloane Square.

Paul Smith, 40-44 Floral St., WC2. Tel. 0171/379-7133. Tube: Covent Garden.

Prada, 44-45 Sloane St., SW1. Tel. 0171/235-0008. Tube: Knightsbridge.

Ralph Lauren, 143 New Bond St., W1. Tel. 0171/491-4967. Tube: Bond Street/Green Park.

Thierry Mugler, 134 New Bond St., W1. Tel. 0171/ 629-7020. Tube: Bond St.

Tiffany & Co, 25 Old Bond St., W1. Tel. 0171/409-2790. Tube: Green Park.

Valentino, 174 Sloane St., SW1. Tel. 0171/235-0719. Tube: Sloane Square.
Branch: 160 New Bond St., W1. Tel. 0171/629-3181. Tube: Bond Street/Green Park.

Vivienne Westwood, 6 Davies St., W1. Tel. 0171/629-3757. Tube: Bond St.

149

Shopping by Subject

ANTIQUES / COLLECTIBLES

There are several distinct antiques districts in London. If you're searching for high-end classical furnishings, Bond Street, W1 (tube: Bond Street) is the place for you. The top-end originals sold here furnish the country's swankiest palaces.

Portobello Road, W11 (tube: Notting Hill Gate) is far more egalitarian. Although it is busiest on Saturdays, when the famous market is in full swing, there are plenty of arcades along the road that stay open throughout the week. Practically everything you can imagine is sold here (along with plenty of stuff you can't). Haggling is the norm.

Antiquarius (131 King's Rd., SW3; tel. 0171/351-5353), the antiques arcade on King's Road, stocks well-kept collections of objects d'art that run the gamut from pocket watches and playing cards to clothing, jewelry and everything art deco.

AUCTIONS

Christie's

8 King St., SW1. Tel. 0171/839-9060. Open hours vary, depending on what's on show. Tube: Green Park.

The fine art auctioneers were founded in 1766 by James Christie, a former midshipman in the Navy. Art and antiques dominate this bastion of British auction houses.

Sotheby's

34-35 New Bond St., W1. Tel. 0171/493-8080. Open Mon-Fri 9am-430pm. Tube: Bond Street.

Antiques and fine arts are the specialties of this house. Phone to find out what's on display while you're in town.

COMMERCIAL ART GALLERIES

When it comes to the commercial art world, London lags far behind New York. Contemporary galleries are few and far between and some of the world's biggest names are without representation in this city. That said, the city's galleries excel at promoting home-grown art by young British artists like Tracey Emin, Jake, Dinos Chapman and local superstar Damien Hirst, whose bisected, pickled cows thrust him onto the world stage. Cork Street, W1 is the axis of London's commercial art scene. Galleries to check-out here include **Boukamel Contemporary Art** (9 Cork St.; Tel. 0171/734-6444); **Entwistle** (6 Cork St.; Tel. 0171/734-6440); **Mayor** (22 Cork St.; Tel. 0171/734-3558); **Victoria Miro** (21 Cork St.; Tel. 0171/734-5082) and **Waddington's** (11/12 and 34 Cork St.; Tel. 0171/437-8611).

Recently, galleries have been gravitating toward the East End, where rents are lower and exhibition spaces are larger. Important names include **E1** (10 White's Row, E1. Tel. 0171/721-8687); **Interim Art** (21 Beck Rd, E8. Tel. 0171/254-9607) and **Jibby Beane** (66 St John St., EC1. Tel. 0171/723-5531). Note that most galleries close in August.

BOOKS – NEW

Books Etc.

120 Charing Cross Rd., WC2. Tel. 0171/379-6838. Open Mon and Wed-Sat 930am-8pm, Tue 10am-8pm, Sun noon-6pm. Tube: Tottenham Court Road.

This is the flagship store of a soon-to-be mega chain owned by Borders. They have a helpful staff, excellent book organization and a great selection of the UKs best sellers.

Books for Cooks

4 Blenheim Crescent, W11. Tel. 0171/221-1992. Open Mon-Sat 930am-6pm. Tube: Ladbroke Groove/ Notting Hill Gate.

Probably the most extensive collection of culinary books ever assembled. You can eat here, too.

Dillons the Bookstore

82 Gower St., WC1. Tel. 0171/636-1577. Open Mon and Wed-Fri 9am-7pm, Tue 930am-7pm, Sat 930am-6pm, Sun noon-6pm. Tube: Goodge Street.

The largest store of one of the largest book chains in Britain has extensive selections of both new and used titles. The location, adjacent to the University of London, explains the extraordinary depth of their literature collection.

Foyles

113/119 Charing Cross Rd., WC2. Tel. 0171/437-5660. Open Mon-Wed and Fri, Sat 9am-6pm, Thurs 9am-7pm. Tube: Tottenham Court Road.

One of the most august of London mega-booksellers, Foyles mixes pop with a decent selection of hard-to-find books.

Forbidden Planet

71/75 New Oxford St., WC1. Tel. 0171/836-4179. Open Mon-Wed and Sat 10am-6pm, Thurs, Fri 10am-7pm. Tube: Tottenham Court Road.

London's leading sci-fi and fantasy book store has a huge selection of everything from Superman to erotic manga. The pierced and peroxided staff look scarier than most of the superheros' nefarious enemies.

Gay's The Word

66 Marchmont St., WC1. Tel. 0171/278-7654. Open Mon-Sat 10am-630pm, Sun 2-6pm. Tube: Russell Square.

The only Lesbian and Gay bookshop in the city. It stocks novels and non-fiction titles along with art cards, videos and magazines, and is also something of a clearinghouse for information on gay goings-on throughout the city.

Hatchards

187 Piccadilly, W1. Tel. 0171/439-9921. Open Mon and Wed-Fri 9am-6pm, Tue, Sat 930am-6pm, Sun noon-6pm. Tube: Piccadilly Circus.

Among all the usual titles you'll find well fortified sections on travel, history and biography.

Talking Bookshop

11 Wigmore St., W1. Tel. 0171/491-4117. Open Mon-Fri 930am-530pm, Sat 10am-5pm. Tube: Bond Street/Oxford Street.

Audiotaped books are just the tip of the iceberg at this excellent shop for spoken-word recordings. Every city needs a store like this.

Motor Books

33/36 St. Martin's Court, WC2. Tel. 0171/836-6728. Open Mon-Wed and Fri 930am-630pm, Thurs 930am-7pm, Sat 1030am-530pm. Tube: Leicester Square.

Side-by-side book shops that specialize in civilian and military transport. Planes, trains and automobiles to your right; fighter jets, rolling stock and tanks to your left.

Stanford's

12/14 Long Acre, WC2. Tel. 0171/836-1915. Open Mon-Wed and Thurs-Fri 9am-730pm, Tues 930am-730pm Sat 10am-7pm. Tube: Leicester Square/Covent Garden.

Easily the best travel bookstore in London, Stanford carries a complete line of all the major guidebook series, plus tons of maps. The entire basement is dedicated to exploring the UK.

Silver Moon Women's Bookshop

64 Charing Cross Rd., WC2. Tel. 0171/836-5376. Open Mon-Wed and Fri, Sat 10am-630pm, Thurs 10am-8pm, Sun noon-6pm. Tube: Leicester Square.

One of the largest feminist booksellers in Europe carries a huge selection of woman-oriented fiction and non-fiction, along with videos, T-shirts, key chains and other crap. Their nonsexist children's books are great. Lesbian-oriented titles are in the cellar.

Waterstone's

121/129 Charing Cross Rd., WC2. Tel. 0171/434-4291. Open Mon-Sat 930am-8pm, Sun noon-6pm. Tube: Tottenham Court Road.

Recently merged with Dillons, Waterstone's is poised to become the UKs largest book retailer. They have branches virtually everywhere, and are opening one of the world's largest bookstores in Piccadilly.

BOOKS — USED/ANTIQUARIAN

Any Amount of Books

62 Charing Cross Rd., WC2. Tel. 0171/240-8140. Open Mon-Sat 1030am-930pm, Sun 1030am-730pm. Tube: Leicester Square.

This is one of the largest second-hand bookshops in the city. There is a complex of rooms on the ground floor, plus an extensive basement of bargains. It's reasonably organized, too.

Bell, Book & Radmall

4 Cecil Court, WC2. Tel. 0171/240-2161. Open Mon-Fri 10am-530pm, Sat 11am-4pm. Tube: Leicester Square.

Shoulder-to-shoulder with a number of other specialist bookshops, BB&R is the authority in the neighborhood for modern first edition literature and poetry. Looking for an author-signed copy of Lewis Carroll's Alice in Wonderland? This is the place to go.

Classic Collection

Galen Pl., WC1. Tel. 0171/831-6000. Open Mon-Sat 9am-530pm. Tube: Holborn/Tottenham Court Road.

Rolleiflexes, Leicas and other used hotrods of the camera world often end up on these stunning shelves, where prices range from reasonable to stratospheric. There's also a good book selection. The shop is located off Bury Place.

Ceta West One

1 Poland St., W1. Tel. 0171/434-1235. Open Mon-Fri 730am-730pm. Tube: Oxford Circus.

This mammoth Soho pro lab can process E6 film in under two hours, make contact sheets and handle B&W as well.

Branches: 45 St. John St., EC1 (tel. 0171/490-0263); and 65 Queen's Gate Mews, SW7 (tel. 0171/584-0064).

Jessop

63/69 New Oxford St., WC1. Tel. 0171/240-6077. Open Mon-Wed and Sat 9am-6pm, Thurs 9am-8pm, Fri 9am-7pm, Sun 11am-5pm. Tube: Tottenham Court Road.

One of the largest photo stores in the country, Jessop stocks everything from disposable Kodaks to large-format Hasselblads. Accessories and processing too.

John Lewis

278/306 Oxford St., W1. Tel. 0171/629-7711. Open Mon-Wed and Fri 930-6pm, Thurs 10am-8pm, Sat 9am-6pm. Tube: Oxford Circus.

We include this department store because of their famous "never knowingly undersold" policy that extends to their extensive electronics department. Wonder if they know that everything they carry is much cheaper in New York.

Spymaster

3 Portman Sq., W1. Tel. 0171/486-3885. Open Mon-Fri 930am-6pm, Sat 10am-5pm. Tube: Bond Street.

Step inside this polished, upscale shop for covert video-camera glasses, bugging devices, bullet-proof briefcases, miniature recording equipment and other James Bondian gadgets. Dress rich.

Anything Left-Handed

57 Brewer St., W1. Tel. 0171/437-3910. Open Mon-Fri 930am-5pm, Sat 10am-5pm. Tube: Piccadilly Circus.

A quirky shop for lefties selling everything from letter-openers and scissors to wrong way address books, knives and pens. It's great for gifts.

Beatles for Sale

8 Kingley St., W1. Tel. 0171/434-0464. Open eight day's a week 10am-7pm. Tube: Oxford Circus.

This ultimate stop for mop top memorabilia hawks an enormous amount of old and new collectibles. The Beatles' mugs are emblazoned on everything from pens and pendants to watches, plates and bags. A great place to browse.

Benjamin Pollock's Toy Shop

44 The Market, Covent Garden, WC2. Tel. 0171/379-7866. Open Mon-Sat 1030am-6pm, Sun noon-5pm. Tube: Covent Garden.

An old-fashioned shop for adults with taste, Pollock's is packed with a jumble of unique, hand-made toys. Most of the original creations are marionettes, puppets, matchbox theaters and the like.

Big Kids Store

394 King's Road, SW10. Tel. 0171/795-0801. Open Mon-Sat 10am-6pm, Sun noon-5pm. Tube: Sloane Square.

The entire line of Tintin adventure books is sold alongside umbrellas, T-shirts, watches, home furnishings and other souvenirs emblazoned with images of the young Belgian detective and his faithful dog. Keeping Tintin company are other European characters including Asterix, Babar and The Little Prince.

Davenport's Magic Shop

7 Charing Cross Underground Shopping Concourse, Strand, WC2. Tel. 0171/836-0408. Open Mon-Fri 930am-530pm, Sat 1015am-4pm. Tube: Charing Cross.

One of the largest, oldest and most respected magic shops in the world, Davenport's sells everything from thumb tips and reels to levitation devices, plus plenty of unique items created exclusively for this store. Ask for demonstrations of everything and get a copy of their catalogue.

Filofax

69 Neal St., WC2. Tel. 0171/836-1977.

Open Mon-Wed 10am-6pm, Thurs-Fri 10am-7pm, Sat 1030am-630pm, Sun noon-5pm. Tube: Covent Garden/Leicester Square.

The ultimate shop for everything Filofax. The brand's entire line of organizers and fillers are here, including super-thin calculators and hole-punchers that make it easy to create your own pages.

Galerie Singleton

40 Theobalds Rd., WC1. Tel. 0171/831-6928. Open Mon-Fri 1030am-630pm, Sat 11am-5pm. Tube: Covent Garden.

The name of this shop refers to the one-of-a-kind nature of their goods original small household items designed by local artists. Cool egg-carton lamps, colorful paper maché clocks... you can never be sure what's in store.

Hamleys

188/196 Regent St., W1. Tel. 0171/494-2000. Open Mon-Wed 10am-7pm, Thurs, Fri 10am-8pm, Sat 930am-7pm, Sun noon-6pm. Tube: Oxford Circus/Piccadilly Circus.

This play palace is so awesome that most kids believe their parents when told they're actually in a toy museum. Five floors of frivolity include enormous stuffed animals, mini-Porche automobiles that actually work, a wall of M&M chocolate candies sorted by color, and all manner of toys and games.

Just Fish

Cucumber Alley, Shorts Gardens, WC2. Tel. 0171/240-6277. Open Mon-Sat 1130am-7pm. Tube: Covent Garden/Leicester Square.

A little hole of a shop stocked with an impressive variety of fish-related kitsch you know—trout ties, "time to fish" watches, pike clothes hangers and the like.

Kokon Tozai

57 Greek St., W1. Tel. 0171/434-1316. Open Mon-Sat 11am-8pm. Tube: Tottenham Court Road.

Fun Tokyo style comes to Soho in the form of this tight and bright shop selling pink furry alarm clocks, rubber calculators, inflatable plastic toys and a large selection of Sanrio stuff. There is a limited selection of small-size clothes and Japanese dance disks too.

Beanos

7 Middle St., Croydon, Surrey. Tel. 0181/680-1202. Open Mon-Fri 10am-6pm, Sat 9am-6pm. Rail: East Croydon.

It's not the easiest place to get to, but if you're a serious collector you absolutely must go to this amazing three-story music shop. Tons of old vinyl includes sizable collections from the 60s.

HMV

150 Oxford St., W1. Tel. 0171/631-3423. Open Mon-Thurs, Sat 930am-8pm, Fri-Sat 930am-7pm, Sun noon-6pm. Tube: Oxford Circus.

The oldest and least celebrated of the city's trio of music megastores, HMV stocks everything they do, and often bests them when it comes to world beat and off-beat jazz.

Ray's Jazz Shop

180 Shaftesbury Ave., WC2. Tel. 0171/240-3969. Open Mon-Sat 10am-630pm. Tube: Leicester Square.

Like the name says, Ray's is all about jive, from the 1920s to the present. Their huge stock is augmented by a large vinyl selection, used cd's and a smattering of world, folk and blues.

Tower Records

1 Piccadilly Circus, W1. Tel. 0171/439-2500. Open Mon-Sat 9am-midnight, Sun noon-6pm. Tube: Piccadilly Circus.

The best of the chain stores stocks plenty of indie stuff along with major labels and plenty of imports. It's a huge space, with a separate classical area where overstocked items are priced under a pound.

Virgin Megastore

14/30 Oxford St., W1. Tel. 0171/631-1234. Open Mon 9am-9pm, Tues and Thurs-Sat 930am-9pm, Wed 10am-9pm, Sun noon-6pm. Tube: Tottenham Court Road.

You could easily spend hours combing through CDs, books, videos and CD-ROMs in this expansive complex in the heart of Oxford Street. There are lots of listening booths to hear new music, but beware of the greasy headphones.

SPORTS EQUIPMENT

The Kite Store

48 Neal St., WC2. Tel. 0171/836-1666. Open Mon-Fri 10am-6pm, Sat 1030am-6pm. Tube: Covent Garden.

The Kite Store spans the world of flying objects from Chinese dragons to Australian boomerangs. It's a fun place, if only to peek at the state of the art in aerial toys.

Lillywhite´s

24/36 Lower Regent St., SW1. Tel. 0171/930-3181. Open Mon-Fri 10am-8pm, Sat 9am-7pm, Sun 11am-5pm. Tube: Piccadilly Circus.

From darts to yoga, Lillywhite's carries clothing and equipment for almost every imaginable activity. In short, it's the best sporting goods shop in the city.

CLOTHING – DESIGNER BOUTIQUES

Agnès B

35/36 Floral St., WC2. Tel. 0171/379-1992. Open Mon-Wed and Fri, Sat 1030am-630pm, Thurs 1030am-7pm, Sun noon-5pm. Tube: Covent Garden

London's schmashion mavens have embraced this epitome of basic Parisian style as their own. The classic styling and sturdy construction is designed to last a lifetime.

Branches: 111 Fulham Rd., SW3 (tel. 0171/225-3477); 235 Westbourne Grove, W11 (tel. 0171/792-1947); 56 Heath St., NW1 (tel. 0171/431-1995).

APC

40 Ledbury Rd., W1. Tel. 0171/229-4933. Open Mon-Sat 1030am-7pm. Tube: Notting Hill Gate.

Parisian basics for men and women include top-quality cotton T-shirts, great turtleneck sweaters, black leather jackets and oiled motorcycle jeans in a variety of colors.

159

Browns

23/27 South Molton St., W1. Tel. 0171/491-7833.
Open Mon-Wed and Fri-Sat 10am-6pm, Thurs 10am-7pm. Tube: Bond Street.
Browns made its name discovering young designers and foisting them onto the forefront of the city's fashion scene. Their trio of shops, which practically take over the entire block, mixes both new and established names, priced for all pocketbooks. It's a great place to talent scout.

Calvin Klein

53 New Bond St., W1. Tel. 0171/491-9696. Open Mon-Wed and Fri-Sat 10am-630pm, Thurs 10am-7pm. Tube: Bond Street.
Not top-of-the-line, only the CK collection is sold here, along with all those branded accessories.

Comme des Garçons

59 Brook St., W1. Tel. 0171/493-1258. Open Mon-Wed and Fri-Sat 10am-6pm, Thurs 10am-7pm. Tube: Bond Street.
Comme des Garçons is so funky that their bridge line looks like other designer's haute couture. The intricate designs are positively wild in contrast to the shop's spare, concrete cube-like interior.

Donna Karan

19 New Bond St., W1. Tel. 0171/495-3100. Open Mon-Wed and Fri-Sat 10am-6pm, Thurs 10am-7pm. Tube: Bond Street/Green Park.
The DK collection is straight out of NY: everything's in black, white and gray. The more popularly-priced **DKNY** collection is across the street (27 Old Bond St., W1. Tel. 0171/499-8089).

Emporio Armani

57 Long Acre, WC2. Tel. 0171/917-6882. Open Mon-Tue and Thurs-Sat 10am-6pm, Wed 10am-7pm. Tube: Covent Garden.
Armani's Covent Garden shop features those trademark crisp suits and less-pricey lines. For the mainline collection, head to Sloane Street (see High-End Hotlist).

Iceberg

10 Sloane St., SW1. Tel. 0171/225-0767. Open Mon-Tues and Thurs 10am-630pm, Wed 10am-7pm, Fri-Sat 10am-6pm. Tube: Knightsbridge.
The Italian designer's relatively new Sloane Street store stocks the full line of Iceberg goodies including clothing, perfume, accessories and even some housewares.

Jones

13-15 Floral St., WC2. Tel. 0171/240-8312. Open Mon-Sat 10am-630pm, Sun 1-5pm. Tube: Covent Garden.
Jones' twin shops stock casual and formal wear of local and international men's labels. It's become a one-stop shop for the dandy who doesn't want to hunt all over town.

Joseph

23 Old Bond St., W1. Tel. 0171/629-3731. Open
Mon-Wed and Fri-Sat 10am-630pm, Thurs 10am-7pm. Tube: Bond Street.
Joseph's perfect designs continue to be some of the city's most coveted. The
store is as famous for its clean and simple lines as it is for its frequent
half-price sales.

Branches: 16 Sloane St., SW1 (tel. 0171/235-1991); 26 Sloane St., SW1
(tel. 0171/235-5470); 77 Fulham Rd., SW3. (tel. 0171/ 823-9500).

Katharine Hamnet

20 Sloane St., SW1. Tel. 0171/823-1002. Open Mon-Tue and Thurs-
Fri 10am-630pm, Wed 10am-7pm, Sat 10am-6pm. Tube:
Knightsbridge.

Hamnet has an uncanny ability of appealing to both LA and London
with collections that are a little bit high-fashion and a little bit
rock'n'roll. Think sequined skirts, leather pants and famous Hamnet
denim.

Miu Miu

125 New Bond St., W1. Tel. 0171/409-0900. Open Mon-Wed
and Fri-Sat 10am-6pm, Thurs 10am-7pm. Tube: Bond Street.
Prada's next wave is a bridge-line that's just a bit funkier
and a wee bit less expensive than its parent.

Moschino

28/29 Conduit St., W1. Tel. 0171/318-0555. Open Mon-Wed and Fri-Sat 10am-6pm, Thurs 10am-7pm. Tube: Piccadilly Circus.

Definitely a store to explore, this five-story emporium is stuffed with couture, diffusion and sport lines, plus jeans, boots and accessories.

Patrick Cox

129 Sloane St., SW3. Tel. 0171/730-8886. Open Mon-Tue and Thurs-Sat 10am-6pm, Wed 10am-7pm, Sun 11am-5pm. Tube Knightsbridge.

This home-grown designer's up-to-the-moment derivations mean moderately-priced spin-offs of top designer styles. Look for well-tailored dresses, suits, tops and other savvy wearables that will get you past the velvet ropes.

Red or Dead

41/43 Neal St., WC2. Tel. 0171/379-7571. Open Mon-Fri 1030am-7pm, Sat 10am-630pm, Sun noon-530pm. Tube: Covent Garden.

With their finger still very much on the fashion pulse, Red or Dead is expert in absorbing current trends and taking them to the next level. Great footwear too. Branch: 38 Kensington High St., W8 (tel. 0171/937-1649).

Vexed Generation

3 Berwick St., W1. Tel. 0171/381-6009. Open Mon-Sat 1130am-630pm. Tube: Piccadilly Circus.

Vexed Gen's totally fashion-forward look includes micro skirts, vinyl tops, coats with faux fur embellishments and real cool shoes. The racks are cluttered with dance-clubby youth-infected fashions.

Vivienne Westwood

6 Davies St., W1. Tel. 0171/629-3757. Open Mon-Wed and Fri-Sat 10am-6pm, Thurs 10am-7pm. Tube: Bond Street.

Vivienne Westwood paved the way for London designers on the international scene. At her ready-to-wear shop you can find both men's and women's clothes from Queen Viv's empire.

Many of the olde Englishe clothiers that line the streets of St. James's are famous for their long histories of service to aristocratic clients. Savile Row, Jermyn Street and St. James's Street are littered with Royal Warrants; coats of arms from the house of Windsor that are granted to the royal family's favorite retailers. Recently, a few hot young interlopers have moved into the neighborhood, tailoring handmade creations for the latest crop of inter-national smashion mavens.

Gieves & Hawkes (1 Savile Row, W1. Tel. 0171/434-2001) is one of the city's top shirt- and suit-makers, offering hand-tailored Oxfords for about £120, and 3-piece outfits from £1,800. your paper pattern is kept on the premises and can be added to or cut away, depending on whether you add or lose some pounds. Other old-time tailors on the Row include **Anderson & Shepherd** (30 Savile Row, W1. Tel. 0171/734-1420), **Dege** (10 Savile Row, W1. tel. 0171/287-2941), Henry Poole (15 Savile Row, W1. Tel. 0171/734-5985) and **H. Huntsman & Sons** (11 Savile Row, W1. Tel. 0171/734-7441).

Ozwald Boateng (9 Vigo St., W1. Tel. 0171/734-6868), one of the newbies in the neighborhood, has been tailoring a lot lately for nouveau riche like Billy Zane and Lisa Stansfield. He's especially known for striking colors and great linings.

Richard James (31 Savile Row, W1. Tel. 0171/434-0605), another hot young talent, has been winning tons of media attention for his funky creations for the likes of Robert De Niro, Dustin Hoffman and Tom Cruise, who he outfitted for the Oscars. A handmade suit here begins at £1,200.

James Lock (6 St Jame's St., SW1. Tel. 0171/930-5849), was the city's preeminent hatter in 1676, and still holds the title to this day. Famous customers read like a history of Britain itself. Lord Nelson once ordered a hat with a built-in eye patch. The Duke of Wellington came here for a plumed cap he wore at the battle of Waterloo and the top hat is said to have been invented here in 1797.

James Smith & Sons (53 New Oxford St., WC1. Tel. 0171/836-4731), the umbrella maker to the rich and famous, resembles something of a gentlemen's club. Traditionally the shop supplied the city gent with his black brolly. These days the clientele is far more inter-national, and women are also catered to.

John Lobb (9 St Jame's St., SW1. Tel. 0171/930-3664) holds three royal warrants as the bootmaker to Queen Elizabeth, The Duke of Edinburgh and The Prince of Wales. When you place an order, the shop will make a molding of your feet, then store them in vaults beside other rich folks like Charles, the Queen and Prince Philip.

CLOTHING — DESIGNER DISCOUNT

Amazon

1/22 Kensington Church St., W8. Tel. 0171/937-4692. Open Mon-Wed and Fri 10am-6pm, Thurs 10am-7pm, Sat 9am-6pm, Sun noon-5pm. Tube: High Street Kensington.

A fashion zoo if ever there was one, Amazon is famous with bargain hounds for last season's designer collections at massively reduced rates. Intrepid shoppers elbow their way through unorganized racks and bins of Romeo Gigli, Helmut Lang, D&G, Jil Sander and others, priced 50%, and more, off original retail.

Browns Labels for Less

50 South Molton St., W1. Tel. 0171/491-7833. Open Mon-Wed and Fri-Sat 1030am-630pm, Thurs 1030am-730pm. Tube: Bond Street.

Unsold stock and irregular merchandise with designer labels often finds its final resting place in one of this city's best-known fashion shops. It's great for unusual designs by up-and-comers (as well as came-and-wenters) that can be found for up to a third off regular retail.

CLOTHING — BASICS

Esprit

82 King's Rd., SW3. Tel. 0171/589-7211. Open Mon-Tue and Thurs-Sat 10am-630pm, Wed 10am-7pm, Sun noon-5pm. Tube: Sloane Square.

Fun sporty clothes and an upbeat atmosphere make it a pleasure to swing through this King's Road shop.

French Connection

99/103 Long Acre, WC2. Tel. 0171/379-6560. Open Mon-Wed and Fri-Sat 1030am-7pm, Thurs 11am-8pm, Sun noon-6pm. Tube: Covent Garden/Leicester Square.

If it's on the street, it's in this up-to-the-moment shop, where classic colors and tight fits are the rule of the day. Prices are great.

Jigsaw

126/127 New Bond St., W1. Tel. 0171/491-4484. Open Mon-Wed and Fri 1030am-7pm, Thurs 1030am-730pm, Sat 930am-630pm. Tube: Bond Street.

Another street-wise chain reflecting youth culture right back at the masses, Jigsaw can be counted on for well-styled clothes that keep up with mainstream trends for both men and women.

Kookai

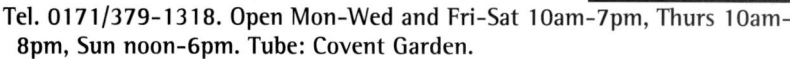

Unit 13, The Piazza, Covent Garden, WC2.
Tel. 0171/379-1318. Open Mon-Wed and Fri-Sat 10am-7pm, Thurs 10am-
8pm, Sun noon-6pm. Tube: Covent Garden.
France's best affordable-clothes exporter is known for tiny dresses and tight
sweaters floating on steel hangers in clean minimalist shops. Here's their full
line of youthful skirts, trousers and blouses for casual and upscale occasions.

Laura Ashley

256/258 Regent St., W1. Tel. 0171/437-9760. Open Mon-Tue 10am-
630pm, Wed, Fri 10am-7pm, Thurs 10am-8pm, Sat 930am-7pm, Sun
noon-6pm. Tube: Oxford Circus.
Flowery dresses are still the mainstay of this home-grown fashion
powerhouse. But the stock has been augmented in recent years to
include classic women's dresses and suits, all decently priced.

Morgan

7 Oxford St., W1. Tel. 0171/437-2768. Open Mon-Wed and Fri-Sat 10am-
7pm, Thurs 10am-8pm, Sun noon-6pm. Tube: Tottenham Court Road.
Of all the Oxford Street shops selling trendy interpretations of
name-brand designs, Morgan is one of the most creative for men's and
women's clothes in a huge variety of synthetic fabrics.

Oasis

13 James St., WC2. Tel. 0171/240-7445. Open Mon-Wed and Fri-
Sat 10am-7pm, Thurs 10am-8pm, Sun 11am-6pm. Tube: Covent
Garden.
Always a good place to look for stylish fashions, Oasis aims to put at
least one of their catchy items in every closet in the UK. Designs run
the gamut from conservative to flamboyant with prices well on this side
of the stratosphere.

Warehouse

24 Long Acre, WC2. Tel. 0171/240-8242. Open Mon-Wed and Fri-
Sat 10am-7pm, Thurs 10am-8pm, Sun noon-6pm. Tube: Covent
Garden.
When you're ready to get glam, there are few better places to do it than
this Covent Garden shop brimming with colorful clubwear. Racks of
future schlock include transparent plastic tops, PVC pants, micro skirts and
plenty of glitterwear.

Woodhouse

99 Oxford St., W1. Tel. 0171/437-2809. Open Mon-Wed and Fri-
Sat 10am-630pm, Thurs 10am-8pm, Sun noon-6pm. Tube:
Oxford Circus.
Top-quality men's basics have long been the specialties of this
accessible Oxford Street shop. Once you get past the Armani
and D&G, you'll find lots of great casualwear from Stone Island
and Katharine Hamnet.

New Look

309 Oxford St., W1. Tel. 0171/499-8497. Open Mon-Wed and Fri-Sat 10am-7pm, Thurs 10am-8pm, Sun noon-6pm. Tube: Oxford Circus. Most clothes sold here are made as if they're not supposed to last a second season, but prices can be low, low, low. Stock shifts as fast as the trends, so you can always find something on the edge.
Branch: 175 Oxford St., W1 (tel. 0171/535-2005).

Top Shop/Top Man

214 Oxford St., W1. Tel. 0171/636-7700. Open Mon-Wed and Fri-Sat 10am-7pm, Thurs 10am-8pm, Sun noon-6pm. Tube: Oxford Circus.
Thoroughly rummaging through this massive Oxford Street emporium is the best education we can think of to learn about what's happening on the country's high streets. Sure, most designs are horrible, but there are always a couple of eye-catching items at prices that can't be beat.

CLOTHING — LINGERIE / FETISH

Agent Provocateur

6 Broadwick St., W1. Tel. 0171/439-0229. Open Mon-Sat 11am-7pm. Tube: Oxford Circus/Tottenham Court Road. The best all-around erotic lingerie shop in town is a luxuriously naughty upper class affair with a large selection of post-party clothes.
Branch: 16 Pont St., SW1 (tel. 0171/235-0229).

Expectations

75 Great Eastern Et., EC2. Tel. 0171/739-0292. Open Mon-Fri 11am-7pm, Sat 11am-8pm, Sun noon-5pm. Tube: Old Street.
In what just might be the largest fetish shop in the world, you'll find stocks of clothing and equipment so extensive it practically defies belief. Latex vests, romper suits, jockstraps and sheets vie for attention with all manner of bondage furniture. Ask to see the peice called Barbie is Sorry.

Cover Girl

44 Cross St., N1. Tel. 0171/354-2883. Open Mon-Wed 10am-5pm, Thurs 11am-7pm, Fri 11am-5pm, first Sat of the month 10am-4pm. Tube: Angel/Highbury & Islington. The place in London for lace-up, thigh-high stiletto boots and sexy platforms, Cover Girl creates made-to-measure footwear for fetish enthusiasts.

Wolford

3 South Molton St., W1. Tel. 0171/499-2549. Open Mon-Wed and Fri-Sat 10am-6pm, Thurs 10am-630pm, Sun noon-6pm. Tube: Bond Street. Top of the line hosiery is Wolford's stock in trade. Their tights and leggings are some of London's most wanted, along with a good selection of lingerie and sexy body suits and swimwear.
Branch: 28A Kensington Church St., W8 (tel. 0171/937-2995).

Buffalo Boots

47/49 Neal St., WC2. Tel. 0171/379-1051. Open Mon-Sat 1030am-7pm, Sun 2-6pm. Tube: Covent Garden.
Chunky party platforms are the current rage at Buffalo, many with shiny reflex colors and vertigo-inducing heels. All the latest street styles are sold at very down-to-earth prices.

The Clarks Shop

476 Oxford St., W1. Tel. 0171/629-9609. Open Mon-Wed and Sat 10am-630pm, Thurs 10am-8pm, Fri 10am-7pm, Sun 11am-5pm. Tube: Marble Arch. Clarks Wallabees, once the ugliest comfort shoes around, are now considered to be style-hound staples. Their classic suede lace-ups are now sold alongside dozens of creative styles, all of which are popularly priced.

Dr. Marten Department Store

1/4 King St., WC2. Tel. 0171/497-1460. Open Mon-Wed and Fri-Sat 10am-7pm, Thurs 1030am-8pm, Sun noon-6pm. Tube: Covent Garden.
Doc Martens have come a long way from their clunky steel-toe roots. This five-story superstore is filled with DM branded footwear that runs the gamut from suede boots to sandals.

Office

57 Neal St., WC2. Tel. 0171/379-1896. Open Mon-Wed and Fri-Sat 10am-7pm, Thurs 10am-8pm, Sun noon-6pm. Tube: Covent Garden.
In addition to plenty of straight officewear, this top chain specializes in hip footwear for those looking to step out. Moderate prices are commensurate with quality.

Pied a Terre

31 Old Bond St., W1. Tel. 0171/629-0686. Open Mon-Wed and Fri-Sat 10am-630pm, Thurs 10am-7pm. Tube: Green Park. Very cool shoes for the urban jungle. Funky mid-priced women's styles for club and streetwear. There always seem to be a lot of Japanese tourists here, so it must be stylish.

R Soles

109A King's Rd., SW3. Tel. 0171/351-5520. Open Mon-Sat 930am-7pm, Sun noon-6pm. Tube: Sloane square. Primarily selling cowboy boots, this King's Road standby earns mention here because of their great name. R Soles. There, we said it again.

CLOTHING — ACCESSORIES

Button Queen

19 Marylebone Lane, W1. Tel. 0171/935-1505. Open Mon-Wed 10am-5pm, Thurs-Fri 10am-6pm, Sat 10am-4pm. Tube: Bond Street. This quirky shop has buttoned up Londoners for nearly four decades. With its vast stock of fasteners from cheap plastic to precious stones it's hard to imagine coming here and not getting buttonholed.

Connolly

32 Grosvenor Crescent Mews, SW1. Tel. 0171/235-3883. Open: Mon-Sat 10am-6pm. Tube: Hyde Park Corner.

The best-known motorcar leathermaker also manufactures leather auto accessories, the entire line of which is available in this very upscale shop. Stock includes stylish overalls, trendy toolkits, leather goggles and even umbrellas.

The Great Frog

10 Ganton St., W1. Tel. 0171/439-9357. Open Mon-Sat 1030am-630pm. Tube: Oxford Circus.

Creating funky, chunky jewelry for street and stage, The Great Frog is a favorite of rockers and bikers for their oversized precious metal rings and bracelets. Branch: 51 Carnaby St., W1 (tel. 0171/734-1900).

Mulberry

41/42 New Bond St., W1. Tel. 0171/491-3900. Open Mon-Wed and Fri-Sat 10am-6pm, Thurs 10am-7pm. Tube: Bond Street.

The Mulberry travel bag is a British institution, as venerable as the Queen and crumpets. Other traditionals include wallets, cigar cases and desk accessories, all sure to appeal to the aristocrat in your life.

Branches: 11/12 Gees Court, W1 (tel. 0171/493-2546); 185 Brompton Rd., SW3 (tel. 0171/225-0313).

Paul Smith

40-44 Floral St., WC2. Tel. 0171/379-7133. Open Mon-Wed and Fri 1030am-630pm, Thurs 1030am-7pm, Sat 10am-630pm. Tube: Covent Garden.

Paul Smith's distinctive British designs have catapulted him to the top of the men's fashion world with everything from suits and shoes to underwear and jeans. But for those in the know, he's really about accessories. And check-out the Paul Smith Sale Shop, 23 Avery Row, W1 (tel. 0171/493-1287).

Philip Treacy

69 Elizabeth St., SW1. Tel. 0171/259-9605. Open by appointment only. Tube: Sloane Square.

When it comes to British milliners, Philip Treacy is tops. His ready-to-wear hats and hairpieces have graced the finest heads, and his wild couture collection is worthy of any runway in the world. This shop also sells Treacy accessories scarves, gloves and the like.

EYEWEAR

Auerbach & Steele
129 King's Rd., SW3. Tel. 0171/349-0001. Open Mon-Sat 10am-630pm, Sun noon-5pm. Tube: Sloane Square/South Kensington.

The trendiest eyewear shop in the city, A&S sells all the hippest brands like Yohji Yamamoto and Boz & Theo. The perfect place to change your look.

Bromptons
306 Old Brompton Rd., SW5. Tel. 0171/373-5753. Open Mon-Sat 930am-630pm. Tube: Earl's Court.

When you need a quick fix, Bromptons delivers fast service and budget frames that start at about £50. They also offer contact lens replacement. Lots of other branches around town too.

Kirk Originals
36 Earlham St., WC2. Tel. 0171/240-5055. Open Mon-Wed and Fri-Sat 1030am-630pm, Thurs 1030am-7pm. Tube: Covent Garden.

Like the name says, all frames sold here are all original designs by Jason Kirk, London's eyewear maker to the stars. Glasses range from about £75 to £250 and are handmade. Famous faces get fitted in the private downstairs lounge.

DEPARTMENT STORES

Fortnum & Mason
181/185 Piccadilly, W1. Tel. 0171/734-8040. Open Mon-Sat 930am-6pm. Tube: Green Park/Piccadilly Circus.

Except for endless throngs of tourists who overwhelm the ground floor food department F&M is a thoroughly wonderful shop in which to browse. The store itself is the star, built with intricately enameled ceilings, trompe l'oeil floors, and marvelous wooden staircases. With a recent expansion into the building next door, now there's even more store to cheer about.

Harrods
87/135 Brompton Rd., SW1. Tel. 0171/730-1234. Open Mon-Tue and Sat 10am-6pm, Wed-Fri 10am-7pm. Tube: Knightsbridge.

Harrods is an institution only because it calls itself one. The store is huge to the point of being unnavigable with precious little to offer that you can't get elsewhere (at better prices). And it's horribly crowded with all the same tourists who, earlier in the day, were standing on line outside Madame Tussaud's. That said, the incredible ground-floor food halls are unparalleled and definitely worth a gawk; but for shopping, hunt somewhere else.

Harvey Nichols

109-125 Knightsbridge, SW1. Tel. 0171/235-5000. Open Mon-Tue and Thurs-Sat 10am-7pm, Wed 10am-8pm, Sun noon-6pm. Tube: Knightsbridge.

Once one of Princess Diana's favorite hunting grounds, "Harvey Nicks," as it is affectionately known, is the Capital's current darling of upscale consumerism. Behind the famed window displays are six floors of great shopping for both men and women. The fifth floor restaurants are destinations all their own, with everything from a pint and crisps to lobster thermador. The Aveda Spa is the shop's latest addition (see Chapter 6/Exercising).

John Lewis

278/306 Oxford St., W1. Tel. 0171/629-7711. Open Mon-Wed and Fri 930am-6pm, Thurs 10am-8pm, Sat 9am-6pm. Tube: Oxford Circus.
A sensible department store for the masses, John Lewis offers an enormous variety of conservative-styled merchandise at relatively honest "Never Knowingly Undersold" prices. Strengths include linens, fabrics and hats, as well as some of the city's best prices for Levi's 501s.

Liberty

210/220 Regent St., W1. Tel. 0171/734-1234. Open Mon-Wed and Fri-Sat 10am-630pm, Thurs 10am-730pm. Tube: Oxford Circus.
Forget Harrods, Liberty is the true London department store shopping experience. A bewigged attendant welcomes visitors to the handsome old world store, where traditional Arts & Crafts originals vie with contemporary cool. The shop is justifiably famous for its dress fabrics and boasts the best scarf collection in the city. The designer labels for men are especially impressive, and the antiques department is worth a trip in itself.

Marks & Spencer

458 Oxford St., W1. Tel. 0171/935-7954. Open Mon-Fri 9am-8pm, Sat 9am-7pm, Sun noon-6pm. Tube: Marble Arch.
The British underwear giant's flagship store also attracts crowds clamoring for women's fashions, groceries and cosmetics.

Selfridges

400 Oxford St., W1. Tel. 0171/629-1234. Open Mon-Wed and Sat 10am-7pm, Thurs-Fri 10am-8pm, Sun noon-6pm. Tube: Marble Arch/Bond Street.
With a recent image change and revamp, Selfridges now aims for the stylish value of Harvey Nichols. Although plenty of serious gaps remain, there is still plenty to coo about. Namely, Europe's largest perfume department, an extensive luggage section and an entire floor devoted to mid-price women's fashions. The cellar bookstore and kitchen shop are also worth a peek. The shop is best on rainy days, when a free machine stationed at the entrance wraps shoppers wet umbrellas.

Outdoor markets are where knowledgeable Londoners and bargain hunters shop for fashions, furniture, antiques and all sorts of rubbish. Dozens of little markets dot the city, most catering to individual communities selling produce and household junk. Portobello Road and Camden are the market Methuselahs; enormous affairs that draw thousands of browsers weekly.

The Camden Markets

Camden Market, Camden High St (at Buck St), NW1. Open Thurs-Sun 9am-530pm.
Camden Lock Market, Camden Lock Place (at Chalk Farm Rd), NW1. Open Sat-Sun 10am-6pm.
Stables Yard Market, Chalk Farm Rd (at Hartland Rd), NW1. Open Sat-Sun 8am-6pm.
Camden Canal Market, Chalk Farm Rd (at Castle Haven Rd), NW1. Open Sat-Sun 10am-6pm.
Electric Market, Camden High St (at Dewbury Terrace), NW1. Open Sun 9am-530pm.
Tube: Camden Town.

Originating as a small counter-culture market in the 1970s, the Camden markets have sprawled into five emporia, all within close proximity to one another. Once the essential Sunday destination for any fashionista with street cred, we're sorry to report that the Camden-area markets are past their prime. The market stalls are now more likely to peddle tourist droppings than edgy alternative gear. Their sheer size is what continues to make these markets something of an attraction; worth a quick nip should you have a morning to spare. Designer seconds and vintage clothes can still be found at both Camden Market and the Electric Ballroom. Interesting furniture is on display at the newer Stables Yard warehouse, and you can dig up some unique decorative pieces at Camden Lock.

Portobello Road Market

Portobello Rd., W10 and W11. Golborne Rd., W10. Open: Antiques, Sat 4am-6pm; Fashions, Fri 7am-4pm, Sat 8am-5pm, Sun 9am-4pm. Tube: Ladbroke Grove/Notting Hill/Westbourne Park.

Portobello Road is the quintessential London market. Antiques are closest to Notting Hill underground, where you'll find hundreds of stands hawking all manner of fabricated fossils, from ancient swords and silverware to retro pocket watches, bottles, binoculars, fountain pens, medallions, coins... you name it. The relative high demand translates into few bargains, but haggling is (almost) always in order. Further along the road, past the produce stalls and under the overpass, you'll come to the fashion market, where unknown designers sell their handmade creations along with terrific unique handicrafts, bootleg tapes and lots of second-hand clothes. Pop into the arcades along the way to the Ladbroke tube, where you'll encounter more of the same.

Bayswater Road Art Market

Bayswater Road (btw Lancaster Terrace/Queensway). Open Sundays 930am-4pm.

Each Sunday hundreds of local artists set up their oils, watercolors, etchings and collages along a mile-long road on the north side of Hyde Park. Although most of the offerings are substandard tourist fodder, there are some gems to be found.

FOOD & DRINK

Berry Bros. & Rudd

3 St James's St., SW1. Tel. 0171/396-9600. Open Mon-Fri 9am-530pm, Sat 10am-4pm. Tube: Green Park.

Berry Bros, the Queen's bottle shop, has been purveying wine and spirits to royalty and the rich for centuries. In addition to their wealth of wines, it's worth checking out the shop's giant scales that once weighed coffee as well as customers like Lord Byron, Lord Nelson, and King William IV (who weighed 189 lbs. in boots). You can find the Berry Bros. & Rudd name on every bottle of Cutty Sark Whiskey.

Cadenhead´s Covent Garden Whisky Shop

3 Russell St., WC2. Tel. 0171/379-4640. Open Mon 11am-630pm, Tues-Sat 11am-7pm, Sun noon-430pm. Tube: Covent Garden/Holborn.

Stocking over 200 whiskies, Cadenhead's is Mecca for single-malt lovers. All of Scotland is represented, with special emphasis on unusuals like vatted malts, cask-strength and rare bottles. Irish whiskies and Caribbean single-cask rums are here too.

Gerry's

74 Old Compton St., W1. Tel. 0171/734-4215. Open Mon-Fri 9am-630pm, Sat 9am-530pm. Tube: Leicester Square/Piccadilly Circus.

When we wanted to track down an African liqueur distilled from peanuts there was only one choice: Gerry's. If it's strange, ancient or rare, this place has it. For the bartender who thinks she knows everything, visit Gerry's and think again. This is the place to fulfill your duty-free allotment.

Rococo

321 King's Rd., SW3. Tel. 0171/352-5857. Open Mon-Sat 10am-630pm, Sun noon-5pm. Tube: Sloane Square then bus 11, 19, 22 or 49.

Rococo is one of the very best chocolate shops anywhere. Period. Their secret is freshness, quality and creative flavorings such as cardamom, chili, and Earl Grey tea. Buy for immediate gratification only, as truffles don't travel well.

The Spice Shop
1 Blenheim Crescent, W1. Tel. 0171/
221-4448. Open Mon-Sat 930am-6pm.
Tube: Ladbroke Grove/Notting Hill Gate.
We ve traveled the world and never found a
better-stocked spice shop. Every flavorful leaf, bark
and berry seems to be here, along with every
international chef worth his or her salt.

The Tea House
15A Neal St., WC2. Tel. 0171/240-7539. Open Mon-
Sat 10am-7pm, Sun noon-6pm. Tube: Covent Garden.
This perfectly located Covent Garden shop proves single-
handedly that the Brits are tops when it comes to tea. About
five dozen varieties from around the world are always
available, attractively packaged either loose-leaf or bagged.
Get a whiff of one of their smoked teas and check out their
exhaustive list of herbal and fruit admixtures.

Twinings
2105. Open by appointment only. Tube: Sloane Square.
When it comes to British milliners, Philip Treacy is tops. His
ready-to-wear hats and hairpieces have graced the finest heads,
and his wild couture collection is worthy of any runway in the world.
This shop also sells Treacy accessories scarves, gloves and the like.

CIGARS

Alfred Dunhill
48 Jermyn St., SW1. Tel. 0171/290-8602. Open Mon-Fri
930am-6pm, Sat 10am-6pm. Tube: Green Park/Piccadilly
Circus.
Both cigar store and gallery, this august shop boasts one of
the world's largest walk-in humidors, chock-full of stogies from
Cuba, the Dominican Republic and elsewhere. The Dunhill
museum is a small collection of ancient pipes and accessories,
some of which are amazing works of art.

Davidoff of London
35 St James's St., SW1. Tel. 0171/930-3079. Open Mon-
Fri 9am-6pm, Sat 930am-6pm. Tube: Green Park.
Jonesing for a Cubano? Head to this upscale corner
cigar store with one of the broadest selections of
singles in the country. A fresh Montecristo A will
set you back about £30.

08 THE RESTAURANT SCENE

London has become a major destination for "restaura-tourists" and the foodies of the world. The past dozen years have seen a gastronomic revolution in this formerly bland city, and today London is widely recognized as one of the restaurant capitals of the world. The concept of eating out was only recently integrated into the city's infrastructure, and already London boasts 27 Michelin-starred restaurants, more than any other city outside Paris (Chez Nico and The Oak Room are both three-starred, and La Tante Claire, Pied á Terre, and Gordon Ramsay are two-starred.). The capital of Britain is finally taking full advantage of its multi-cultural past, extracting the best elements of the world's cuisines and tossing them together in new, inventive ways.

"Modern British" cuisine means classic English working-class food, updated with inventive sauces and surprising flavor combinations that are never completely incomprehensible to the English workers in question. In other words, Britain's new cooking is basically the same chow that's been brewing in the kitchens of New York and California for the last ten years: internationally-influenced meals made with fresh, local ingredients. True cosmopolitans won't get too excited about another plate of grilled tuna with wilted field greens, but here it's celebrated as an entirely novel concept.

Likewise, chefs have become celebrities in their own right, interviewed in the Sunday magazines and sometimes even pursued by tabloid press paparazzi. Marco Pierre White is the hottest chef of the moment, and restaurateur/designer Terence Conran, who now operates over a dozen major eateries, continues to be the single biggest influence on the city's dining scene (*see* London's Major Multi-Restaurateurs, below). In the 1960s, Conran's Habitat stores persuaded middle-class Brits to pretend they all lived in Provençal farmhouses. Ten years later, Conran was credited with single-handedly pulling London out of recession by developing previously neglected areas and instilling enough confidence in the locals to dine out. One of Conran's most particular creations is the "mega-restaurant," 200-plus seat warehouses designed to bring the culture of dining out to the masses. Quaglino's, Bluebird, and Mezzo are among a growing list of behemoths vying for the palates and wallets of Britain's common men and women.

It's safe to say that some of the best dining in the world is in London; the result of a confluence of hyperlatives: some of Europe's best chefs, finest ingredients and prettiest people converge nightly in the capital's top restaurants.

The Reservations Game

As sure as death and taxes, there's always a restaurant of the moment; one in which every night is like a movie premiere, filled with film stars, models, musicians, the media elite, athletes, restaurateurs, garmentos and generic rich people. Within the first two weeks of opening everyone will trample through, before quickly heading off to the Next New Thing. If you want to be there too, it's time to use some muscle, work the phones and call in favors. When white-hot slows to simmering, street wise mortals can get reservations about a week in advance. Unless you have connections, or don't mind being seated at 6pm or 11pm, we advise you to reserve a table as far in advance as possible (the country code for England is 44; the city code for central London is 171. From the US dial 011-44-171 plus the local number).

COVETED TABLES:
AVANT*guide TO GETTING ONE

For a Tough Reservation:

Restaurant: Good afternoon, Haute Restaurant, may I help you?

Avant-Guide: Hello, who am I speaking to?

Restaurant: (caught slightly off-guard) This is Joanne.

Avant-Guide: (with feigned recognition) Oh, hi Joanne! This is (your name). I need a table for four tonight at nine-o'clock, can you do it? Say yes.

Restaurant: (laughs) Well, we're booked solid, Ms. (your name), but I'll see what I can do. Can you hold-on a moment?

Avant-Guide: Thank you very much, it's really important. (Short pause)

Restaurant: Ms. (your name), we can fit you in at 8:30, is that OK?

For a Really Tough Reservation:

Restaurant: Good afternoon, Haute Restaurant, may I help you?

Avant-Guide: Hello, who am I speaking to?

Restaurant: (caught slightly off-guard) This is Joanne.

Avant-Guide: (with feigned recognition) Oh, hi Joanne! This is Randy Thomas at CKA Talent. I'm calling for my client (your name). She needs a table for four tonight at nine-o'clock, can you do it? Say yes. (continue with above script).

Tipping:

London waiters expect to be tipped about 10 to 15 percent of the total bill, though it is becoming more common these days for restaurants to tack on an obligatory 12.5% service charge. Beware unscrupulous waiters who make the service charge, then leave the final total open on the credit card slip. Hee hee.

Kibbles & Bits

- Lunch is usually 25-50% cheaper than dinner.
- Although we may say some nasty things in the reviews below, we enthusiastically recommend all the restaurants we list.
- You can drink the water.

Our reviewers have no connection with any establishment listed in this guidebook or on the Avant-Guide Web site. All restaurant visits are anonymous, and expenses are paid by Avant-Guide.

RESTAURANTS BY AREA & PRICE

The cost (£) reflects the average price of an entree

£	= Under £10
££	= £10–£15
£££	= £16–£20
££££	= Over £20

WHO'S WHO:
LONDON'S MAJOR MULTI-RESTAURATEURS

Terence Conran
Bibendum
Blue Print Cafe
Bluebird
Butlers Wharf Chop House
Cantina del Ponte
Coq d'Argent
Le Pont de la Tour
Mezzo
Quaglino's
Sartoria
The Orrery
Zinc Bar & Grill

Nico Ladenis
Simply Nico
Simply Nico Barbican
Simply Nico Chelsea
Chez Nico

Alastair Little
Alastair Little
Alastair Little at Lancaster Rd

Jean-Christophe Novelli
Maison Novelli
Les Saveurs
Novelli EC1
Novelli W8

Oliver Peyton
Mash
Isola
Coast

Gordon Ramsay
Gordon Ramsay
Petrus

Gary Rhodes
City Rhodes
Rhodes in the Square

Marco Pierre White
Cafe Royal Grill Room
Mirabelle
MPW
Oak Room MPW
Quo Vadis (with Damien Hirst)
The Criterion

Antony Worrall Thompson
WOZ
WIZ

Aldo Zilli
Signor Zilli
Zilli Fish

Chez Nico

90 Park Lane, W1. Tel. 0171/409-1290. Reservations essential. Lunch Mon-Fri noon-2pm; dinner Mon-Sat 7-11pm. Main courses £24-£30; Set dinner £53 (2-course), £65 (3-course), £75 (10-course); set lunch £25 (2-course), £40 (3-course). AE, MC, V. Tube: Hyde Park Corner/Marble Arch.

One of the very best restaurants in London, with three Michelin stars and prices to prove it, Nico Ladenis' celebrated, eponymous dining room is a classic French affair that straddles the fence between serene and stuffy. the atmosphere is elegant and civilized at dinner, and more lively at lunch. Nico's specialty is classic French peasant food, updated with inventive sauces and surprising flavor combinations that are never completely incomprehensible to the French peasants in question. Here, foie gras—a dish that has made its way onto the menu at practically every expense-account restaurant in town—is paired with caramelized oranges or a sweet-and-tart poached pear. It's a memorable appetizer that has become something of a signature dish here. Grilled sea scallops and leeks is another excellent starter from Nico's seasonal menus. Entrees run the gamut from Dover sole with a sharp cream sauce to veal in a dense red wine and porcini reduction. The French-heavy wine cellar is excellent, with the best on the budget end around £30. Chez Nico is known for a particularly generous fixed-price lunch, the back door to an otherwise very expensive meal.

Gordon Ramsay

68 Royal Hospital Rd., SW3. Tel. 0171/352-4441. Reservations essential. Kitchen open Mon-Fri noon-245pm and 645-11pm. Set dinner £50-£65; set lunches £28-£50. AE, MC, V. Tube: Sloane Square.

In his time Gordon Ramsay has worked for a pantheon of top chefs, including Joel Robuchon, Marco Pierre White and Pierre Koffmann, whose own La Tante Claire occupied this same space, before it moved to the Berkeley Hotel (see below). He is legendary in London for both his out-of-this-world food, and his very temporal temperament that has lead to the summary execution of his staff and random acts of unkindness to his customers.

The food, in a word, is sensational. Meals might begin with roasted scallops on cauliflower purée with white raisin vinaigrette, a salad of crispy pig's trotters with calves sweetbreads, or fried quail's eggs with cream vinaigrette, which appears on the menu as a bow to Koffman. Mains can be complicated, like turbot poached in red wine and served with a sumptuous claret-rich reduction, or pigeon that's poached then grilled, and served with a pizza of foie gras and truffle sauce.

The classic cuisine is matched by exacting service, and a subdued, pale dining room infused with a whiff of deco. The best seats are at window tables 5, 6 and 7. But getting one of these coveted spots is another story. Tables must be booked one month in advance; if you want to eat on the 9th of September, you have to telephone the morning of August 9th. Try to call just one minute after midnight.

La Tante Claire

in the Berkeley Hotel, Wilton Pl., SW1. Tel. 0171/823-2003. Reservations essential. Kitchen open Mon-Fri noon-2pm and 7-11pm, Sat 7-11pm. Main courses £24-£35. AE, MC, V. Tube: Hyde Park Corner/Knightsbridge.

After 21 years in Chelsea, chef Pierre Koffmann moved his show to Knightsbridge's stylish Berkeley Hotel, where it competes with the intensely successful Vong (see below). While Vong attracts younger rich people, this august establishment is the domain of older foreign foodies; the kind who subscribe to Gourmet Magazine.

The mauve and green dining room is so vrai Francais you practically expect a dog under the next table. The menu is in French, the food is serious, and jackets are required. And prices are in the stratosphere. Accordingly, Koffmann's signature starter is foie gras galette, and lots of dishes incorporate high-priced ingredients like lobster and truffles. Koffmann's classics include a delicious white bean soup flavored with slices of chorizo, delectable lobster risotto, and grilled Dover sole with béarnaise sauce. The well-versed staff are auditioning for nothing, and can describe each dish right down to the last sprig of parsley. Make reservations, and don't forget to bring a date.

Nobu

in the Metropolitan Hotel, 19 Old Park Lane, W1. Tel. 0171/447-4747. Reservations essential. Kitchen open Mon-Sat 6-1030pm, Sun 6-945pm. Main courses £17-£25. AE, MC, V. Tube: Hyde Park Corner.

Chef Nobu Matsuhisa, a Japanese-Peruvian-Los Angeleno, is perfectly pedigreed to introduce a new kind of fusion artistry to London. The stunningly delicious results are perfect ying-yang combinations like raw yellowtail with jalepeño peppers, barely-cooked sashimi drizzled with garlic-and-ginger-flavored olive oil, and monkfish-liver paté with soy dressing and a gleaming dollop of caviar. Squid pasta—delicate segments of squid and asparagus glazed with butter and garlic sauce—is an extraordinary taste treat you won't soon forget. The stylish minimalist dining room is at once stunning and stereotyped, mixing contemporary Japanese architecture with a model waitstaff dressed by Comme des Garçons. Meals are served with flourish; saké (chilled) is poured from exquisite bamboo flasks. And there are terrific views of Park Lane and Hyde Park. Needless to say, A-list personalities fill this space nightly, many of whom are sleeping upstairs in the swanky Metropolitan Hotel. The main complaint about Nobu is the difficulty of getting a table. Make reservations as far in advance as possible, come for lunch, or arrive alone with your eye on a single seat at the sushi bar.

The Oak Room

in the Meridien Hotel, 21 Piccadilly, W1. Tel. 0171/437-0202. Reservations essential. Lunch Mon-Fri noon-215pm; dinner Mon-Sat 7-1115pm. Set dinner £80; set lunch £30. AE, MC, V. Tube: Piccadilly Circus.

The Oak Room is the premiere showcase for Marco Pierre White, London's most celebrated chef. Michelin's staffers have bestowed this establishment with a coveted three stars, amply warranted by both the cooking and ambiance. Classic French cooking and top ingredients converge nightly in this amazing kitchen, turning

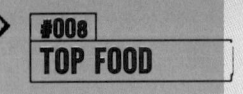
out dishes that are so fragrant they threaten to levitate off the table. To start, you might indulge in a juicy seared scallop, served in its shell with a garlicky cream sauce. Follow that with herb-encrusted roast cod or tender roast pork with mash. Of course it's delicious, but portions are also uncharacteristically generous.

The imposing dining room actually looks like the temple to high cuisine it is. The food, the ambience and the bill will take your breath away.

Pied à Terre

34 Charlotte St., W1. Tel. 0171/636-1178. Reservations recommended. Lunch Mon-Fri 1215-215pm; dinner Mon-Sat 715-1030pm. Main courses £22-£28. AE, MC, V. Tube: Goodge Street/Tottenham Court Road.

Forget about the bland modernist setting because, first and foremost, Pied à Terre serves great food. Intensely-flavored meats and fish are the specialties of this house, served to a good cross-section of suits and sporty types. Chef Tom Aikens consistently earns his two Michelin stars with flavorful and creative renditions of brasserie classics. There are ebbs in the kitchen's flow, but most meals are winners, including the house's specialty starter, roasted veal sweetbreads paired with a garlicky green parsley sauce. Entrees might include saffron scented pan fried mullet, or fricassee of rabbit in an intense stock reduction. Desserts are tops, and a gratis plate of petits fours helps soften the blow of the bill.

Vong

in the Berkeley Hotel, Wilton Pl., SW1. Tel. 0171/235-1010. Reservations essential. Lunch Mon-Fri noon-230pm; dinner Mon-Sat 6-1130pm, Sun 6-10pm; brunch Sat-Sun 1130am-2pm. Main courses £11-£16. AE, MC, V. Tube: Hyde Park Corner/ Knightsbridge.

Vong is the first European outpost for New York-based chef Jean-Georges Vongerichten, one of the century's great masters of contemporary cooking. His East/West combinations are so extravagantly inventive they're almost mystifying. Witness, for example, seared sea scallops in a sweetish raisin-caper emulsion served with grilled, caramelized cauliflower. Or Muscovy duck with spicy sweet-and-sour jus—unlikely but wonderful tag teams of ingredients. Of course, the master himself is rarely in the kitchen, but his presence is felt everywhere, from the creative menus to the stylish metropolitan atmosphere of the spacious basement dining room. Local cognoscenti know Vong for weekend brunches, when some of the world's most unusual fusion-style dim sum are served.

Zafferano

15 Lowndes St., SW1. Tel. 0171/235-5800. Reservations essential. Lunch Mon-Sat noon-230pm; dinner Mon-Sat 7-11pm. Set dinner £27-£37. Set lunch £18-£21. AE, MC, V. Tube: Knightsbridge.

Often referred to as "the best Italian restaurant in London," Zafferano is as superb as it is busy. The draw is awesomely flavorful classic Italian cooking, chummy service and portions that are far larger than they need to be. Staples include wind-dried tuna on top of a mound of crunchy French beans, wild herb ravioli, and chargrilled anything—vegetables/chicken/fish. Veal chops are reminiscent of Jurassic Park, and seafood specials really are. Regulars swear by roast rabbit with parma ham and polenta, and the pan-fried calf's liver with balsamic vinegar. The book of Italian wines is as lengthy as it is expensive.

Physically, Zafferano is standard new-wave Italian, with exposed-brick walls, brightly colored wall-hangings, and a florabundance of cut stems. The dining room is very noisy and always crowded—even those with reservations have to wait for tables. There is often a limo or two parked out front (Joan Collins, Margaret Thatcher, Eric Clapton), and locals tend to get down to business early here, snug in their seats by 730pm. Window tables are the most coveted, but if you don't have reservations at least a week in advance, fugetaboutit.

Connaught Restaurant & Grill Room

Connaught Hotel, Carlos Pl., W1. Tel. 0171/491-0668. Reservations essential. Kitchen open daily 630-1045pm. Main courses £26-£32. AE, MC, V. Tube: Bond Street/Green Park.

From the tailcoated career waitstaff to the green Georgian wallpaper, The Connaught is as far from avant as it gets. The look is retro nothing: the paneled bar and the wing-back ar chairs speak of the real McCoy. And if you think the dining room is dated, just get a look at the food. Forget fusion. Culinarily, The Connaught is that rare and wonderful thing: a rigorously unambitious restaurant. It's a masculine, old world grill with crystal chandeliers, banquette seating and a meaty menu of carteological no-no's that seems terminally locked in the 50's. The 1850s. The restaurant-that-time-forgot is so out of fashion that it's actually in vogue, packed with power-lunching suits by day, and a full complement of tourists and locals by night. While some restaurants update their menus nightly, The Connaught's might not have changed in a quarter of a century. Witness Sole Jubilee, created for the Queen's 1977 Silver Jubilee, or Tourte de Cailles "Noce d'Or," invented for the occasion of the monarch's golden wedding anniversary. Along with steaks and grills, the kitchen turns out excellent coquille St. Jacques, kipper paté, and filet mignon Stroganoff. Go hungry, with a bulging wallet, and your tongue firmly in cheek.

Rules

35 Maiden Lane, WC2. Tel. 0171/836-5314. Reservations recommended. Kitchen open Mon-Sat noon-1130pm, Sun noon-1030pm. Main courses £14-£19. AE, MC, V. Tube: Covent Garden/Charing Cross.

Opened in 1798, Rules is one of London's oldest restaurants, and smells like it. This is "Olde Englande" in full monty. The specialty here is "feathered and furred"; if it's hunted, it's on the menu. Game players are best catered for in autumn and winter, when the seasonal specialties might include wild highland deer with bitter chocolate sauce, roast breast of squab with cherry tomato compote, and roast lamb with basil mash, butter beans and Madeira sauce. Duck, partridge and other wild birds make regular appearances, as does some shell and fin fish. The thoroughly old-skool decor includes requisite dark wood paneling and a plethora of hunting prints. Jackets and ties are required and the room feels exclusive, though one look around lets you know it's not. Rules is best for lunch, when the strong sense of Edwardian comfort is not diminished by all the American accents.

Sweetings

39 Queen Victoria St., EC4. Tel. 0171/248-3062. Reservations not accepted. Kitchen open Mon-Fri 1130am-3pm. Main courses £10-£19. No cards. Tube Cannon Street.

Venerable Sweetings is best defined by what it's not. There's no dinner, no reservations, no coffee, no credit cards and almost no meat. There is healthy doses of ancient Englishness, lots of 19th-century mementos, and plenty of perfectly-cooked fish. The atmosphere is traditional to the point of eccentricity, sprawling across three separate rooms set with stools fronting a series of counters. Well-dressed business-types, and the more-than-

occasional anglophile visitor come to slurp up real turtle soup, smoked cod roe, or fried whitebait, followed by smoked haddock with poached eggs, sea bass in Pernod sauce, or grilled Dover sole. The "Bill of Fare" changes just twice a year: once when oysters go off the menu and again when they come back on. Wash them down with Black Velvet (Guinness and champagne) served in half-pint tankards, some of which date back to the Victorian era.

Simpson's in the Strand

100 Strand, WC2. Tel. 0171/836-9112. Reservations recommended. Breakfast Mon-Fri 7-11am; lunch daily noon-230pm; dinner Mon-Sat 530-11pm, Sun 6-9pm. Main courses £15-£20. AE, MC, V. Tube: Covent Garden/Charing Cross.

Serving from splendid silver trolleys since 1828, Simpson's is synonymous with verrry, verrry traditional English meals like roast beef with horseradish sauce, lamb with mint sauce and red currant jelly, and pork with crackling (roasted pork fat) and apple sauce. The restaurant opened in 1828 as a citadel of male chauvinism, and didn't admit women into the Great Cigar Divan until 1979. Alas, times change. These days, Simpson's is wooing ladies who lunch with a lighter modern British menu in the West Dining Room. Traditionalists head straight for the Old World dining rooms, upstairs, where the gentleman's club image is further cultivated by tailcoated waiters and surroundings that feel aristocratic, as long as you don't look too closely at the diners at the next table. Last, but not least, Simpson's is perhaps the best place in London to have the Great British Breakfast, an opulent multi-course meal that comprised of fruit, porridge, eggs, bacon, grilled trout, sausages, chops and steak.

iN-StYLE SCENES

Axis

One Aldwych Hotel, 1 Aldwych, WC2. Tel. 0171/300-0300. Reservations recommended. Lunch Mon-Fri noon-3pm; dinner Mon-Sat 6-1115pm. Main courses £15-£20. AE, MC, V. Tube: Covent Garden/Temple.

The split-level, modernist dining room buried under Gordon Campbell Gray's fashionable hotel is appropriately popular with the black-clothes crowd. Customers include the usual smattering of famous faces, along with plenty of people who are simply generically rich. Needless to say, the best table is No. 15, set between two pillars at center-stage. The food, you may have guessed, is almost an afterthought. Tasty starters include king prawn cocktail, and poached haddock and cheese soufflé tart. The best mains are boneless hare with creamed turnips, fresh-water prawn and crayfish ravioli, and hay-baked leg of Welsh lamb with gravy and fresh mint sauce. Prices are refreshingly reasonable, and reservations are well within the reach of mere mortals.

Bank

1 Kingsway, WC2. Tel. 0171/379-9797. Reservations recommended. Breakfast Mon-Fri 730-1030am; lunch Mon-Fri noon-3pm; dinner daily 530-1130pm; brunch Sat-Sun 1130am-330pm. Main courses £11-£17. AE, MC, V. Tube: Charing Cross/Holborn/ Temple/ Covent Garden.

Inserting a trendy restaurant into a former NatWest bank seems at once both high-concept and oh so 1980s. Despite the

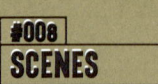

contrivance, this place works. It's a huge, noisy place with high ceilings and reasonable prices that are meant for the masses: the local media mob and suits from The City. The rigorously designed mega-interior is meant to wow, with a glazed walkway that leads into a red and yellow dining room where the primary architectural elements are seemingly endless rows of glass "fins" suspended from the ceiling, part of a 26-ton cut-glass chandelier. Bank is big, very big.

The food is Modern British tossed with brasserie classics. Fish and chips is a big seller here, but you'd do just as well to choose seared mullet, roast rabbit leg, or Cajun blackened chicken. It's all good, though nothing on the menu can compete with the space itself. Put your mobile phone on the table if you want to look like a local, or sit at the bar for breakfast.

Belgo Centraal

50 Earlham St., WC2. Tel. 0171/813-2233.

Reservations recommended. Kitchen open Mon-Sat noon-1130pm, Sun noon-1030pm. Main courses £8-£15. AE, MC. V. Tube: Covent Garden.

Until 1999, when they opened a branch in Manhattan, Belgo was the London restaurant we dreamed of whenever we were away. It's a theme restaurant of the best kind, with waiters in monk's habits serving Belgian comfort food in a cavernous, post-modern "monastery." An industrial chic elevator drops guests into a vast, brick-vaulted cellar. To your left is the restaurant, for which a reservation is recommended. To your right is the beer hall, for which you cross your fingers that you'll find a seat. Both sides are perpetually heaving with twentysomethings and thirtywhatevers feasting on spit-roasted chicken, steak tartare, and wild boar sausages. The most popular meal is mussels, frites and beer. One hundred different kinds of Belgian brews are on offer and, weekdays from 6-8pm you pay the price for your set meal according to the time it is ordered. So if you order chicken, fries and beer at 615pm, you pay £6.15. Smart.

Branches: Belgo Noord, 72 Chalk Farm Road NW1; Belgo Zuid, 124 Ladbroke Grove.

Bibendum

Michelin House, 81 Fulham Rd., SW3. Tel. 0171/581-5817. Reservations essential. Lunch Mon–Fri 1230-230pm, Sat–Sun 1230-3pm; dinner Mon–Sat 7-11pm; Sun 7-1030pm. Main courses £22-£28; lunch £16-£22. Tube: South Kensington.

One of the first restaurants in the Conran empire, Bibendum remains one of the best. The restaurant occupies an amazing early 20th-century building that was once the UK headquarters for the Michelin Tyre Company. It's a swoony art deco space, with spectacular tiling, plenty of stained glass, and depictions of the Michelin Man on everything from plates and glasses to walls and windows. The second thing you'll notice is the prices which, appropriately enough for this themery, are "inflated." But the relatively traditional British and European menu rarely misses its intended marks. Winning starters include yogurt-marinated herring, brioche with bone marrow, and black-ink risotto with grilled squid and caviar. Main courses include both surf (fillet of sea bass with saffron and tarragon cream) and turf (calf's sweetbreads en croête), paired with a good selection of wines. Suits arrive in droves at lunch, while dinner draws rich diners who live in the neighborhood. If you just want a snack and a peek at the architecture, head for the ground-floor oyster bar.

Bluebird

350 King's Rd., SW3. Tel. 0171/559-1000. Reservations essential. Lunch Mon–Fri noon-330pm; dinner Mon–Sat 6-1130pm, Sun 6-1030pm; brunch Sat–Sun 11am-4pm. Main courses £11-£28. Tube: Sloane Square, then bus 19 or 22.

This 1920s garage-turned-gastro complex is one of the newer jewels in the Conran crown. The ground floor is an upscale produce market and grocery selling top-quality cheese, poultry, breads and wine (see Food Markets, below). Upstairs is a relaxed, warehouse-sized restaurant, with blue-shirted waiters darting back and forth beneath exposed I-beams. It's a bright space that looks best during the day, with a lighthearted menu to match. Quality food and decent prices translates into dishes like soy-glazed reef fish, and kangaroo on sweet potato mash. The best dishes come from the wood-fired oven, including squab, lobster and rabbit.

Birdcage

110 Whitfield St., W1. Tel. 0171/383-3346. Reservations essential. Kitchen open Mon–Fri noon-11pm, Sat–Sun 6pm-11pm. Set meals £24-£35. AE, MC, V. Tube: Goodge Street/Warren Street.

At Birdcage, that holy trinity of trendy, stylish and delicious come together to make a really great restaurant. Culinarily, the restaurant represents the epitome of haute Asian cooking. Chef/owner Michael von Hruschka, formerly of The Oriental in Bangkok, regularly wows diners with amazing dishes like creamy tom yam soup, chicken curry with jasmine rice, and parchment wrapped fish, which is lifted onto the plate with a dramatic puff of steam. This is not fusion food, it's a sophisticated take on Thai cuisine, created with top ingredients. The restaurant's colorful decor and central location pulls in a youngish crowd that's attracted to attitude-free service and respectable noise levels. It's a fun spot that often devolves into one of the most rollicking parties in town. Eat dessert elsewhere.

Coast

26B Albemarle St., W1. Tel. 0171/495-5999.
Reservations recommended. Lunch Mon-Fri noon-3pm; dinner Mon-Sat 6pm-midnight, Sun 6-1030pm; brunch Sat-Sun noon-330pm. Main courses £15-£20. AE, MC, V. Tube: Green Park.

Coast is the largest poseur place in Britain. Customers dress up and come to Oliver Peyton's cavernous eatery to ogle each other. There's nothing else to do, since it's way too loud for any serious conversation. Formerly a Volvo showroom, Coast is now a different kind of exhibit hall. It's an adventurous, futuristic place, with enormous plate-glass windows, corners that have been rounded to seamlessly blend floors into walls, and some of the best bathrooms in the city. The multi-million pound interior leaves some diners cold, but even they warm to the exceptional cooking, which shows occasional flashes of brilliance. The menu is fusion fru-fru, and offers something for everyone. Reserve a table on the ground floor to avoid cellar Siberia and learn sign language if you plan to converse.

Great Eastern Dining Room

54 Great Eastern St., EC2. Tel. 0171/613-4545. Reservations essential. Lunch Mon-Fri noon-3pm; dinner Mon-Sat 630-11pm. Main courses £8-£14. AE, MC, V. Tube: Liverpool Street/Old Street.

Not to be confused with the nearby Great Eastern Hotel, which includes a half-dozen restaurants of its own, this popularly-priced bar and eatery occupies a smart-looking corner building right in the heart of Shoreditch. The food is vaguely rustic Northern Italian, and includes dishes like lemon pasta with caper berries and battered lemon, spicy tomato-and-mussel stew, and grilled lamb steak with garlic and white-bean mash. Few meals top £10. Paper-clothed tables are as tiny as the prices, but the wood floors and hard surfaces make for big noise. Dress is casual, but tie-wearers won't be turned away.

The Ivy

1 West St., WC2. Tel. 0171/836-4751. Reservations essential. Lunch Mon-Sat noon-3pm, Sun noon-330pm; dinner daily 530pm-midnight. Main courses £10-£22. AE, MC, V. Tube: Covent Garden/Leicester Square.

The Ivy is packed each night not because it's new, but because it's great. Ten years running, and this restaurant remains one of the toughest reservations in town, attracting politicians and media stars with unusual loyalty. Even those who arrive without a limo are received graciously. The ground-floor dining room is dressed in Regency style; dark, oak paneled, and fitted with stained glass windows that create a private interior world. You can feel comfortable eating anything here, from bacon and eggs to caviar; the waiter won't bat an eye. The food is both familiar and excellent, and includes perfectly-made corned beef hash, crispy haddock and chips, and dreamy shepherds pie. There are more complicated Italian meals too, followed by delicious desserts that run the gamut from cinnamon fritters to baked Alaska.

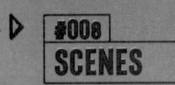

Mash

19-21 Great Portland St., W1. Tel. 0171/637-5555. Reservations recommended. Breakfast Mon-Fri 8am-noon; lunch Mon-Fri noon-3pm; dinner daily 6pm-1am; brunch Sat-Sun 11am-430pm. Main courses £8-£14. AE, MC, V. Tube: Great Portland Street/Oxford Circus.

Oliver Peyton's very hip restaurant and brew-pub is one of the most heavily hyped tickets in town. It's a suitably stylish place, with high noise levels, colorful site-specific artwork, designer staff uniforms, twin wood-fired ovens, and a humidor. You get the picture. The barley pop is good, the food is agreeable, and the total effect is greater than the sum of the parts. Caesar salad and designer pizzas (i.e. chili, ginger and lime-marinated swordfish) make the best beer ballast. Wood-baked fish, suckling pig, chicken, and lamb are somewhat less successful, but few diners seem to mind. Women might pop in just to see the video screen in the lavatory that shows distorted goings-on in the men's room via hidden camera. See Chapter 9/Bars for complete information.

The Pharmacy Restaurant & Bar

150 Notting Hill Gate, W11. Tel. 0171/221-2442. Reservations recommended. Lunch daily noon–245pm; dinner Mon-Sat 645-1145pm, Sun 7-1030pm. Main courses £13–£19. AE, MC, V.

The main thing to know about Pharmacy is that no self-respecting local Notting Hillbilly would ever go there. Designed by pop-art hero Damien Hirst, and endlessly promoted by the fawning media, the restaurant opened to a mob of self-conscious poseurs who have already left for the Next New Thing. Drugs are the high concept here; or rather the store that sells them. Pharmacy is a theme restaurant, decorated with medical instruments, pill-shaped bar stools, and a waitstaff in Prada-designed surgical gowns. Thankfully the food is far less fussy. Decent meals can be made of roast suckling pig, sea bass with Nobu sauce (sashimi slivers in a Japanese style citrus dressing), and sweetbreads with cooked lettuce hearts and mash.

Mezzo/Mezzonine

100 Wardour St., W1. Tel. 0171/314-4000. Reservations recommended. Mezzo: Lunch Mon-Fri noon-3pm, Sun 1230-3pm; dinner Mon-Thurs 6pm-midnight, Fri-Sat 6pm-1am. Main courses £15-£21. AE, MC, V. Mezzonine: Lunch Mon-Fri noon-3pm, Sat noon-4pm; dinner Mon-Thurs 530pm-1am, Fri-Sat 530pm-3am. Main courses £8-£14. AE, MC, V. Tube: Leicester Square/Piccadilly Circus/Tottenham Court Road.

Once the location of the Marquee Club where everyone from Elton John to REM played, this enormous space is now home to twin restaurants Mezzo and Mezzonine. Food, service, atmosphere... there's nothing really great about this place. But the ground zero location and 700-plus seats makes this buzzy Conran spot the perfect standby when all other Soho doors are closed to you.

Mezzo, the bustling restaurant in the basement, features a surprisingly light, double height interior that feels nouveau Jazz Age schmoozy. The Frenchish-Mediterranian menu is somewhat nouveau, offering everything from grilled chicken in vegetable broth to baked salmon with a Thai style sauce.

Mezzonine, the brasserie and bar on the ground floor, is just as good as the restaurant below, at a cheaper price. The menu is split equally between large and small dishes, making this the perfect stop for a full dinner or some light snacks. Winners include seared salmon on delicately spiced eggplant, and glass noodle salad loaded with fresh herbs and a fabulous sour dressing. The menu warns that you may be ordered into the bar with your dessert and coffee if other people are waiting for a table. Ouch!

Momo

25 Heddon St., W1. Tel. 0171/434-4040. Reservations recommended. Lunch Mon-Fri 1230-215pm; dinner Mon-Sat 645-1145pm. Main courses £11-£17. AE, MC, V. Tube: Piccadilly Circus.

So what if food of the Maghreb was last year's cuisine of the moment? Momo continues to rock with both food and atmosphere that's outrageously appealing. Often called the city's "best North African restaurant," Momo evokes the complex atmosphere of Marrakech, without the danger of the real thing. A non-descript entrance belies little about the goings-on inside, where French servers weave around low tables occupied by trendy romantics. The best tables, on the raised dais in the upstairs dining-room, are usually occupied by Prada-wearing waifs and their fashionably-dressed dates. It's a devastatingly sexy interior, but on warm nights, the dining room should be renounced in favor of the sidewalks, on which huge rugs are rolled out for surreal al fresco dining. Parisian DJs spin classical Arab music, which transforms into rocking World music after 10pm. All this and terrific meals too. Try vegetable couscous served with side plates of sultanas and chickpeas, or coriander spiced monkfish tagine.

Quaglino's

16 Bury St., SW1. Tel. 0171/930-6767. Reservations essential. Lunch daily noon-3pm; dinner Mon-Thurs 530pm-midnight, Fri-Sat 530pm-1am, Sun 530-11pm. Main courses £16-£22. AE, MC, V. Tube: Green Park.

Situated in a former hotel ballroom and inspired by the great brasseries of Paris, Quaglino's feels like a landlocked Carnival cruise ship self-consciously infused with the spirit of the 1930s (a cigarette girl!). Like Conran's other mega-restaurants, this one feels like a destination place, meant to be the culmination of one's evening, and not just a prelude to another event. Indeed, the atmosphere is far more memorable than the food. It's a huge place with an artificial skylight that's artfully lit to mimic the change in light from day to night. Almost everything—from the classic wooden cafe chairs right down to the ashtrays—has been specially crafted for the space. And it's perpetually buzzing with train station acoustics.

Remarkably for such a corporate restaurant, standards in the kitchen remain high. Fish and chips are an essential element of an otherwise upscale menu that offers great seafood and decent grills. Shoulder of pork with crunchy crackling and the fresh shellfish platter are high on our list of reccommendables.

Yo! Sushi

52 Poland St., W1. Tel. 0171/287-0443. Reservations not accepted. Kitchen open daily noon-midnight. Sushi £2-£4 for 2 pcs. AE, MC, V. Tube: Oxford Circus/Piccadilly Circus.

Conveyor-belt sushi is taken to the next level in this rock 'n' roll Japanese, where green tea is dispensed from barside taps, tableside buttons summon the waitstaff, and drinks are delivered by robotic trolleys. The high tech, stainless steel interior, pulsating with televisions and techo music, is just oh so Tokyo. And the low-priced, low-quality sushi is often just what the doctor needs at 11pm. It's popular with Soho's fashion people, workers from area post-production houses, and visiting tightwads from around the globe.

The Sugar Club

21 Warwick St., W1. Tel. 0171/437-7776. Reservations recommended. Kitchen open Mon-Sat noon-230pm and 6-1130pm, Sun 1230-230pm. Main courses £12-£18. AE, MC, V. Tube: Oxford Circus/Piccadilly Circus.

One of our most favorite restaurants in London, The Sugar Club has both a sophisticated kitchen and aggressively fashion conscious dining room that has earned a prestigious two Michelin stars. Australian chef Peter Gordon whips up avant fusion cuisine that combines thought-provoking combinations of taste and texture that are unique and delicious. The simple, bi-level dining rooms are often something of a scene. But even the appearance of Madonna can't take the wind out of the kitchen's sails. Spicy carrot, red lentil and coconut soup with minted yogurt is about as good as anything we've ever put in our mouths. Yellowtail sashimi with black-bean-and-ginger salsa is a multiethnic jambalaya that just somehow really *works*. As does kangaroo with mint, peanuts and chili-and-lime dressing.

PUb GRUb

Pub food can vary from snacks at the bar to a complete restaurant meal. The best, as far as we're concerned, are traditional English affairs serving the kind of stick-to-your-ribs comfort food that made Britain the laughing stock of the world's foodies. Popular items include bangers and mash (sausages and mashed potatoes), meat pies (including cottage pie, made with ground beef and a potato topping), pasties (meat-filled pastries), and ploughman's lunch (a plate of bread, cheese, salad, and chutney). Wash it all down with a beer. Some of the best pubs display their casseroles so you can choose by sight. When they don't, ask the barkeep for a menu and expect an inferior meal.

For some strange reason, food and drink at pubs are usually kept as separately from one another as vigilantly as a rabbi keeps milk from meat. Order and pay for each independently.

And beware of pub conversions, former Victorian-style pubs gussied-up to serve modern British, fru-fru fusion, and even Thai and Indonesian meals.

Fox & Anchor

115 Charterhouse St., EC1. Tel. 0171/253-4838. Kitchen open Mon-Fri 7am-3pm. AE, MC, V.

While the vast majority of London's pubs can't open until 11am, the F&A is early-licensed to cater to workers at the adjacent Smithfield meat market, thus making it the people's choice for a boozy breakfast. Each morning, after-hours partiers rub shoulders with early-rising beef porters while washing down banger-and-egg fry-ups with pints of Fuller's London Pride.

The Guinea

30 Bruton Pl., W1. Tel. 0171/499-1210. Reservations recommended. Lunch Mon-Fri 1230-230pm; dinner Mon-Sat 630-11pm. Main courses £12-£19. AE, MC, V. Tube: Green Park/Bond Street/Oxford Circus.

Perhaps the best pub food in Soho, The Guinea is justly famous for it's steak and kidney pie, a hearty and hefty affair that's repeatedly been voted "Best in Britain." At these prices, it better be. English lamb and grilled steaks are also popular and, like most everything else, are drenched in delicious gravy and served with mountains of potatoes and vegetables. The crowd is a balanced mix of well-spoken visitors and local business types, none of whom seem to mind the inevitable short wait for a table.

fish & ChiPS

▼

Fish and Chips are Britain's most famous junk food cliché. You can find battered and fried seafood on nouveau menus all over town, but there's nothing like the big greasy portion you pick up at a "chippy," wrapped in a newspaper and drenched with vinegar and salt. Cod is the cheapest and most popular fish, while haddock and skate are the connoisseurs' choices. The chip, a French invention, arrived on these shores in the early 19th century for the classic pairing with deep-fried fish. There are few remaining traditional fish and chip shops in London. Fast-fooderies have taken their toll, and Middle Eastern "kebob" places have picked up the slack.

Geale's

2 Farmer St., W8. Tel. 0171/727-7969. Reservations not accepted. Lunch daily noon-3pm, dinner Tues-Sat 6-11pm. Main courses £7-£9. AE, MC, V. Tube: Notting Hill Gate.

Geale's is not the cheapest place, but it's the one favored by locals such as John Cleese, and has been around forever. Their secret? The freshest fish is fried in beef drippings for extra carteological fun. The crust is deliciously crisp while the meat remains juicy and tender. If you're famous, bring a photo for their wall.

North Sea Fish Restaurant
7-8 Leigh St., WC1. Tel. 0171/387-5892. Reservations accepted. Kitchen open Mon-Sat noon-230pm and 530-1030pm. Main courses £8-£10. MC, V. Tube: Russell Square/Kings Cross.
North Sea serves great fish and chips. Period. There are almost a dozen kinds of filets to choose from, and they will fry them traditionally or grill them avant. The seafood platter comes piled high with cod, plaice, haddock, scampi, squid and sardines, sided with tartar sauce and a first-rate basket of chips.

Rock & Sole Plaice
47 Endell St., WC2. Tel. 0171/836-3785. Reservations recommended. Kitchen open Mon-Sat 1130am-10pm, Sun 1130am-9pm. Main courses £5-£7. No cards. Tube: Covent Garden.
The finest chippy in the West End dishes up BIG portions of plaice, cod, haddock and rock salmon coddled in a golden batter, and paired with terrific wedge-shaped chips. The dining room is far from beautiful, but there are outside tables in summer.

Upper Street Fish Shop
324 Upper St., N1. Tel. 0171/359-1401. Reservations not accepted. Lunch Tues-Fri noon-215pm, Sat noon-3pm; dinner Mon-Thurs 6-1015pm, Fri-Sat 530-115pm. Main courses £7-£9. No cards. Tube: Angel. Lots of punters think that Upper Street Fish Shop cooks the best fish in London. And not just fried fish. Their unusually creative kitchen is as comfortable dishing out poached halibut and smoked haddock as it is fresh plaice in a puffy light batter. Top it all with a mountain of chips.

Cafe Spice Namaste

16 Prescot St., E1. Tel. 0171/488-9242. Reservations essential. Lunch Mon-Fri noon-3pm; dinner Mon-Fri 615-1030pm, Sat 630-10pm. Main courses £9-£13. AE, MC, V. Tube: Tower Hill/Aldgate East.

Soaring ceilings and contemporary surroundings complement some of the very best Indian food in London. That's no easy task in a city that takes its curry as seriously as its fish and chips. The arms-length menu is all over the sub-continent, offering fantastic food that's both beautifully prepared and expertly presented. Venison tikka is full with fine-grained meat, Tandoori duck arrives amazingly tender, and the pork vindaloo is one of the best hot dishes we've ever put to tooth. Breads are great too, including Peshawari nan, which packs a coconut, cardamom and dried fruit surprise. As you can see, this is no ordinary post-lager curry house, and experts are well catered for. Arrive hungry and sober and settle in for a treat.

Chutney Mary

535 King's Rd., SW10. Tel. 0171/351-3113. Reservations recommended. Lunch Mon-Sat 1230-230pm, Sun 1230-3pm; dinner Mon-Sat 7-1130pm, Sun 7-1030pm. Main courses £11-£16. AE, MC, V. Tube: Fulham Broadway.

Another top restaurant serving multi-regional Indian cuisine, Chutney Mary is a large basement restaurant squeezed amongst antique shops near the bottom of King's Road. The Raj interior, complete with potted ferns and neocolonial ceiling fans, won't distract you from the delicious Anglo-Indian food that seems to move from strength to strength. Specialties include diced leg of lamb with coriander, layered with saffron rice and cooked slowly in a sealed pot; and fiery Mangalore prawn curry cooked with spices in an earthenware pot. The best tables for intimacy and discretion are located in the Conservatory, where Liz Hurley and Hugh Grant have been spotted. Richard Branson, Christy Turlington, Pamela Anderson and lots of other famous faces have also graced these premises. The bar is famous for its fruity mango daiquiris, though we prefer Goa on the rocks, a lively blend of vodka, crushed limes and sugar.

Dakota

127 Ledbury Rd., W11. Tel. 0171/792-9191. Reservations recommended. Lunch Mon-Fri noon-330pm; dinner Mon-Thurs 7-11pm, Fri-Sat 7-1130pm, Sun 7-1030pm; brunch Sat-Sun noon-330pm. Main courses £12-£17. AE, MC, V. Tube: Notting Hill.

This bastion of the American Southwest is known for lively surroundings, great drinks and good food—in that order. It's a fun, upbeat place, attracting well-dressed hipsters out for a night on the town. Most of the patrons who have probably never tasted real Southwestern cuisine will honestly swear that Dakota serves the best tequila-cured mahi mahi on the planet. And if you're not fresh from New Mexico, you might even agree. Other hits include corn and sweet potato chowder with crayfish tails, and pecan encrusted rump of lamb with roasted corn and chipotle mash.

Daquise

20 Thurloe St., SW7. Tel. 0171/589-6117. Reservations accepted. Kitchen open daily 10am–11pm. Main courses £7–£9. MC, V. Tube: South Kensington.

A South Kensington institution since before you were born, Daquise is a Polish restaurant that time forgot. It's a "pre-gentrified" space with Formica fittings, Soviet-era decor and cobwebs on everything, including the waiters. The thorough menu reads like a survey of stick-to-your-ribs Slavic cooking and includes staples like borscht with sour cream, cheese blini, potato pirogi and cabbage leaves densely stuffed with rice, meat and vegetables. Plenty of customers look like they're part of the furniture, and nobody seems to mind if you come just to idle some time away and kick back a few shots of vodka. The restaurant's location, just outside the South Ken underground, makes it the perfect lunch stop when visiting the area's museums.

East One

175 St. John Street, EC1. Tel. 0171/566-0088. Reservations recommended. Lunch Mon–Fri noon–

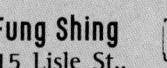

Fung Shing

15 Lisle St., WC2. Tel. 0171/437-1539. Kitchen open daily noon-1130pm. Main courses £10-£15. AE, MC. V. Tube: Leicester Square/Piccadilly Circus.

One of the best restaurants in Chinatown, Fung Shing is equally as adept at turning out traditional pork and poultry meals as they are at new creations like venison in a spicy yellow bean sauce and veal in peppercorns. It's the more adventurous dishes that continue to draw the crowds, and this is one place where you can confidently order an unfamiliar dish and float away to a new culinary dimension. Chief among these might be cold herb boiled chicken with jelly fish, or crispy spicy eel, both of which are outstanding. Ask for the short menu of "Chef's Recommendations," and try to get a recommendation from the manager, Jimmy Jim.

Granita

127 Upper St., N1. Tel. 0171/226-3222. Reservations recommended. Lunch Wed-Sun 1230-230pm; dinner Tues-Sat 630-1030pm, Sun 630-10pm. Main courses £9-£14. MC, V. Tube: Angel/Highbury & Islington.

Despite becoming famous as the place where Tony Blair hatched New Labour, Granita remains a seriously good restaurant catering to enthusiastic foodies. The space itself is rigorously uncluttered; basically a spare blue box with upholster-less furnishings, wooden floors, and a well dressed all-female staff. And the food is just as straightforward, and much of it is pescatori. Look for chargrilled cod with Spanish butter beans, or salmon fillet served on a bed of lentils. Celebrity diners show up with regularity, especially at lunch, when three courses can be had for under £15.

3pm; dinner Mon-Sat 5pm-midnight. All-you-can-eat £10-£13. AE, MC, V. Tube: Farringdon/Angel.

London's version of a Mongolian Barbecue is a modern, minimalist (some say spare) place with a short menu, pleasant staff, and interesting wooden bench seating that's said to be inspired by Hong Kong's Star Ferry. Here's the rap: Load up a bowl with strips of raw meat and chopped vegetables, then hand it to a chef on the post-post-modern stainless-steel podium for some showy flash frying. It's such a fun, filling way to eat you can almost overlook the automatic 12.5% service charge.

Hunan

51 Pimlico Rd., SW1. Tel. 0171/730-5712. Lunch daily noon-230pm; dinner Mon–Sat 6-11pm. Main courses £11-£15. AE, MC. V. Tube: Sloane Square.

Hunan is the spiciest of Chinese foods, and a welcome alternative to the relatively bland Cantonese fare that's served over in Chinatown. The chef here is great, creating exotic foods with rich meaty broths and scattered with lotus seeds, wolfberries and other magical medicinal Chinese things. Cognoscenti drive across town for lettuce leaf dumplings cradling spicy minced meat with crunchy nuts and vegetables, or succulent scallops in fish-fragrant sauce. Of course, there's chilies with everything. Regulars order the "feast," a multi-course extravaganza that changes daily according to what's in the kitchen. It's hard to make specific suggestions because it's not unusual that the dish you ordered has little to do with the one that's delivered. But marinated octopus, tea-smoked duck, and beef in Hunan sauce are all good and, suffice to say, we've never had a bad meal here.

Livebait

21 Wellington St., WC2. Tel. 0171/836-7161. Reservations recommended. Lunch daily noon-3pm; dinner Mon–Sat 530-1130pm. Main courses £14-£19. AE, MC. V. Tube: Covent Garden.

We find it endlessly amusing that, despite being surrounded by water, Britain never developed a taste for fish—vinegary deep fried filets notwithstanding. Livebait strives to change all that with a bold attempt to combine the sea with being seen. A great West End location and an amazingly extensive oyster bar play to all manner of fish-lovers and shellfish-ionados. Good chefs and top ingredients converge daily in Livebait's hard-working kitchen where fresh ocean catch like halibut, cod, monkfish and tuna are brought in each morning and handled with utmost care. Preparations can be unusual. Witness pan-roasted Ecuadorian tuna served with a sashimi of Kentish cured mackerel, horseradish sauce and a sunny-side-up egg. Of course, you can also choose your poisson and have it cooked to your specifications: baked, poached or grilled. There's a good selection of whites by the glass, and an appetizing fish display and exhibition kitchen in the rear. And because it's wrapped in green and white bathroom tiling, the restaurant serves decibels with everything.

Branch: 41-45 The Cut, SE1 (tel. 0171/928-7211).

Mirabelle

56 Curzon St., W1. Tel. 0171/499-4636. Reservations recommended. Lunch daily noon-3pm; dinner Mon–Sat 6pm-midnight, Sun 6-1030pm. Main courses £15-£18. AE, MC, V. Tube: Green Park

Lots of foodies consider Mirabelle to be chef Marco Pierre White's best restaurant. It's a voguish place that has all the flavor of the Oak Room (see above), with none of the stodginess. The food, in a word, is brilliant, and the dining rooms are plainly elegant, glamorous and inviting. Best of all, food this great is accessible to gourmets on a budget. The menu reads like a list of MPW classics, and includes the chef's signature truffled parsley soup with smoky bacon broth and poached egg, braised pork cheeks with spices and fresh ginger, and smoked haddock with Jersey royals and beurre blanc. The waitstaff is great, the sommeliers are knowledgeable, and Mirabelle is set to take its rightful place as one of the best restaurants in town.

Oxo Tower Restaurant & Brasserie

Oxo Tower Wharf, 8th Fl., Barge House St., SE1. Tel. 0171/803-3888. Reservations essential. Lunch Mon-Fri, Sun noon-3pm; dinner Mon-Sat 6-11pm, Sun 630-1030pm. Main courses £16-£21. AE, MC, V. Tube: Blackfriars/ Waterloo.

There is so much hype surrounding these riverfront South Bank restaurants that it can be hard to distinguish truth from fantasy. One thing's for certain, Oxo Tower Restaurant & Brasserie serves up one of the best views in the city. Step off the elevator and turn left towards the restaurant, or right, into the brasserie. The two spaces are almost identical—only the menus, and prices, diverge. The glass-wrapped eateries feature floor-to-ceiling windows that run the length of their respective dining rooms, offering unobstructed views over the Thames to St. Paul's, the City and Houses of Parliament. Inside is stunning too. Topped with a double-height aerofoil roof, the entire mood of the restaurant can be changed as the louvered ceiling is turned on its white side during the day, and sea-blue at night. Both meals attract lots of business types and precious few funky folk. Meals on both sides of the divide are good, fusion affairs (read: marinated skirt steak with roast shallots, roast sirloin with Thai noodle salad). But ultimately it's the view you'll remember, so go on a clear day, visit the Brasserie side, and splurge on a good bottle of wine.

The People's Palace

Royal Festival Hall, South Bank Centre, SE1. Tel. 0171/928-9999. Reservations recommended. Kitchen open daily noon-3pm and 530-1045pm. Main courses £12-£18. AE, MC, V. Tube: Waterloo.

Located above the main foyer of Royal Festival Hall, The People's Palace has matured into an excellent restaurant of massive proportions. Despite its arts complex location, the dining room has become a destination restaurant in which the majority of diners aren't concert-goers. Physically, it's a huge place, built with theatrical effects that vaguely echo the concert hall downstairs. And the great views across the Thames are rivaled only by nearby Oxo Tower. Food here is that ubiquitous Continental melange, offering up dishes like pan fried mullet with saffron cream, warm chicken livers with baby spinach and walnut dressing, and seared escalope of salmon with lemon oil mash.

Porters

17 Henrietta St., WC2. Tel. 0171/836-6466. Reservations recommended on weekends. Kitchen open Mon-Sat noon-1130pm, Sun noon-830pm. Main courses £8-£14. AE, MC, V. Tube: Covent Garden.

We include Porters here as our single nod to unabashed tourism. The Covent Garden restaurant is an English theme eatery serving the quintessential pies and puddings of Old Blighty. Fish and chips, steak and mushroom pie, and bangers and mash are served in a faux-Victorian wood-and-brass dining room. The food is good, portions are decent and prices are touristy.

Rasa

6 Dering St., W1. Tel. 0171/629-1346. Reservations recommended. Kitchen open Mon-Sat noon-3pm and 6-11pm, Sun 6-11pm. Main courses £7-£12. AE, MC, V. Tube: Oxford Circus.

The South Indian state of Kerala is one of the most celebrated regions of the Sub-continent. And Rasa, a colorful little Keralan vegetarian eatery, is one of London's most venerated Indian restaurants. Food here is the Real McCoy, cooked by native chefs who appear to be fresh off the airplane. Order acchapam and pappadavadai—poppadum taken to new heights of crunch—while deciding on your main courses. Recommended meals include Vendakka cheera kozhambu, a particularly excellent combination of okra, spinach, shallots and spices cooked in coconut milk and yogurt; and vegetable curries sweetened with green banana and green papaya. Reservations are a must.

Branch: 55 Stoke Newington Church Street, N16 (tel. 0171/249-0344).

Royal China

13 Queensway, W2. Tel. 0171/221-2535. Kitchen open Mon-Thurs noon-11pm, Fri-Sat noon-1130pm, Sun 11am-10pm. Dim Sum £1.50-£3.50; main courses £12-£17. AE, MC. V. Tube: Queensway.

People come here for the great selection of dim sum, pure and simple. Stashed away in Bayswater, Royal China is one of those exotic and wonderful Hong Kong-style hideaways (translation: crowded, noisy, bullet service, and lazy susans in the middle of big round tables) that you would have a hard time finding on your own. A huge variety of dim sum, piled high on carts, is piloted around the dining room by middle-aged, no-nonsense waitresses. Hail one, and start pointing to the little treats you want: Steamed meat-filled dumplings, sautéed soft-shell crab, bacon-wrapped shrimp, rice-noodle rolls, Peking duck, savory pork triangles and much more. Other items are available from a vast Cantonese menu, but they somehow seem superfluous.

Veronica's

3 Hereford Rd., W2. Tel. 0171/229-5079. Reservations recommended. Lunch Mon-Fri noon-3pm; dinner Mon-Sat 6-1115pm. Main courses £14-£19. AE, MC, V. Tube: Bayswater/Queensway.

We love Veronica's because it's a unique and original place that's not duplicated anywhere else. Veronica Shaw is a masterful chef with a passion for historical British fare. Her modest restaurant is something of a living culinary museum, dedicated to classical meals created from recipes that date from as far back at the 14th century. As you might imagine, many of the meals are unusual meaty affairs like spring lamb with crabmeat, calf's liver and beetroot, and steak grilled on an oak plank, but there are always fish and vegetable dishes, too. This is no kitschy theme restaurant: some of the food is so good we felt as though we dined and went to Devon.

Wódka

12 St. Alban's Grove, W8. Tel. 0171/937-6513. Reservations recommended. Lunch Mon-Fri 1230-230pm; dinner daily 7-1115pm. Main courses £10-£15. AE, MC, V. Tube: Gloucester Road/High Street Kensington.

An post-contemporary Polish restaurant—as anyone who has been to Warsaw knows—is the ultimate contradiction. The truth is, however, that Wódka is just far ahead of its time. Specializing in surprisingly light classics served in swanky minimalist surroundings, this is as upscale and professional as Polish gets—anywhere. The best dishes are blend ingredients and techniques from both sides of the Iron Curtain. Char-grilled swordfish is paired with couscous, and roast suckling pig is stuffed with kasha and wild mushrooms. And one of London's greatest vodka selections, featuring about three dozen varieties, assures that most diners leave happy.

Cafe in the Crypt

Crypt of St. Martin-in-the-Fields, Trafalgar Square, WC2. Tel. 0171/839-4342. Reservations not accepted. Kitchen open daily noon-315pm and 5-730pm. Main courses £5-£7. Tube: Leicester Square/Embankment/Charing Cross.

A sanctuary of tranquillity in the middle of the bustle, this cellar eatery is located beneath the most famous church in Trafalgar Square. Choose your own salads from the multitude of offerings along a lengthy counter, or order a warm meal along the lines of vegetable rigatoni or pork escalope in cider sauce. Classical music and classic desserts round out the offerings.

Cafe Emm

17 Frith St., W1. Tel. 0171/437-0723.
Reservations not accepted. Lunch
Mon–Fri 1230-230pm; Dinner Mon–
Thurs 530-1030pm, Fri 530pm-
1230am, Sat 5pm-1230am, Sun 530-
1030pm. Main courses £5-£7. Tube:
Leicester Square/Tottenham Court
Road.

While Cafe Emm hardly stands out,
either physically or gastronomically, it
packs a powerful one-two punch of huge
portions and small prices that's one of
Soho's most coveted combinations. Good
music creates an upbeat atmosphere for
chowing down Cajun chicken with fries,
salmon and cheese crepes, and smoked
salmon salad with rice.

Food for Thought

31 Neal St., WC2. Tel. 0171/836-
0239. Reservations not accepted.
Kitchen open Mon–Sat 930-1130am
and noon-815pm. Main courses £3-
£5. No cards. Tube: Covent Garden.

A ground-breaking vegetarian
restaurant when it opened, Food for
Thought has matured into one of the
most successful eateries in Covent Garden.
The simple downstairs dining room
is perpetually packed with local
salespeople and visitors in the know who
come for big portions of well-prepared
meals that are both cheap and delicious.
There are always a half dozen hot
entrees to choose from (i.e. leek quiche,
polenta with wild mushrooms, lasagna),
as well as a couple of really tasty soups
and salads. If the weather is cooperating,
order everything to take away and head
to nearby Covent Garden
Market.

Ikkyu

7 Newport Pl., WC2. Tel. 0171/439-
3554. Reservations recommended on
weekends. Kitchen open Mon–Wed,
Sun noon-1030pm, Thurs–Sat noon-
1130pm. Main courses £5-£7. AE,
MC, V. Tube: Leicester Square.

This Chinatown eatery is a great
choice for some of the best-value
Japanese food in London. Of course
there's sushi and sashimi, but the real
deals are on shabu shabu set meals
featuring beef teriyaki and tonkatsu
(pork chops on rice).Ramen and soba noodles are also on offer, though real aficionados might find the broth too thin.
Raw fish is good here as is the
selection of yakitori, skewered sticks of
tongue, heart, liver, gizzard or chicken
skin—all at about £1 a stick.

   Branch: 67A Tottenham Court Road,
W1 (tel. 0171/636-9280).

Jenny Lo's Tea House

14 Eccleston St., SW1. Tel. 0171/259-0399. Reservations not accepted. Lunch Mon-Fri 1130am-3pm, Sat noon-3pm; dinner Mon-Sat 6-10pm. Main courses £5-£7. No cards. Tube: Victoria.

Great entrees and a terrific selection of Chinese teas served in excruciatingly plain surroundings pretty much sums up this Victorian-area Chinese. Jenny Lo's consistently wows diners with fair prices, friendly service and consistently good Chinese cooking. Once seated in the bright, sparse dining room, waiters will walk you through a menu of Chinese hits that sound familiar but taste far better than the glutinous rice toppers dished out by most other places. Recommended dishes include chili-beef soup hofun, black-bean seafood noodles, and long-cooked pork and chestnuts. The herbalist-blended teas are meant to be therapeutic: try "long-life" or "cleansing tea."

Pollo

20 Old Compton St., W1. Tel. 0171/734-5917. Reservations not accepted. Kitchen open daily noon-midnight. Main courses £3.50-£5. Tube: Leicester Square/Tottenham Court Road.

When your wallet is crying "uncle" and your stomach is not far behind, Pollo comes to the rescue with Chef Boy-R-Dee Italian-ish cooking right in the heart of the Soho hustle. There are a reckless number of dishes, and few top £5. Despite the name, pasta is the main meal, available in a myriad of shapes and sizes, and sauced with a choice of over a dozen red and white toppings. Bullet service and uncomfortable wooden seats ensure that nobody lingers too long.

Prêt À Manger
77 St. Martin's Lane, WC2. Tel. 0171/379-5335. Open: Mon-Fri 8am-10pm, Sat 8am-11pm, Sun 10am-8pm. Sandwiches £3-£4. No credit cards. Tube: Leicester Square. The working-class hero turns haute at this upscale sandwich shop, where designer breads are filled with an astounding choice of delicacies that range from smoked meats and fishes to gourmet vegetables and cheeses. Customers line up cafeteria style, then take their meals to stylish matte-black tables. It's a zoo at the height of lunch hour, but after the midday rush, you can enjoy a fantastic meal surrounded by local office workers pretending they don't have real jobs.

Branches: 12 Kingsgate, Victoria Street, SW1 (tel. 0171/828-1559); 17 Eldon St., EC2 (tel. 0171/628-9011); 28 Fleet St., EC4 (tel. 0171/353-2332); and 298 Regent St., W1 (tel. 0171/637-3836).

Wagamama
101 Wigmore St., W1. Tel. 0171/409-0111. Reservations not accepted. Kitchen open Mon-Sat 1230-11pm, Sun 1230am-1030pm. Main courses £5-£7. AE, MC. V. Tube: Bond Street. This quick and cheap nouvelle noodle warehouse offers hip dining for the de-jobbed in trendy Soho. A high-tech slurpateria, Wagamama is intensively designed to serve as many light-and-healthy meals as they can in as short a time as possible. Diners are seated at communal tables on uncomfortable benches enveloped with an atmosphere of high-energy efficiency. Very good, fresh food makes the functional ambiance palatable. The best of the pan-Asian-inspired meals-in-a-bowl are chicken tama rice (Malaysian chicken with coconut, lime & lemongrass sauce) and koi sen udon (a thin seafood noodle dish). Meat and vegetable dumplings (gyoza) make good starters, and there's a small selection of Asian beer. Large portions and low prices draw crowds nightly.

Branches: 4 Streatham St., WC1 (tel. 0171/323-9223); 10 Lexington St., W1 (tel. 0171/292-0990).

Balans

60 Old Compton St., W1. Tel. 0171/437-5212. Reservations recommended. Kitchen open Mon-Fri 8am-5am, Sat 8am-7am, Sun 8am-1am. Main courses £8-£13. AE, MC, V. Tube: Leicester Square/Piccadilly Circus.

This trendy and sleek dining room with tightly-spaced tables and a good sound-system is one of the brightest late-night bites in Soho. The menu is all over the culinary map with items ranging from blackened salmon with broccoli and hollandaise sauce, to a Greek plate of houmous, baba ganoush and taramasalata.

The vibe here is very male and very young; plenty of people come here just to ogle the other customers.

Brick Lane Beigel Bake

159 Brick Lane, E1. Tel. 0171/729-0616. Open nonstop. Bagel with lox £1. No cards. Tube: Liverpool Street/ Shoreditch.

The Beigel Bake has long be a late night pilgrimage for everyone from sleepy taxi drivers to avant partiers. The dense round breads sold here are far smaller than those made Stateside, and are pre-made into sandwiches filled with cream cheese, salt beef, cheese and egg, chopped herring, or smoked salmon. There are two adjacent bagel shops on Brick Lane, and this one is best. Ironically, both are located near the corner of Bacon Street.

Cafe Boheme

13 Old Compton St., W1. Tel. 0171/734-0623. Reservations accepted. Kitchen open Mon-Wed 7am-3am, Thurs-Sat nonstop, Sun 7am-1130pm. Main courses £9-£14. AE, MC, V. Tube: Leicester Square.

Although we wouldn't choose this faux Parisian brasserie with smoke-stained walls during daylight hours, after midnight it's one of the best games in town. The varied and well-cooked food is the attraction: decent meals that range from grilled tuna with lime dressing to baby squid on red pepper purée with deep-fried spinach. The location's great too, right in the heart of Soho.

Istanbul Iskembecisi

9 Stoke Newington Rd., N16. Tel. 0171/254-7291. Reservations not accepted. Kitchen open daily noon-5am. Main courses £6-£10. AE, MC, V. Bus: 38/67/149/242/243.

Day or night, Istanbul Iskembecisi is one of the very best Turkish restaurants in London. The restaurant's legendary tripe soup is said to be a hangover cure, and the kebabs and grilled meats are the perfect cures for hunger. Charcoal-grilled intestines are another house specialty, served as crisp, golden shreds with salads and spices that are meant to be mixed in.

Little Italy

21 Frith St., W1. Tel. 0171/734-4737. Reservations accepted. Kitchen open Mon-Sat noon-4am, Sun noon-1130pm. Main courses £8-£13. AE, MC, V. Tube: Leicester Square/Tottenham Court Road.

Owned by the Pollidri family of Bar Italia fame, Little Italy is another golden success that seems to buzz at all hours. Nobody we know comes here during "normal" hours, but late at night this authentico trottoria is unbeatable. It's neither cheap nor quiet, and the service is as variable as the English weather. But nowhere else in the city can you get such good pasta, meatloaf, or fish at 2am.

Mr. Kong

21 Lisle St., WC2. Tel. 0171/437-7341. Reservations accepted. Kitchen open daily noon-3am. Main courses £7-£10. AE, MC, V. Tube: Leicester Square/Piccadilly Circus.

There's no getting around it, Mr. Kong is a divvy Chinese diner with anti-decor that begins with a nondescript exterior and only gets worse inside. But the food! This is one late-niter that we're happy to eat in even during scheduled mealtimes. The menu is exhaustive, encompassing all the South China traditionals, and prices are well within this world. The best dishes come from the "Cantonese Specials" menu.

Tinseltown

44/46 St. John St., EC1. Tel. 0171/689-2424. Reservations not accepted. Kitchen open nonstop. Main courses £5-£7. MC, V. Tube: Farringdon.

This funky bar and burger joint has been serving the city's clubbers for years. Nothing's cheap and the menu is banal—burgers, grills, and breakfast served anytime. But food and service are decent, and after midnight there's little else open in the vicinity anyway. It's a large, loud diner complete with celeb photos, private booths, and plenty of televisions. And they serve booze till midnight.

Vingt-Quatre

325 Fulham Rd., SW10. Tel. 0171/376-7224. Reservations not accepted. Kitchen open nonstop. Main courses £6-£8. AE, MC, V. Tube: Gloucester Road/Fulham Broadway.

Looking like a greasy spoon that serves cocktails, Vingt-Quatre is a great place for a late night Caesar salad, steak frites, or plate of pasta. Breakfast is also served throughout the night. It can be quite a scene on weekends, when it seems as though half of Chelsea is here.

Coffee houses arrived in The City in 1652, but the coffee bar as we know it is a relatively new phenomenon in London. Today there are Aroma, Starbucks (formerly Seattle Coffee Company) and Coffee Republic shops all around town.

Bar Italia

22 Frith St., W1. Tel. 0171/437-4520. Open Mon-Sat nonstop, Sun 7am-5am. Desserts £1.50-£3. No cards. Tube: Leicester Square/Tottenham Court Road.

For decades, Bar Italia was the only place in Soho you could count on for properly made espresso. It's a small and always-crowded institution through which everyone, it seems, passes through at least once during each week. Bar Italia is basically a traditional Italian coffee bar—just like thousands in Italy. There's a giant Rocky Marciano poster over the bar, a TV that's always turned to Sky Sports, and a sound-system that's particularly partial to Frank Sinatra.

Maison Bertaux

28 Greek St., W1. Tel. 0171/437-6007. Open daily 830am-830pm. Desserts £2.50-£3.50. No cards. Tube: Leicester Square/Tottenham Court Road/ Piccadilly Circus.

Soho's most celebrated cafe is a very French affair with the tricolor in every corner and cobwebs on everything, even the waitresses. They've got good coffee and great pastries and cakes baked fresh daily. Insiders show up just past 1pm for the freshest new batch of goodies.

Patisserie Valerie

44 Old Compton St., W1. Tel. 0171/437-3466. Open Mon-Fri 8am-8pm, Sat 8am-7pm, Sun 930am-6pm. Desserts £2.50-£3.50. AE, MC, V. Tube: Leicester Square/Tottenham Court Road/Piccadilly Circus.

Opened in 1926, Patisserie Valerie is one of the best places we can think of for moist cakes and perfect pastries. Unfortunately, we're not alone in thinking so, and getting a table at any hour is close to impossible. They've got light meals too, including croque monsieur, filled and grilled croissants, mini-pizzas, and a variety of quiches.

AFTERNOON TEAS

The tradition of high tea has mostly gone the way of Empire, but some indulgent locals, and plenty of visitors, still enjoy the ritual daily in many of the city's top Victorian-era hotels. A pot of high-quality tea is usually served with a spread of sandwiches with the crusts removed, pastries, scones, preserves and clotted cream. Live music is *de rigeur*, jackets and ties are required, and reservations are recommended.

The Ritz Hotel, Piccadilly, W1 (tel. 0171/493-8181), is probably London's most famous spot for afternoon tea but, for our money, it's not the best.

Brown's Hotel, 33 Albermarle St., W1 (tel. 0171/518-4108), is more our speed. For £19 you can set in one of three wood-paneled, stained-glass lounges and feel like a millionaire. Tailcoated waiters will make sure that you don't leave hungry, as they fill your table with tomato, cucumber, and meat sandwiches, as well as scones and pastries. Served daily from 3pm to 545pm.

The Lanesborough, Hyde Park Corner, SW1 (tel. 0171/259-5599), is another top choice. They're known for great service, delicious triple-decker sandwiches, and home-made scones with lemon curd, jam and clotted cream. Tea costs £19-£24 (the higher-priced option includes champagne), and is served daily from 330pm to 6pm.

FOOD MARKETS

Sure, you can get decent picnic staples at supermarkets all over town. But for something really special, stop into one of the city's gourmet food shops, veritable museums of cuisine that will make you wish you lived nearby.

Bluebird, 350 King's Rd., SW3 (tel. 0171/559-1000), is a food emporium worth exploring, featuring top-quality produce, meats, cheese, baked goods and prepared foods. It's open Mon-Wed 10am-8pm, Thurs-Fri 10am-9pm, Sat 9am-9pm, Sun noon-6pm (Tube: Sloane Square then bus 11, 19 or 22).

Neal's Yard Dairy, 17 Shorts Gardens, WC2 (tel. 0171/379-7646) has been selling some of the city's best cheeses since 1979. Their specialties are British and Irish cheeses like Cheddar, Double Gloucester, and Stilton, and there are lots of rarer varieties on hand too. The shop also sells terrific, haute bread. It's open Mon-Sat 9am-7pm, Sun 10am-5pm (Tube: Covent Garden).

Planet Organic, 42 Westbourne Grove, W2 (tel. 0171/221-7171), is an amazing place offering a terrific range of fresh produce, cooked meats and delicious cheeses. There's an in-store juice bar too. It's open Mon-Sat 9am-8pm, Sun 11am-4pm (Tube: Bayswater).

192

192 Kensington Park Rd., W11. Tel. 0171/229-0482. Open Mon-Sat 1230-11pm, Sun 1230-1030pm. AE, MC, V. Tube: Ladbroke Grove/Notting Hill Gate.

Popular with Notting Hill trustfunders, media darlings and plenty of famous faces, 192 attracts some of the city's best-dressed socialites. The sleek restaurant/bar sports a black-and-white, banquette-wrapped interior that, some nights, turns into a virtual catwalk. is still one of the best places in town for a perfectly made cocktail. Jackets are required of men, but drink prices are reasonable, and bar snacks are plentiful. Head bartender Peter Dorelli is probably the most famous barkeep in the land, and his assistant, Salim Khouri, is known far and wide for great Bloody Mary's.

Alphabet

61-63 Beak St., W1. Tel. 0171/439-2190. Open Mon-Sat 11am-11pm. MC, V. Tube: Oxford Circus.

Alphabet is a great bar populated by fashionable youngsters drinking well-priced wines and bottled beers. The best place to hang is downstairs, where a street map of Soho is painted onto the floor, and lounging is on surprisingly comfortable car seats. There's good food too.

American Bar

Savoy Hotel, Strand, WC2. Tel. 0171/836-4343. Open Mon-Sat 11am-11pm, Sun noon-3pm, 7-1030pm. AE, MC, V. Tube: Charing Cross.

Opened by an American fleeing Prohibition in the Thirties, the shabby-chic Savoy Hotel piano bar has attracted plenty of celebs in its day, and

Atlantic

20 Glasshouse St., W1. Tel. 0171/ 734-4888. Open Mon-Sat noon-3am, Sun 6-1030pm. AE, MC, V. Tube: Piccadilly Circus.

No London bar made a bigger splash in the late 1990s than Atlantic. And now that the scene has cooled, this place has gotten better. Looking something like the interior of a 1930s cruise liner, this decadent, swoony spot is a timelessly fashionable cocktail zone offering plenty of deck space for serious drinking and people-watching. Lots of punters who don't know any better come here for dinner. Don't. The restaurant is for suckers. And wear Prada to get past the apes at the door

Atlantis

114-117 Crawford St., W1. Tel. 0171/224-2878. Open Mon-Sat 5-11pm. AE, MC, V. Tube: Baker Street.

This watery-themed cellar bar is one of the coolest places in Marylebone. They have one of the best vodka selections in the city.

Connaught American Bar

16 Carlos Pl., W1. Tel. 0171/499-7070. Open Mon-Sat 11am-3pm, 530-11pm, Sun noon-230pm, 7-1030pm. AE, MC, V. Tube: Bond Street/Green Park.

A smokers bar long before the word "trendy" ever preceded "cigar," the Connaught is a terrifically posh spot to visit the humidor and kick back for some quiet conversation. It's a wonderful Victorian-style spot with a gentleman's club atmosphere, complete with leather sofas, wingback armchairs and a wealthy-looking middle-aged crowd. Jackets and ties are required.

Detroit

35 Earlham St., WC2. Tel. 0171/240-2662. Open Mon-Sat 5pm-midnight. AE, MC, V. Tube: Covent Garden.
This dark, low-ceilinged, basement bar is one of the hot spots of Covent Garden. There's no dance floor but that doesn't stop anyone from dancing. A lengthy cocktail menu and decent prices attracts everyone, from loud tourists to locals on the pull.

Kemia Bar at Momo

25 Heddon St., W1. Tel. 0171/434-4040. Open Mon-Sat 7pm-1am. AE, MC, V. Tube: Piccadilly Circus.
The best Casablanca restaurant in the city (see Chapter 8/In-Style Scenes) is such a great place to hang, it's worth booking a table just so you can hang out here. It's hard to say which is more beautiful, the fashion/media crowd or the space itself, which is decked-out with imported Moroccan furnishings right down to the ashtrays.

La Belle Epoque

151 Draycott Ave., SW3. Tel. 00171/460-5000. Open Mon-Sat 530pm-midnight. AE, MC, V. Tube: South Kensington.
One of the largest restaurant complexes in Europe is best experienced from the bar. True to its name, the restaurant recreates a period in French cultural life that embraced good living. Le Bar, situated in the massive cellar, is filled with beveled mirrors, mahogany surfaces, objects d'art and lots of good-looking rich people. It's not the most comfortable place to linger, but this place is a scene that shouldn't be missed.

The Library Bar

Lanesborough Hotel, Hyde Park Corner, SW1. Tel. 0171/259-5599. Open Mon-Sat 11am-11pm, Sun noon-1030pm. AE, MC, V. Tube: Hyde Park Corner.
Calm and sophisticated, and perfect for traditionalists, the Lanesborough Library Bar is the quintessential hotel watering hole. Lined with *trompe l'oeil* bookshelves, it's a great place to eavesdrop on multi-million dollar business deals.

Lupo

50 Dean St., W1. Tel. 00171/434-3399. Open Mon noon-midnight, Tues noon-1am, Wed-Sat noon-2am. AE, MC, V. Tube: Leicester Square/Tottenham Court Road.

It's hard to know who's better looking at Lupo, the clients or the bar staff, all of whom are so fashionable you can hardly tell the media types from the meet-and-greeters. It's a great space too, with a trio of bars and lots of little nooks and crannies for sitting. It's best after 11pm, when the pubs close and the amateurs head home.

Mash

19-21 Great Portland St., W1. Tel. 0171/637-5555. Open Mon-Sat 8am-2am, Sun 10am-1030pm. AE, MC, V. Tube: Oxford Circus.

The city's best-known brew-pub gets high marks for its beer, food and atmosphere. Opened by über-restaurateur Oliver Peyton, who's responsible for the mega-restaurants Atlantic and Coast, has put just as much emphasis on the design of this theatrical bar and restaurant (see Chapter 8/In-Style Scenes).

Navajo Joe's

34 King St., WC2. Tel. 0171/240-4008. Open Mon-Sat noon-11pm. AE, MC, V. Tube: Covent Garden.

The best Mexican restaurant in London isn't saying much, but we can thoroughly recommend this rollicking place for its well-stocked south-of-the-border bar. A terrific selection of tequilas is the main draw, along with plenty of newbies getting drunk on the stuff. Unfortunately, the same can't be said about the food: even the tortilla chips should be skipped.

Notting Hill Arts Club

21 Notting Hill Gate, W11. Tel. 0171/460-4459. Open Mon-Sat 5pm-1am, Sun 4-11pm. No cards. Tube: Notting Hill Gate.

The feeling is that anything goes in this fashionable, yet laid-back, Notting Hill basement. There are two rooms: one for drinking and one for events, which run the gamut from movies and book readings to game-playing and dancing.

Riki-Tik

23-24 Bateman St., W1. Tel. 0171/437-1977. Open Mon-Sat noon-130am. MC, V. Tube: Leicester Square/Tottenham Court Road.

Still trendy after all these years, Riki-Tik is a very cool bar and modish lounge attracting a great, suitless crowd. As stylish as it is busy, this is the place to go when you're looking for a laid-back scene with in-the know locals.

Roadhouse

Jubilee Hall, 35 The Piazza,
WC2. Tel. 0171/240-6001. Open
Mon-Sat 530pm-3am, Sun 530pm-1am.
AE, MC, V. Tube: Covent Garden.
We include the Roadhouse because it's one of the
few places in Covent Garden where you can get a drink
after 11pm. It's a fun spot that's great for first timers.

Saint

8 Great Newport St., WC2. Tel. 0171/240-1551. Open Mon-Thurs
530pm-1am, Fri 530pm-2am, Sat 730pm-2am. AE, MC, V. Tube:
Leicester Square.
Descend the sweeping staircase to Saint's sexy underground. The
post-modern design is favored by the city's fashion crowd. Wednesday's
are best, as weekends here are for amateurs. And Wear Vivienne Westwood
if you want to have a dress as nice as the one on Terry, the doorman.

Tactical

26-27 D'Arblay St., W1. Tel. 0171/287-2823. Open Mon-Fri 9am-11pm,
Sat noon-11pm, Sun noon-1030pm. No cards. Tube: Oxford Circus, Piccadilly
Circus, Tottenham Court Road.
Bar meets club meets bookstore is the strange mixture that makes Tactical
unique. There are regular poetry and book readings, as well as jazz
nights and DJ shows.

Windows Bar

Hilton Park Lane, W1. Tel. 0171/493-8000 ext. 4564. Open Mon-Fri noon-
3pm, 530pm-2am, Sat 530pm-2am, Sun noon-3pm. AE, MC, V. Tube:
Green Park, Hyde Park Corner.
Our most unlikely recommendation is the rooftop bar 28 floors above Hyde
Park, in the hotel that's one of London's greatest architectural disasters.
In-the-know locals join the Wisconsin tourists in hardy drinks at Herculean
prices. The view is spectacular in all directions, and even offers a
birds-eye glimpse into the back garden of Buckingham Palace.

Zinc Bar & Grill

21 Heddon St., W1. Tel. 0171/255-8899. Open Mon-Wed
noon-11pm, Thurs-Sat noon-midnight, Sun noon-6pm. AE,
MC, V. Tube: Piccadilly Circus.
Zinc Bar is one of the newer additions to the Conran
empire. Like lots of others in town, this one is also a
restaurant, but is most successful as a suitably
upscale watering hole. When touring Soho on
a night of intemperance, add Zinc Bar
to the crawl.

As culture shifts towards leisure, London is witnessing a redefinition of the pub. In many of the city's public houses, the old Victorian trappings are being eliminated in favor of a cleaner look: bare wood floors, clear-glass windows, and wide open rooms that won't scare away women. The food is changing too, moving away from traditional English beer ballast towards lighter, internationally-influenced meals.

A small clutch of breweries now control the majority of pubs, and most of the large chain pub/bars (Pitcher & Piano, Slug & Lettuce, All Bar One and Firkin) are designed to cater to a younger, more affluent crowd.

Of course, beer is the main drink; don't even try to order a martini in most places. Sold in Imperial half-pints and pints (20% larger than US measures), the choice is usually between lager and bitter. Many pubs serve particularly good "real" ales, distinguishable at the bar by hand-pumps that must be "pulled" by the barkeep. Real ales are natural, "live" beers, allowed to ferment in the cask.

As a rule, there is no table service in pubs, and drinks (and food) are ordered at the bar. Tipping is unusual and should be reserved for exemplary service. Most pubs are open Monday through Saturday from 11am to 11pm and on Sunday from noon to 3pm and 7 to 1030pm.

BAYSWATER/ PADDINGTON

Archery

4 Bathurst St., W2. Tel. 0171/402-4916. Open Mon-Sat noon-11pm, Sun noon-1030pm. AE, MC, V. Tube: Lancaster Gate.

A 19th-century country-style pub, the Archery is a genuinely old-fashioned place with excellent beer and good food. It's a great choice in the neighborhood.

Mitre

24 Craven Terrace, W2. Tel. 0171/262-5240. Open Mon-Sat noon-11pm, Sun noon-1030pm. MC, V. Tube: Lancaster Gate.

The most famous pub in Bayswater occupies a beautiful Victorian building and contains three bars with marble fireplaces, handsome furnishings, and a maze of little drinking areas tucked under low ceilings. There's plenty of atmosphere, and even a resident ghost.

Victoria

10A Strathern Pl., W2. Tel. 0171/724-1191. Open Mon-Fri 11am-11pm, Sat noon-1am, Sun noon-1030pm. MC, V. Tube: Lancaster Gate.

A huge horseshoe-shaped bar, a good selection of traditional ales, and terrific pan-fried steaks are the draws of this well-known pub. Dance disks spin each Saturday until 1am.

CHELSEA

Chelsea Ram

32 Burnaby St., SW10. Tel. 0171/351-4008. Open Mon-Thurs, Sat 11am-3pm, 530-11pm, Fri 11am-11pm, Sun noon-1030pm. MC, V. Tube: Sloane Square then bus 19 or 22.

Local antique dealers and King's Road shoppers rub shoulders at this bright and handsome pub with big arched windows and a reputation for good food. The best seats are in back, under the skylight.

Orange Brewery

37 Pimlico Rd., SW1. Tel. 0171/730-5984. Open Mon-Sat noon-11pm, Sun noon-1030pm. AE, MC, V. Tube: Sloane Square.

This good-looking four-story Victorian pub makes all its own ale directly beneath the bar. The beers are great, and the room seems not to have changed in a hundred years. It even has a gas light.

Lamb & Flag

33 Rose St., WC2. Tel. 0171/497-9504. Open Mon-Thurs 11am-11pm, Fri-Sat 11am-1045pm, Sun noon-1030pm. No cards. Tube: Covent Garden/Leicester Square.

A throwback to the 17th-century, this beautiful wood-framed ale house has a long history of serving Londoners. Charles Dickens was a customer, as was the poet Dryden, who was almost beaten to death here after being too witty at someone else's expense. Fights were once so common that the pub is know known as the "Bucket of Blood." Today, however, the only real danger is of suffocating in the crowd, which often overflows onto the pavement. It's a minuscule, charming pub tucked in an alley between Floral and Garrick streets.

COVENT GARDEN

Faun & Firkin

18 Bear St., WC2. Tel. 0171/839-3252. Open Mon-Sat 11am-11pm, Sun noon-1030pm. MC, V. Tube: Leicester Square.

A rollicking pub with a stellar location, the Faun & Firkin is a fun place to get drunk and sing along with a roomful of other revelers. They brew their own real ale and food is served all day.

KENSINGTON

Churchill Arms

119 Kensington Church St., W8. Tel. 0171/727-4242. Open Mon-Sat 11am-11pm, Sun noon-1030pm. MC, V. Tube: High Street Kensington/Notting Hill.

Despite an Irish landlord, a parade of Aussies behind the bar, and a kitchen specializing in Thai food, the Churchill feels so very English. Named for Winston, the walls are cluttered with pictures of every prime minister since 1721.

There's an enormous collection of butterflies, and all manner of things hang from the ceilings. The place is always crowded, and looks for any excuse to throw a party.

Windsor Castle
114 Campden Hill Rd., W8. Tel. 0171/727-8491. Open Mon-Sat noon-1130pm, Sun noon-1030pm. AE, MC, V. Kensington High Street/Notting Hill Gate.

When you're looking to rub shoulders with Eton grads, look no further than Windsor Castle, one of the most upmarket pubs in London. There's a garden out back, the kitchen is good, and there's actually a no-smoking section at lunchtimes.

KING'S CROSS/EUSTON

The Backpacker
126 York Way, N1. Tel. 0171/278-8318. Open Fri-Sat 8pm-2am, Sun 330pm-midnight. No cards. Tube: King's Cross.

Drinking in the Backpacker is practically a right of passage for any traveling Australian worth his or her rucksack flag. The myth is true: Aussies love to party, and this place proves it. Weekends are absolutely heaving.

Friar & Firkin
120 Euston Rd., NW1. Tel. 0171/387-2419. Open Mon-Sat noon-11pm, Sun noon-1030pm. No cards. Tube: King's Cross/Euston.

Begun with an old Southwark pub in 1979, the Firkin chain has grown into one of the biggest in London. The hook? Plain wood furnishings, bare floorboards, a little stage with a piano, and lots of party games. And, oh yeah, an on-site brewery too. It's not uncommon for the entire pub to become a huge party with everyone singing along with the piano player. But the Firkin jokes can wear a little thin (the Firkin food! the Firkin toilets! The Firkin beers!).

KNIGHTSBRIDGE

Bunch of Grapes
Brompton Rd., SW3. Tel. 0171/589-4944. Open Mon-Sat 11am-11pm, Sun noon-1030pm. AE, MC, V. Tube: Knightsbridge/South Kensington.

This is hardly the first travel guide to laud the Bunch of Grapes, one of the most beautiful Victorian pubs in the city. It's a sophisticated place, with Corinthian columns, etched glass, painted mirrors, a cast iron balcony, and four polished mahogany bars. And like the sign on the door says, "The management regrets that people in dirty clothing will not be served."

Marquis of Granby

51 Chandos Pl., WC2. Tel. 0171/836-7657. Open Mon-Sat 11am-11pm, Sun noon-1030pm. MC, V. Tube: Leicester Square.

Formerly known as the Hole in the Wall, this ancient, wedge-shaped tavern is popular with actors and workers from the nearby theaters and opera-goers from London Coliseum. The pub was where the infamous 19th century highwayman and ladies' man Claude Duval was caught napping. After his execution he was buried in St. Paul's Church under a stone that reads: "Here lies Duval. Reader, if male thou art look to thy purse; if female to thy heart."

The Salisbury

90 St. Martin's La., WC2. Tel. 0171/836-5863. Open Mon-Sat 11am-11pm, Sun noon-1030pm. AE, MC, V. Tube: Covent Garden/Leicester Square.

All marble, cut-glass, and brass, the Salisbury is often referred to as the most beautiful Victorian-era pub in London. Needless to say, it's a very popular place indeed, packed with theatergoers and the more than occasional actor from the West End playhouses that surround it.

MAYFAIR

The Audley

41 Mount St., W1. Tel. 0171/499-1843. Open Mon-Sat 11am-11pm, Sat noon-3pm, 7-1030pm. AE, MC, V. Tube: Green Park.

If you want to see the grandest pub in London, you should go no further than The Audley, a large glittery public house built in red brick and pink terra-cotta. Inside you'll find oak paneling, original chandeliers, and one of the best-dress crowds in pubdom.

SOHO

French House

49 Dean St., W1. Tel. 0171/437-2799. Open Mon-Sat noon-11pm, Sun noon-1030pm, AE, MC, V. Tube: Leicester Square/Tottenham Court Road.

The unofficial headquarters of the French Resistance in exile during World War II, this small, single-room pub continues to attract a fiercely loyal French-speaking clientele. General de Gaulle wrote his historic declaration of defiance to the Nazis in the room above the bar. Aside from beer, Gitanes and Ricard are the drugs of choice.

The Moon Under Water

105-7 Charing Cross Rd., W1. Tel. 0171/287-6039. Open Mon-Sat 11am-11pm, Sun noon-1030pm. AE, MC, V. Tube: Leicester Square/Tottenham Court Road.

Named after a fictitious pub created by George Orwell, The Moon under Water is one of the simplest, and cheapest, pubs near Leicester Square. There are several real ales and food is served all day. It's also extraordinarily popular.

Pitcher & Piano

69-70 Dean St., W1. Tel. 0171/434-3585. Open Mon-Sat noon-11pm. AE, MC, V. Tube: Leicester Square.

This chain pub points the way to the future: clean, bright and decidedly unstuffy. It's a big, open place with a couple of sofas that appeals to women as well as hard-drinking lads.

WESTMINSTER

Red Lion

48 Parliament St., SW1. Tel. 0171/930-5826. Open Mon-Sat 11am-11pm, Sun noon-1030pm. MC, V. Tube: Westminster.

This Parliament Square pub is the choice of MPs, who regularly pop in for a quick one. The handsome bar and restaurant even has its own division bell to call the legislators back to vote.

THE CITY

Filthy McNasty's

68 Amwell St., EC1. Tel. 0171/837-6067. Open Mon-Sat noon-11pm, Sun noon-1030pm. No cards. Tube: Angel/Farringdon.

Sporting a reputation as grubby as its name, Filthy's is a real Irish pub, not some wannabe plastic shamrock joint. Ex-Pogue Shane MacGowan is said to down martinis here, along with other hard-drinking bohemians. The occasional Vox 'n' Roll nights feature local writers reading their own works, interspersed with liberal doses of music.

The Hoop & Grapes

47 Aldgate High St., EC3. Tel. 0171/2656-5171. Open Mon-Wed 11am-10pm, Thurs-Fri 11am-11pm. AE, MC, V. Tube: Aldgate.

Unscorched in the Great Fire of 1666, the Hoop and Grapes is the only surviving 17th-century timber-framed building in the City of London. The spacious main bar sports lots of exposed timbers, and everything is perfectly kept to look old. It's usually packed at lunch and virtually empty by night.

Old Bank of England

194 Fleet St., EC4. Tel. 0171/430-2255. Open Mon-Fri 11am-11pm. AE, MC, V.

Far more egalitarian than Bank, another financial institution turned

drinking room, this magnificent pub is London's most striking. The building was erected a century ago as the Law Courts' branch of the Bank of England. Built with sturdy columns, and huge chandeliers that have to be winched down to change a bulb, the interior still looks like a high Victorian banking hall. It's popular with lawyers and bankers who work upstairs.

Old Cheshire Cheese

145 Fleet St., EC4. Tel. 0171/353-6170. Open Mon-Fri 1130am-11pm, Sat 1130am-2pm, 530-11pm, Sun noon-4pm. AE, MC, V. Tube: Blackfriars.

You probably wouldn't make the Old Cheshire Cheese your local, but it is so great to see *once* that it's even worth fighting all the tourists to get in there. The tavern is an authentic 17th-century chophouse—all wood, with small, cozy rooms and even smaller doorways. The sawdust-covered floorboards creak loudly as you pass from bar to bar, and twice as loudly as you go up the worn steps to the dark paneled restaurant and various function rooms.

SOUTH/NORTH

George Inn

77 Borough High St., SE1. Tel. 0171/407-2056. Open Mon-Sat 11am-11pm, Sun noon-1030pm. AE, MC, V. Tube: Borough, London Bridge.

Built in 1676 and owned by the National Trust, the George is one of London's oldest surviving pubs. Set in a narrow alley on the South Bank, it's a galleried coaching inn; a hostelry that once offered room and board for travelers. Charles Dickens was a frequent former customer, and makes reference to the George in his novel *Little Dorritt*. Dickens' life insurance policy is displayed inside; the novelist gave it to the inn's landlord to secure a loan and settle a drinking bill.

The Flask

14 Flask Walk, NW3. Tel. 0171/435-4580. Open Mon-Sat 11am-11pm, Sun noon-1030pm. MC, V. Tube: Hampstead.

Once a house which bottled the supposedly medicinal waters that sprung from Hampstead, The Flask is a traditional neighborhood pub in this untraditionally prosperous neighborhood. The yellow house is guarded by big gas lanterns. The interior remains divided by its original Victorian screen, erected to separate the plebeian Public Bar from the upper-classes-only Saloon Bar.

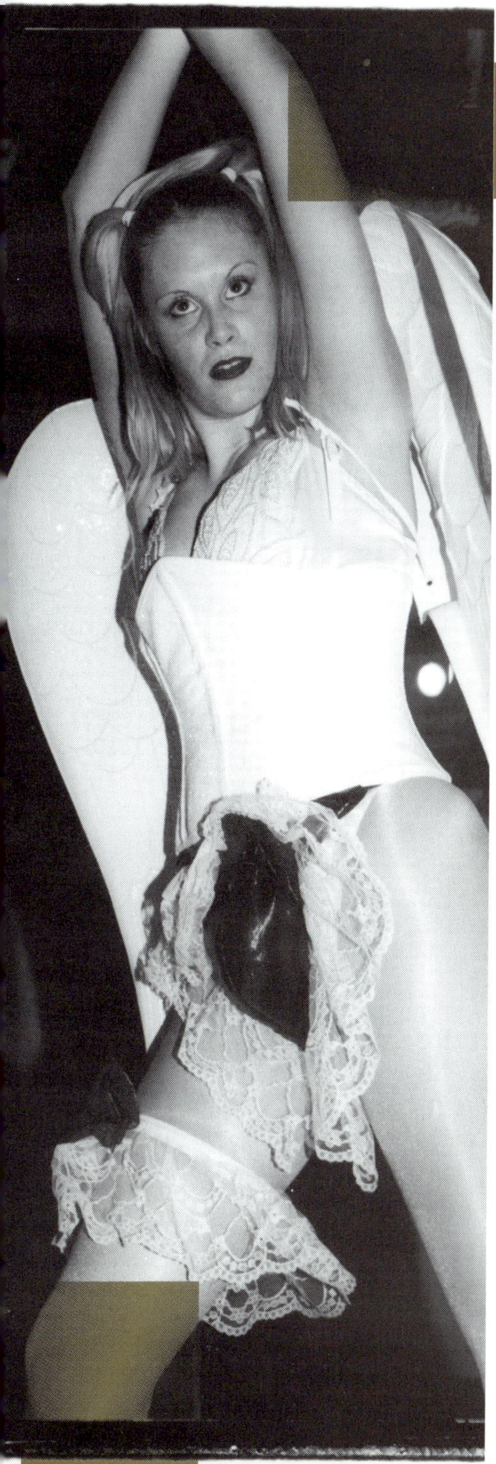

dANCE CLUbS

London is the clubbing capital of the world. Every weekend a half-million revelers hit the city, heading for one of the capitol's 100-plus venues. Physically, London's megaclubs are some of the nicest in the world. The sound and light systems are generally top-of-the-line, and most places have two or more dance floors grooving simultaneously. Even drug use has become elaborate. The trend is multi-substance usage rather than one signature high: CK One (a cocaine and ketamine mix) is currently a popular combination. Some of the most fashionable nights are on early in the week, and the club scene is constantly changing. A venue featuring hip-hop on Wednesday can easily host a roots night on Friday. Check avantguide.com or the listings magazine *Time Out* before traipsing across town in your dancing shoes.

The Arches

53 Southwark St., SE1. Tel. 0171/207-2980. Open Fri-Sat 10pm-3am. Admission £5-£8. Tube: London Bridge.

Great design keeps this shabby-chic spot at the top of the clubbers' agenda. Look out for disco theme nights.

Bar Rumba

36 Shaftesbury Ave., W1. Tel. 0171/287-2715. Open Mon 1030pm-3am, Tues-Wed 9pm-3am, Thurs 10pm-330am, Fri 9pm-4am, Sat 10pm-6am, Sun 8pm-130am. Admission £3-£12. Tube: Piccadilly Circus.

A small club with big DJs serving up everything from salsa and Latino deep house and techno. There's a great sound system and an eclectic, dressy crowd.

Café de Paris

3 Coventry St., W1. Tel. 0171/734-7700. Open Mon-Fri 5pm-4am, Sat 8pm-4am. Admission £10-£20. Tube: Piccadilly Circus.

A stylish cosmopolitan party crowd enjoys soulful house anthems in this spectacular 1920s ballroom.

Camden Palace

1A Camden High St., NW1. Tel. 0171/387-0428. Open Tues-Wed 9pm-2am, Fri 10pm-6am, Sat 10pm-8am. Admission £5-£15. Tube: Camden Town.

One of the best and biggest dance clubs in London attracts top DJs who play a mix of indie pop and alternative tunes to a relatively straight young crowd.

Chunnel Club

101 Tinworth St., Albert Embankment, SW1. Tel. 0171/820-1702. Open Fri-Sat 9pm-6am. Admission £5-£10. Tube: Vauxhall.

Great house music and a friendly, laid-back vibe are the hallmarks of this long-running late-night venue. There's usually something good on.

The Complex

1-5 Parkfield St., N1.
Tel. 0171/288-1986. Open Fri
10pm-7am, Sat 10pm-5am.
Admission £10-£12. Tube: Angel.
One of the largest nightclubs around,
The Complex is a multilevel disco theme
park, with a quartet of dance floors, a
chest-thumping sound system, and a
laser show that would make a Vegas
hotel proud. From reggae and rock
to acid-jazz, hip-hop and techno,
there's usually something for
everyone.

The End

16A West Central St.,
WC1. Tel. 0171/419-9199.
Open Fri 10pm-6am, Sat 10pm-
7am. Admission £8-£13. Tube:
Holborn.
There are lots of rooms to dance and
chill at this beautifully designed club.
There's a great sound system, cool
bathrooms, and the trendy AKA
restaurant is next door.

The Cross

King's Cross Freight Depot, off York Way, N1. Tel. 0171/837-0828. Open Fri-Sat 10pm-6am. Admission £10-£15. Tube: King's Cross.

A small venue that's big on fun, The Cross attracts sophisticated clubbers with some of the biggest DJs in the business. It's best in summer when the party spills into the club's large outdoor dance space.

The Fridge

Town Hall Parade, Brixton Hill, SW2. Tel. 0171/326-5100. Open Fri-Sat 10pm-6am. Admission £8-£12. Tube: Brixton.

A long-time fixture on the city's club scene, The Fridge is actually two venues in one: a club and bar. The club is huge, and most always heaving. Saturday's "Love Muscle" is one of the biggest gay nights in the city. The bar is man-heavy too.

Gardening Club

4 Covent Garden Piazza, WC2. Tel. 0171/497-3154. Open Mon-Thurs 10pm-330am, Fri-Sat 10pm-6am. Admission £4-£10. Tube: Covent Garden.

Uplifting house and dance anthems superbly mixed by resident DJs is a surprising find right in the heart of touristy Covent Garden.

Gossips

69 Dean St., W1. Tel. 0171/434-4480. Open Mon-Thurs 10pm-3am, Fri-Sat 1030pm-330am. Admission £4-£8. Tube: Piccadilly Circus, Tottenham Court Road.

The crowd is so different each night of the week that this cavernous cellar club might as well be six clubs in one. Check the listings magazines.

Hanover Grand

6 Hanover St., W1. Tel. 0171/499-7977. Open Wed-Thurs 10pm-330am, Fri 1030pm-5am, Sat 11pm-430am. Admission £3-£10. Tube: Oxford Circus.

A former theater, Hanover Grand is now a glamorous club and one of the most beautiful venues in the land. Two floors of deep, funky house shakes a dressy crowd.

Heaven

The Arches, Craven St., WC2. Tel. 0171/930-2020. Open Tues-Sat 10pm-late, times vary on Sun. Admission £1-£12. Tube: Charing Cross.

Hands down, this is the most famous gay club in the city. A stage, where live bands sometimes perform, overlooks a huge dance floor. The crowd varies, but the sound system is always great. The club entrance is on a small street between Charing Cross and Embankment underground stations.

Limelight

136 Shaftesbury Ave., WC2. Tel. 0171/434-0572. Open Mon-Thurs & Sun 10pm-5am, Fri 10pm-330am, Sat 9pm-330am. Admission £5-£12. Tube: Leicester Square.

There's music on at least two floors every night of the week in this former Welsh chapel. An excellent sound system belts out house, garage, rap, and ragga to a mixed crowd.

Ministry of Sound

103 Gaunt St., SE1. Tel. 0171/378-6528. Open Fri 1030pm-630am, Sat midnight-9am. Admission Fri £10-£12, Sat from £15 . Tube: Elephant & Castle.

The best regular weekend raver has worked hard to keep their underground atmosphere and warehouse style. The vast main floor is frenetic and debauched. MoS is well known around the world for attracting the world's top DJs. Too bad about the T-shirts, emblazoned bags and other sell-out gear.

Turnmills

63 Clerkenwell Rd., EC1. Tel. 0171/250-3409. Open Mon 7pm-2am, Thurs 10pm-4am, Fri 10pm-7am, Sat 9pm-330am, Sun 6pm-630am. Admission £5-£10. Tube: Farringdon.

A multi-story disco theme park, Turnmills is a welcoming venue with something for everyone, from reggae and rock to acid-jazz, hip-hop and techno. There are plenty of nooks and crannies to explore and, on any given night, the club attracts the entire spectrum of clubbers, from frat boys to home-boys—both gay and straight.

The Wag Club

36 Wardour St., W1. Tel. 0171/437-5534. Open Wed-Thurs 10pm-3am, Fri 10pm-4am, Sat 10pm-5am. Admission £4-£10. Tube: Piccadilly Circus.

The club of the 1980s is still pulling in crowds with two floors of great music. Look for uplifting, underground garage and house downstairs, and soulful R&B and hip hop up top.

LiVE ROCK, RAP, fUNK & REGGAE

Rock 'n' roll may have been born in the USA, but it came of age on the streets of London. Abbey Road was nowhere, man, until The Beatles walked its pedestrian crossing. Jimi Hendrix lived and died here, as did Mama Cass, Keith Moon, Freddie Mercury, Brian Epstein, and Marc Bolan.

Since the British rock explosion in the 1960s, London hasn't let up on the number of clubs featuring home-grown talent. The West End in general, and Soho in particular, has a number of

intimate places featuring
every kind of music known to
bandkind. Archaic drinking laws require
most late-opening clubs to charge admission.
The best live music venues are listed below.
Check avantguide.com or Time Out magazine for
up-to-the-minute details on what's on.

THE MAJOR ROCK CLUBS ◁ —

The Astoria/LA1 Club, 157 Charing Cross Rd., WC2. Tel. 0171/434-0403. Admission £3-£10. Tube: Tottenham Court Road.

Brixton Academy, 211 Stockwell Rd., SW9. Tel. 0171/924-9999. Admission £9-£22.50. MC, V. Tube: Brixton.

The Forum, 9-17 Highgate Rd., NW5. Tel. 0171/344-0044. Admission £7-£18.50. MC, V. Tube: Kentish Town.

Hackney Empire, 291 Mare St., E8. Tel. 0181/985-2424. Admission £8.50-£18.50. MC, V. Rail Hackney Central, then bus 30/38.

Shepherd's Bush Empire, Shepherd's Bush Green, W12. Tel. 0181/740-7474. Admission £8-£20. MC, V. Tube: Shepherd's Bush.

ROCK PUBS

Bull & Gate, 389 Kentish Town Rd., NW5. Tel. 0171/485-5358. Open Mon-Sat 11am-11pm, Sun noon-1030pm. Music 845-1130pm. Admission £4. No cards. Tube: Kentish Town.

Camden Falcon, 234 Royal College St., NW1. Tel. 0171/485-3834. Open Mon-Sat 5-11pm, Sun 7-1030pm. Music 830-11pm. Admission £3.50. No cards. Tube: Camden Town.

Dublin Castle, 94 Parkway, NW1 Tel. 0171/485-1773. Open Mon-Sat noon-midnight, Sun noon-11pm. Music Mon-sat 9pm-midnight, Sun 830-11pm. Admission £3.50-£4. No cards. Tube: Camden Town.

Hope & Anchor, 207 Upper St., N1. Tel 0171/354-1312. Open Mon-Thurs noon-midnight, Fri-Sat noon-1am, Sun noon-1030pm. Music Mon-Thurs & Sun 9pm-midnight, Fri-Sat 9pm-1am. Admission £3-£4. No cards. Tube: Angel.

Station Tavern, 41 Bramley Rd., W10. Tel. 0171/727-4053. Open Mon-Sat 11am-11pm, Sun noon-1030pm. Music Mon-Sat 9-11pm. Admission free. No cards. Tube: Latimer Road.

The Water Rats, 328 Gray's Inn Rd., WC1. Tel. 0171/837-7269. Open Mon-Sat 11am-11pm, Sun noon-1030pm. No cards. Tube: King's Cross.

LIVE JAZZ & BLUES

Jazz and blues clubs usually start sets at 9pm and 11pm, and add an additional show on weekends after midnight. Most serve dinner, but as long as you down the usual two-drink minimum, no food is required. Phone for show times, reservations and prices before heading out.

Dover Street

8-10 Dover St., W1. Tel. 0171/629-9813. Music Mon-Wed 10.15-11pm, midnight-1am, Thurs-Sat 1030-1120pm. Admission £3-£10. AE, MC, V. Tube: Green Park/Piccadilly Circus.

The biggest jazz bar in town, Dover Street is a first-rate jive room with a terrific booking policy that attracts both mainstream giants and adventurous newcomers. There's R&B and soul nights too.

1130pm. Music Mon-Thurs & Sun 9–1130pm, Fri-Sat 9pm-1230am. Admission £8-£20. AE, MC, V. Tube: Tottenham Court Road.

Jazz will always be in its heyday at this Soho mainstay, where mainstream trios and quartets kick it up nightly before a crowd of hungry pizza-eaters. The space can get dangerously crowded, so it's best on weekdays when a no-name is bopping.

Ronnie Scott's

47 Frith St., W1. Tel. 0171/439-0747. Open Mon-Sat 830pm-3am, Sun 730-1030pm. Music 930pm. Admission £4-£15. AE, MC, V. Tube: Leicester Square/Tottenham Court Road.

Perhaps the most famous jazz club in London, Ronnie Scott's gives a stage to everyone from unknowns to top players. Book a table or stand in the rear.

Jazz Café

5 Parkway, NW1. Tel. 0171/916-6060. Open Mon-Thurs & Sun 7pm-midnight, Fri-Sat 7pm-2am. Admission £6-£15. MC, V. Tube: Camden Town.

Like the name says, this is a restaurant and jazzery serving modern European food and contemporary American music. When the live music stops DJs fill in, spinning everything from drum 'n bass to Latin beats.

Pizza Express

10 Dean St., W1. Tel. 0171/439-8722. Open daily 9-

CLASSICAL MUSIC & OPERA

Classical music has benefited greatly from government arts funding. As a result, the city has four top-class orchestras, and lots of smaller ensembles. The **London Symphony Orchestra**, which plays primarily at the Barbican Centre, is undoubtedly one of

the finest in Europe. The **London Philharmonic Orchestra,** based at the South Bank Centre, is another excellent ensemble. The **Royal Philharmonic Orchestra,** which funds it-self almost entirely through ticket sales is the most populist of the quartet of classical music orchestras. Although the **Philharmonia** is the least known, it usually bests most of the other orchestras in quality and repertoire.

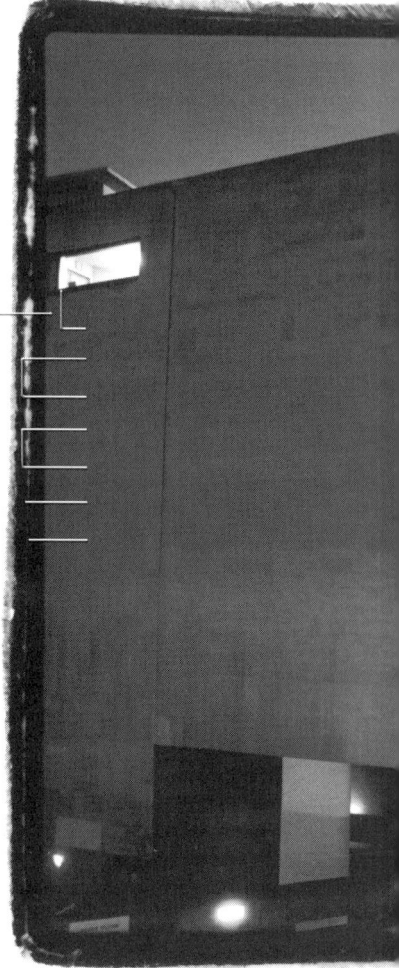

Opera

Not until the 1946 premiere of Benjamin Britten's *Peter Grimes* did British opera gain a serious reception. But since then a host of great composers have lifted British opera onto the world stage. These days there are two major opera companies; the **Royal Opera,** which is desperately trying to change its image as a snobbish dinosaur, and the **English National Opera,** a more user-friendly company that sings all their shows in English. In addition to the big houses, there are literally dozens of small opera companies in the city offering stages to younger singers. Lots of big-time belters are alumni of the city's lesser-known companies, and smaller shows are especially good for hearing lesser-known works. Many critics scoff that pygmy operas are created for the benefit of junior singers and composers, rather than the audiences they perform for. So unless you are a die-hard opera fan, or spot a show in the listings magazines that really piques your interest, it's probably best to spend your time at one of the major houses.

MAjOR CONCERt & THEATER VENUES

Royal Albert Hall

Kensington Gore, SW7. Tel. 0171/589-3203. Box office open daily 9am-9pm. Tube: Knightsbridge/Kensington High Street. When there's no rock concerts or boxing matches, the Hall is often booked by a top symphony. A major refurbishment, due to be completed in 2003, is underway to upgrade facilities for performers and audience. But the question on everybody's lips is "will repairs eliminate the infamous echo?"

London Coliseum

St. Martin's La., WC2. Tel. 0171/836-3161. Box office open Mon-Sat 10am-8pm. Tube: Leicester Square/ Charing Cross.

The 2,000-plus seat Coliseum is home to the English National Opera (ENO), whose season runs from August to May. Traveling dance troupes often here perform during summer months.

Royal Opera House

Bow St., Covent Garden, WC2. Tel. 0171/240-1200. Box office open Mon-Sat 10am-8pm. Tube: Covent Garden.

Home to both the Royal Opera and the Royal Ballet, this posh theater has recently has the wraps removed from a major multi-year face lift revealing a dramatic new piece of architecture in Covent Garden. Cheap seats are usually available on the day of the performance, though they can be pretty far from the stage.

Sadler's Wells Theatre

Rosebery Ave., EC1. Tel. 0171/863-3000. Box office open Mon-Sat 1030am-630pm (until 730pm on performance nights). Tube: Angel.

One of the busiest stages in London, Sadler's Wells is also one of the best. The 1,600-seat theater was recently rebuilt from scratch with state-of-the-art architecture and technology. The theater specializes in dance, featuring renowned companies from around the world. A limited number of very low priced tickets are available on the day of each performance.

Barbican Centre

Silk St., EC2. Tel. 0171/ 638 8891. Box office open Mon-Sat 9am-11pm, Sun and Bank Holidays n o o n –

11pm. Tube: Barbican/Moorgate/ St. Paul's/Bank/Liverpool Street.
Comprising a concert hall, two theaters, three cinemas, two art galleries, a library, and trade exhibition halls, the mazelike Barbican Centre claims to be Europe's largest arts center. It's home base for the London Symphony Orchestra and the Royal Shakespeare Company.

South Bank Arts Centre
South Bank, SE1. Tel. 0171/928-8800. Box office open daily 10am-9pm. Tube: Waterloo/Embankment.
The South Bank Arts Centre is one of the best modern public buildings in London. It contains three well-designed concert halls, all of which work almost nightly. Royal Festival Hall is the usual site for major orchestral performances. The smaller Queen Elizabeth Hall is known for its chamber-music concerts, and the intimate Purcell Room usually hosts advanced students and young performers making their professional debuts.

Wigmore Hall
36 Wigmore St., W1. Tel. 0171/935-2141. Box office open Mon-Sat 10am-830pm. Tube: Bond Street/Oxford Circus.
The best auditorium in London for both intimacy and acoustics, Wigmore Hall presents instrumental and song recitals, chamber music, and early music and baroque concerts. Buy the cheapest seats, as it really doesn't matter where you sit.

LUNCHTIME CONCERTS IN CHURCHES
Lunchtime concerts are regularly scheduled in various churches throughout the city. Church concerts, usually given by young performers, are all free, though it's customary to leave a small donation. The best are listed below.

St. Bride's Church
Fleet St., EC4. Tel. 0171/ 353-1301. Recitals Tues-Wed, Fri 115pm. Tube: Blackfriars.
Completed by Christopher Wren in 1703, St. Bride's tall, tiered spire is said to have inspired the traditional design of wedding cakes. Concerts here feature professional musicians or top students on Tuesday and Friday, while Wednesday is devoted to organ recitals. Arrive early to explore the ancient crypt.

St. James's Church
197 Piccadilly, W1. Tel. 0171/734-4511. Recitals Thurs-Fri at 110pm. Tube: Piccadilly Circus.
Another Christopher Wren-designed church, the architect once described St. James's as the embodiment of what a parish church should be. In addition to regular lunchtime recitals, keep an eye out for the occasional inexpensive evening concert, usually scheduled during the summer months.

St. Martin-In-The-Fields
Trafalgar Sq., WC2. Tel. 0171/930-0089. Recitals Mon-Tues & Wed-Fri at 105pm. Tube: Embankment/Charing Cross.
Now, of course, Trafalgar Square is the heart of London. But when the first church was erected on this spot in the thirteenth century, it was truly "in the fields." Works by Debussy and Schubert are favorites at the weekly hour-long chamber music recitals. This church is also known for its above-average choir, and a visit to a full choral Sunday service is a rare treat.

StAgE

The heart of the West End Theater District, between Shaftesbury Avenue and The Strand, is clogged with English school groups and American tourists heading to see McShows like Miss Saigon, Les Misérables, Cats, The Phantom of the Opera, and Starlight Express—all of which have been playing for more than a dozen years, and Cats almost twice that. This is fast-food "theater," for those who think that Oxford Street is for high fashion and Planet Hollywood is a swanky restaurant. There are about fifty West End theaters and, happily, the best shows are usually less popular than the hit musicals, making tickets easier to come by.

Fringe theater, London's equivalent to off-Broadway, is practically unknown to the masses and often offer better entertainment value. Because they have less to lose financially, fringe houses are usually more adventurous than the big theaters. Nicole Kidman, Kevin Spacey and Liam Neeson have appeared in small London venues. Particularly notable for quality productions are the **Almeida Theatre**, the **Old Vic** and the **Royal Court**.

Most shows begin at 745pm, with matinées on Wednesdays (or Thursdays), and Saturdays. Most theaters are dark Sundays.

INFORMATION & TICKETS

Time Out magazine has excellent, comprehensive theater listings.

West End ticket prices are, on average, almost 50-percent lower than Broadway, and usually cost between £10 and £30.

Tickets can be purchased in advance or on the day of performance at theater box offices. Previews and matinees are often offered at reduced prices, and many theaters offer cheap student standby tickets and discounts for senior citizens.

For a small per ticket service charge, you can purchase tickets by phone or via the Web through Ticketmaster (tel. 0990/344444;

www.ticketmaster.co.uk). You can visit Ticketmaster at HMV Records at Oxford Circus, Tower Records at Piccadilly Circus and the London Tourist Board office in Victoria Station.

The **Half Price Ticket Booth** in Leicester Square (no phone) sells same-day theater tickets to West End and fringe productions for up 50% off box office prices, plus a £2 service charge. The booth opens at noon for matinee shows, and from 230pm to 630pm for evening performances. There is a limit of four tickets per person, and only cash is accepted.

When all else fails, take a deep breath and talk to a hotel concierge or a legalized scalper like **First Call** (tel. 0171/420-0020), **Ticketselect** (tel. 0171/494-5394), or **Net-Tix** (tel. 0171/836-7385).

OTHER THEATER SPACES

Most fringe productions are staged outside of the city center, where rents are cheaper and audiences are more forgiving. Check the listings magazines for program information and show times.

Shakespeare's plays and other classical theater reaches its zenith at the **Royal National Theatre**, South Bank, SE1 (tel. 0171/928-2252), and at **Shakespeare's Globe Theatre**, Bankside SE1 (tel. 0171/401-9919), an outdoor playhouse built with oak beams and thatch according to plans for the original 1799 theater (*see* Chapter 5/The South Bank). The theater only stages performances in summer, and offers standing-room (groundling) tickets for just £5. The adjacent **Inigo Jones Theatre,**

which debuted in late 1999, is a 300-seat indoor playhouse built from the architect's 1617 design.

COMEDY & CABARET

It seems like every comedy club advertises that theirs is the place where Adam Bloom, Phil Nichol and every other British funny bone got their start. None of them are lying: When you're a struggling comedian you play everywhere. All of the clubs below offer essentially the same acts: Comedians are served-up by the half-dozen and, despite the occasional sarcastrophe, quality is tops.

Comedy Spot, The Spot, Maiden La., WC2. Tel. 0171/379-5900. Open Mon 8pm. Performances 9pm. Admission £8 (incl. dinner if you book before 8pm), £6, £3 students/seniors. after 8pm. Tube: Covent Garden.

Comedy Store, Haymarket House, Oxedon St., SW1. Tel. 0171/344-4444. info 01426/914-433. Open Tues-Sun 630pm. Performances Tues-Sun 8pm, Fri-Sat midnight. Admission £10-£12, £6 students/seniors. Tube: Piccadilly Circus.

Jongleurs Camden Lock, Dingwalls, Middle Yard, Camden Lock, Camden High St., NW1. Tel. 0171/564-2500. Open Fri 7pm, Sat 6pm, 1030pm. Performances Fri 815pm, Sat 715pm, 1115pm. Admission £10-£12, £7-£8 students/seniors. Tube: Camden Tower/Chalk Farm.

Comedy Café, 66 Rivington St., EC2. Tel. 0171/739-5706. Open Wed-Sat 7pm. Performances 9pm. Admission Wed free, Thurs £2, Fri £8, Sat £12, £7-£8 students/seniors. Tube: Old Street.

Cosmic Comedy Club, 177 Fulham Palace Rd., W6. Tel. 0171/381-2006. Open Tues & Thurs 8pm, Fri-Sat 730pm. Performances Tues & Thurs 9pm, Fri-Sat 830. Admission Tues & Thurs free, Fri-Sat £8. Tube: Hammersmith.

London's best-kept secret? Cabaret—usually a combination of song, dance and comedy that's one of the city's best nights out. Basically anything goes, and uniformly low prices make this one of London's best bets. Note: Many cabarets are closed during the Edinburgh International Festival in late summer. Check *Time Out* for current offerings.

The Black Cap

171 Camden High St., NW1. Tel. 0171/428-2721. Open Mon-Thurs, Sun noon-2am, Fri-Sat noon-3am. MC, V. Tube: Camden Town.

Camden Town's synagogue of high camp is also the best gay bar in the hood. A loud sound system pumps out the latest beats for men and the men who love them. It's dimly lit and crowded, with a long bar and a small stage at the far end. Come midnight the bar hosts a terrific drag show in which elaborately bewigged sexual dissidents lip-synch to Toni Braxton and comics entertain the audience. And, with so many characters in the audience, it's often hard to distinguish spectators from performers. Upstairs is the sensational Shufflewick's Bar which opens onto a terrific roof garden.

FiLM

London is a city of cinemanics. Big films often open on the capital's screens before they're unveiled anywhere else in Europe, and even where ticket prices approach £10, evening shows constantly sell-out. Most theaters show Hollywood flash and trash exclusively, and sell reserved seats at prices that range from £6 to £9, depending on location.

All the listings magazines and most newspapers have comprehensive movie listings.

The best First Run houses are the mega-screens that in and around Leicester Square. These include **The Empire**, Leicester Square, WC2 (tel. 0171/734-7123); **Odeon Leicester Square**, Leicester Square, WC2 (tel. 0171/930-6111); **Odeon West End**, Leicester Square, WC2 (tel. 0171/930-5252); and **The Plaza**, Lower Regent St., W1 (tel. 0171/930-0144).

IMAX

Just a few years ago, there were no IMAX theaters in London. Today there three. The British Film Institute IMAX Cinema, opened in 1999, features the biggest cinema screen in Europe. Linked to the Museum of the Moving Image, the £20 million cinema shows both 2D and (very cool) 3D films on a ten-story screen. The Science Museum IMAX Cinema (0171/938-8000) features films that are more educational in nature. Conversely, the IMAX Cinema at the Pepsi Trocadero (0171/434-0030) in Piccadilly Circus brings big-screen technology to the masses, showing the most popular titles in heavy rotation.

London's Best Non-Hollywood Screens

Chelsea Cinema, 206 King's Rd., SW3. Tel. 0171/351-3742. Tube: Sloane Square.

Everyman Cinema, Hollybush Vale, NW3. Tel. 0171/435-1525. Tube: Hampstead.

ICA Cinema, Nash House, The Mall, SW1. Tel. 0171/930-3647. Tube: Piccadilly Circus/Charing Cross.

Lux Cinema, 2-4 Hoxton Square, N1. Tel. 0171/684-0201. Tube: Old Street.

National Film Theatre, South Bank, SE1. Tel. 0171/928-3232. Tube: Embankment/Waterloo.

The Phoenix, 52 High Rd., N2. Tel. 0181/444-6789. Tube: East Finchley.

SEX

Pop into almost any phone box, which is usually plastered with flyers advertising "new young models" and you'll see that consentual non-monogamy is alive and well in London. The phone book too contains dozens of pages of ads and listings for personal companions under the heading "Escort." Most of these "houses of horizontal pleasure" are open nonstop and accept credit cards.

The city's few sex clubs are musky, man-only affairs, though there are a few decent venues in which to see cleavage-wielders. The most famous strip club is **Stringfellows**, 16-19 Upper St. Martins La., WC2 (tel. 0171/240 5534), which features women so beautiful there's no way they can be British. Monday through to Thursday is the Cabaret of Angels, featuring tableside dancing. Fridays and Saturdays are normal club nights.

dAY TRiPS & SLEEP-AWAYS

Windsor Castle

Just a few miles from Trafalgar Square you'll be confronted with an England that's strikingly different from the inner city. The air is cleaner, the people friendlier and everything is cheaper.

Getting Around by Train
Seats can be purchased up until the moment of departure, but pre-booking is recommended, especially on weekends and in summer. **Rail Travel Centres**, located in all the major stations, provide information and sell tickets. You can also book by credit card by calling 0345/222333. For train times and ticket prices, call 0345/484950.

Getting Around by Bus
Buses typically cost half the price of trains, and reservations should be made as far in advance as possible. **National Express** (tel. 0990/808080) coaches depart from Victoria Coach Station on Buckingham Palace Road, near Victoria rail and tube stations.

hAMPTON COURt PALACE

Richmond, Surrey. Tel. 0181/781-9500. Open Mar-Oct, Mon 1015am-6pm, Tues-Sun 930am-6pm; Oct-Mar Mon 1015am-430pm, Tues-Sun 930am-430pm. Closed Dec 24-26. Admission £9.25 adults, £6.10 children under 16; The Maze £2.10 adults, £1.30 students/children.

Hampton Court's absolutely amazing palace was built in 1514 by the Catholic Church for Cardinal Thomas Wolsey. But just twenty years after throwing his first garden party, the Cardinal's kingly house was seized by the real monarchy as part of a package deal that also included an official rejection of Catholicism, dissolution of the monasteries, and the requisition of all Church property. This was the time of King Henry VIII, who thought the mansion would make a splendid home for five of his six wives.

The house was designed to impress guests who, today, are still wowed when they snag an invite from one of the residents: retired servants of the Crown.

It's not called a "castle," but it sure looks like one. Vaguely fortlike, the Palace is built with brawny red brick and incorporates lots of towers topped with crenelated walls. The house sprawls across three courtyards and is filled with the Royals' Renaissance art and furniture. Its over-the-top rooms are time capsules of architecture and design displaying the state of the art of the past five hundred years. The Chapel is particularly indulgent, built with a whimsical blue-and-gold ceiling, and fitted with oak screens behind the altar fashioned by Grinling Gibbons, Britain's most celebrated master carver. There's an original Tudor indoor tennis court, a Christopher Wren-built gallery hung with Raphael cartoons (copies!), and cool kitchens that look like they're straight out of Medieval Times.

Set on the banks of the River Thames, the Palace is especially great in summer, when you can install yourself under a tree in the extensive gardens. Any time of year you can pay two quid to pretend you're a rat in the famous maze.

Guided tours are offered from March through September, and are free with admission. There are several itineraries to choose from, the best of which are Henry VIIIs State Apartments (the Tudor Rooms), the King's Apartments, and the Tudor Kitchens. Phone for times.

GETTING THERE: Hampton Court is southwest of London, about 30 minutes by train from Waterloo Station. Just show up: trains run frequently throughout the day.

From April to October, you can reach Hampton Court by boat from Westminster Pier, near the Westminster underground. The trip upstream takes about three hours. Phone 0171/930-4721 for complete information.

WINDSOR CASTLE

Windsor, Berkshire. Tel. 01753/868286. Open Nov–Feb, daily 10am–4pm (last admission 3pm); Mar–Oct, daily 10am–530pm (last admission 4pm). Admission: £9.50 adults, £7 seniors, £5 children 5–17.

An official residence of The Queen and royal residence for 9 centuries, Windsor Castle is one of the largest inhabited castles in the world, set on a site that has been home to monarchs for more than 900 years. When the royal family is away, visitors can explore some of the castle's more opulent rooms, most of which are ceremonial quarters reserved for official occasions. Situated on a bend in the Thames, about 20 miles west of London, the castle sits on 4,800 acres of lawn, woodlands, and lakes, and is furnished with fabulous antiques and paintings, including masterpieces by Holbein, Rembrandt and Van Dyck. The Castle Gallery displays a rotating collection of the royal family's art, including paintings by Dali, Constable and Chagall. Queen Mary's Dolls' House is a three-story

masterpiece in miniature that shouldn't be missed. A mansion built to 1:12 scale, it's faithful to the real thing, right down to running water in the bathrooms. St. George's Chapel, site of Prince Edward's wedding to Sophie Rhys-Jones, is open every day but Sunday.

Weather permitting, the Guard Change at Windsor Castle takes place on alternate days at 11am. Phone for details.

The exclusive **Eton College** is across the river and easily reached by a cast-iron footbridge. The school educates the country's most privileged students, including 18 prime ministers and Prince William among them. Founded in the mid-15th century, the school is also famous for requiring its students to attend classes in high collars and tails. It's open to visitors daily during term from 2-4pm; during Easter and summer holidays from 1030am-4pm. Phone for tour times (tel. 01753/671177).

Windsor is just 20 miles west of London. Trains to Windsor depart from London's Waterloo Station, Monday to Saturday every 30 minutes, Sunday every hour. The journey takes 50 minutes.

bATh

GETTING THERE

By Train BritRail trains depart from London's Paddington Station every 90 minutes and make the trip in about 80 minutes. Round-trip standard-class tickets cost from £30 to £40.

By Bus National Express buses leave daily from London's Victoria Coach Station, and make the trip in about three hours. About twice as slow and half as expensive as the train, round-trip tickets cost £16 to £22.

By Car From London, take the M4 motorway to Exit 18.

ORIENTATION & INFORMATION

Bath (pop. 83,000) is situated along the River Avon, 110 miles west of London. It's traversed by two bridges: North Parade Bridge and Pulteney Bridge, and most of the city's main sights are crowded around the bridgeheads and the centrally located Abbey. Both bus and train stations are located at the end of Manvers Street, within easy walking distance to the city center.

The town's **Tourist Information Centre**, Abbey Chambers, Abbey Church Yard (tel. 01225/477101), is open Jun-Sept, Mon-Sat 930am-6pm, Sun 10am-4pm; Oct-May, Mon-Sat 930am-5pm, Sun 10am-4pm.

Because it's home to the only hot-water spring in Britain, Bath found fame early, and was founded by the Romans in A.D. 43. But its heyday wasn't until the late 18th century, when Bath became a stylish social destination for Europe's society set. Everyone came to Bath; from Johann Strauss and Franz Liszt to Charles Dickens, Jane Austen and Sir Walter Scott, and even that famous vertically-challenged General Tom Thumb. There were plenty of generic old people here too, who considered this spa town to be a fine slope to the grave.

The town's quasi-official Master of Ceremonies was Richard "Beau" Nash, a professional gambler, amateur womanizer, extravagant bon vivant and master of PR who flattered aristocrats with his courtly manners, and made his living from the city's casino profits. Although Bath was heavily bombed by the Germans in 1942, the result of a depraved strategy to demoralize Britons by targeting urban centers and historical sites, the city has been painstakingly restored to its Georgian splendor. And despite the fact that the public may no longer bathe in the town's natural springs, Bath is still an extraordinarily beautiful place, and one of the most popular day trips from London.

The Roman Baths and Museum

Abbey Churchyard. Tel. 01225/477785. Open summer, Mon–Sat 930am–6pm, Sun 10am–4pm; winter Mon–Sat 930am–5pm, Sun 11am–3pm. Dedicated to Sul and Minerva, the Celtic and Roman goddesses of healing, these are the only remains of the town's first bath temples. Over a half-million gallons of stinky thermal mineral water still gush from these grounds at temperatures hovering around 118-degrees Fahrenheit (48(C), but nobody bathes here anymore. It's verboten. Today the baths are but a historical museum, and a monument to a former golden age. The temple is attached to a gallery that displays decayed jewelry and other personal effects lost and forgotten by ancient bathers. In the adjacent Pump Room you can taste the waters.

Bath Abbey

Built for the Bishop of Bath in the 16th century, this is the city's most important church. It's always been an historical site; a church has stood here since A.D. 937, when King Edgar, the first English king, was crowned here. The Abbey was the last of England's big churches to be built in the Perpendicular style, a form of English Gothic architecture characterized by vertical ornamental lines. The usual smattering of gravestones includes a monument to an obscure local named Mary Frampton, inscribed with a verse especially written for it by poet John Dryden.

Guildhall

This 18th-century meeting and eating hall for upper class tradesmen is a spectacular building that's well worth visiting. Walk up to the second-floor Banqueting Hall, a dining room that many critics agree is one of the finest public rooms in England. The elaborate chandelier, comprised of some 15,000 pieces, was commissioned in 1778 at a cost of £270. When some minor defects were discovered upon delivery, the city council deducted three shillings off the final bill.

CAMbRiDGE

55 miles N of London

GETTING THERE

By Train BritRail trains depart from London's Liverpool Street and King's Cross stations every 20 minutes and make the trek in about one hour. The standard round-trip fare is about £20. Once at Cambridge station, take the Cityrail bus link to Market Square, the center of the city.

By Coach National Express buses depart from London's Victoria Coach Station 13 times each day. The ride to Cambridge takes an hour and 50 minutes, and costs from £13 to £18 round-trip.

By Car From London, take the M11 motorway to Exit 11.

ORIENTATION & INFORMATION

There are two main thoroughfares in Cambridge (pop. 103,000). Trumpington Street, which becomes King's Parade, Trinity Street, and finally St. John's Street, runs parallel to the River Cam and is close to several of the city's colleges. The main shopping street starts at Magdalene Bridge, and turns into Bridge Street, Sidney Street, St. Andrew's Street, and finally Regent Street. The **Tourist Information Center**, The Old Library, Wheeler Street (tel. 01223/322640), located behind Guildhall, offers transportation and sightseeing information, as well as maps and accommodations lists. It's open Nov-Mar, Mon-Fri 9am-530pm, Sat 9am-5pm; Apr-Jun and Sept-Oct, Mon-Fri 9am-6pm, Sat 9am-5pm, Sun 1030am-330pm.

Cambridge might just be the prettiest town in all of England. The town came into its own in 1209, when a group of academics migrated here in order to escape from riot-torn Oxford, and by 1475 twelve colleges were affiliated with the school. Each college is a self-governing body, independently responsible for the admission, accommodation, and education of its undergraduates. "Oxford University" is the rubric that unites the colleges, establishes graduation requirements and administers final exams. Since its inception, Cambridge has been competing with Oxford in almost everything. It loses in age, and usually in boat races, but Cambridge wins big on charm. The magnificent town center is filled with stunning architecture and lots of trees, and is mercifully devoid of cars. Walking around the various colleges, and picnicking along the River Cam, is one of the best days out we know.

Emmanuel College

Emmanuel Chapel was designed by master architect Sir Christopher Wren. Inside, the second stained glass window on your left depicts John Harvard, an Emmanuel student and founder of the American university that bears his name. Harvard and other religious puritans migrated to America in the 1630s in order to escape religious and social intolerance in England.

Christ´s College

Fellows Garden is the courtyard of the Fellows Building, a college dormitory. It was laid out in the early 19th century with a small bathing pool and a bust of poet John Milton, who studied and taught here from 1625 to 1632. The author of Paradise Lost and other seminal works of English literature was as unpopular with his Cambridge Fellows as his difficult books are with modern-day students. The Garden is open Mon-Fri 1030am-1230pm and 2-4pm.

Jesus College

Jesus College Hall, originally built as the nuns' refectory, has been in continuous use as a dining chamber for over 800 years. The room features a beautiful three-sided oriel window, antique paneling around the dais that dates from 1703, and an early 16th-century timbered roof. The portrait at the far end of the hall is of Henry VIII.

Gonville and Caius College

"Honoris" Gate is one of the most-photographed monuments in Cambridge. The novel design, which incorporates six sundials, is said to have been inspired by an ancient Roman-era tomb.

Great St. Mary´s Church

Cambridge's best parish church enjoyed its proverbial fifteen minutes of fame in the 16th century, when the trouble-making Protestant bishops Nicholas Ridley, Hugh Latimer and Thomas Cranmer, preached their Reformationist rhetoric here. Subsequently accused of heresy, the trio were burned at the stake. While the church interior is relatively plain, it's definitely worth climbing the 123 steps to the top of the church tower for some terrific views of Cambridge.

Corpus Christi College,

The Old Court, Cambridge's first enclosed quadrangle, has changed little in over 600 years. The student dorms that surround it were not heated, and had floor-coverings made of reeds. The windows are original, and have recessed jams and oversized sills made to hold the oiled linens that kept out the cold before glass panes were invented.

The College Library contains a magnificent collection of ancient manuscripts and imprints from the monasteries that King Henry VIII dissolved in 1538. The most valuable work is the 6th-century Canterbury Gospel, believed to have been given to St. Augustine by Pope Gregory the Great. A portrait in the hall of the library, dated 1585 with the notation, "This was him in the 21st year of his age," is thought to be of playwright Christopher Marlowe, who began school here in 1578 and stayed for almost ten years. He was killed in a tavern brawl in 1593. The Library is usually open Mon-Fri 2-4pm.

Pembroke College

Pembroke Chapel was uber-architect Sir Christopher Wren's first architectural work, designed when he was a professor of Astronomy at Oxford. The Chapel was financed by the architect's nephew, Matthew Wren.

The Parish Church of Little St. Mary's is a great stop for historically-minded Americans. Inside is a memorial to Reverend Godfrey Washington, a great uncle of American President George Washington, who was minister of this church and a Fellow of St. Peter's College. The memorial also includes the Washington family's coat of arms—stars and stripes and an eagle—that is reminiscent of the emblem of the City of Washington D.C., and said to have influenced the design of the American flag.

Peterhouse

Peterhouse Chapel, a dynamic architectural anomaly built in 1628, incorporates the artistic transition from Gothic to Renaissance styles. The spectacular East Window, which is over four hundred years old, competes for your attention with the remarkable ceiling that sparkles with gilded suns. Peterhouse Hall, the college's social headquarters, was constructed in 1268. Almost all the Hall's trimmings—from wall decorations to fireplace tiles and window glass—were designed by William Morris, a pre-Raphaelite who was one of England's most famous interior designers.

King's College

The Fellows Building, made of white Portland stone, is considered by many to be architect James Gibbs' finest work.

King's College Chapel is full of beautiful things to look at. Its hard not to be impressed by the building's delicate fan-vaulted roof. And the Chapel Screen is one of the finest examples of Renaissance woodwork in Europe. The church's most valuable jewel is Rubens' oil-on-wood painting, *Adoration of the Magi*, donated to King's College in 1961. The Chapel floor had to be lowered in order to fit the painting beneath the church's East Window. The Chapel is only open Mon-Fri 930am-345pm.

Trinity College

This is the largest of the Oxbridge colleges, and the alma mater of many of the world's most outstanding intellectuals, including twenty-eight Nobel Prize winners. Established by King Henry VII in 1546, just five weeks before his death, the College of the Holy and Undivided Trinity fulfilled the king's wish to be remembered as the founder of England's greatest college.

Wren's Library, designed by Sir Christopher Wren, is considered to be Cambridge's best example of neo-Classical architecture. At the far end of the library is a statue of Lord Byron that was originally intended for London's Westminster Abbey, but was refused by the Abbey's dean due to the subject's bisexuality and "questionable morals." You can see lots of valuable books in glass showcases, including the original manuscript of A.A. Milne's *Winnie the Pooh*. Both Milne and his son, Christopher Robin, were Trinity men. The Library is usually open Mon-Fri noon-2pm, and Sats during the term 1030am-1230pm.

Trinity College Chapel has many statues of Trinity men, including poets Alfred Lord Tennyson and Sir Francis Bacon, and physicist Sir Isaac Newton holding a prism.

StRATFORd-UPON-AVON
92 miles NW of London

GETTING THERE
By Bus National Express buses depart from Victoria Coach Station, Buckingham Palace Road, almost every hour. The first coach leaves at 10am and arrives in Stratford at approximately 1pm. Their last coach departs Stratford about 6pm.

By Train British Rail trains depart from Paddington Station and take about 2 hours 15 minutes.

ORIENTATION & INFORMATION
Stratford's simple Middle Ages layout and aesthetics has everything to do with its charm. It's a minuscule place, comprised of about three streets running parallel to the river, and three streets at right angles to it. The **Information Center**, Bridgefoot (tel. 01789/293127), offers tourist information, maps and an accommodations booking service. It's open Apr-Oct, Mon-Sat 9am-530pm, Sun 2-5pm; Nov-Mar, Mon-Sat 1030am-430pm.

Recognized by the crown in 1196 when it was granted permission to hold a weekly market, the provincial town of Stratford remained in relative obscurity until the late 16th century, when fame visited its favorite son, William Shakespeare. Born in Stratford in 1564, Shakespeare left for London around 1590; and when he returned home ten years later, Shakespeare was a rich and famous celebrity. But the Bard's popularity doesn't completely explain Stratford's immense popularity with visitors. Even without its famous former resident, this small town on the Avon would still attract sightseers with its picture-perfect, half-timbered houses, statuesque poplar and chestnut trees, and one of the world's most romantic rivers running through it.

Shakespeare´s Birthplace
Henley St. Tel. 01789/204016.
The first public record indicating the presence of the Shakespeare family on this property is a 1552 fine levied against William's father for amassing animal dung outside the house. Before he reached the age of eighteen, William Shakespeare had become involved with Anne Hathaway, a farmer's daughter from the nearby village of Shottery. Anne got pregnant, a hasty marriage was arranged and, on Sunday May 26th, 1583, the young couple's first

child, Susanna, was christened. Less then two years later, William and Anne had twins—a son, Hamnet, and a daughter, Judith. All the Shakespeares lived in this Henley Street home, including William's parents. The house was purchased in 1847 by a private preservation committee that restored the property to its near-original form, and furnished it in period style.

Holy Trinity Church

One of England's stateliest Medieval churches, Holy Trinity contains lots of eye-candy, including William Clopton's tomb, called one of the grandest Corinthian monuments in England. Also on show are records from the church register that certify both the baptism and burial of William Shakespeare; and the Shakespeare Memorial, a bust depicting the bard looking like a well-lunched executive. The face may have been modeled from the playwright's death mask, thus reflecting the body's bloated state just after death. The symbol above the statue, between the pair of cherubs, is the family's Coat of Arms. Shakespeare is buried under the floor beneath the bust.

The Royal Shakespeare Theatre

This is the home of the Royal Shakespeare Company (RSC), one of the best known theater troupes in the world. The company traces its roots to 1875, when local brewer, Charles Edward Flower, donated 10 acres of land and launched a national campaign to build a theater here dedicated to the works of William Shakespeare. The company blossomed in the 1950s, attracting John Gielgud, Vivien Leigh, Laurence Olivier, and other top Shakespearean actors, along with a handful of talented unknowns, like the young Richard Burton.

265

iNFORMAtiON

The www.avantguide.com CyberSupplement™ is the best source for happenings in London during your stay. Visit us for book updates and links to info on current cultural events and other happenings.

See Chapter 2 for a list of information sources in London.

For information and entry requirements, duty-free limits and other foreign concerns, see "For Foreign Visitors," below.

WEAThER

Today's weather in London: scattered clouds with sunny periods and showers, possibly heavy at times. This seems to be the forecast the majority of the time. England's island setting translates into temperamental weather patterns and temperatures that rarely go below freezing in winter, or above 70 degrees Fahrenheit in summer. The best advice: Prepare for every eventuality.

fOR TRAVELERS WiTh diSABiLiTiES

London is not very hospitable to wheelchair-bound and other disabled travelers. Although the terrain is relatively flat, sidewalks are smooth, and most public buildings are ramped, public transport makes almost no accommodation for wheelchair-bound travelers. And few restaurants and hotels are accessible.

It is common in London for theaters, nightclubs, and attractions to offer discounts (concessions) to people with disabilities. Ask for these before paying full-price. For information about disabled access, contact the London Tourist Board

Access in London a painstakingly thorough book detailing wheelchair-accessible sights, theaters, pubs, shops and toilets all over town, is the essential guide for disabled visitors. Request a copy (£8, including postage) from Access Project, 39 Bradley Gardens, West Ealing, London W13 8HE, England.

LONdON'S WEAThER AVERAgES

Month	Daytime Temperature	
January	43°F =	6°C
February	43°F =	6°C
March	46°F =	8°C
April	50°F =	10°C
May	55°F =	13°C
June	61°F =	16°C
July	66°F =	19°C
August	66°F =	19°C
September	61°F =	16°C
October	55°F =	13°C
November	46°F =	9°C
December	45°F =	7°C

Frankly, we don't trust most travel agents to really dig for the lowest fare. They get paid a small percentage of the price of each ticket, so it doesn't benefit them to spend more time trying to make less money. We usually make reservations ourselves, directly with the airlines, then visit our travel agent for ticketing. Here's the secret to getting the best deal: If you don't know airline jargon, don't use it. Just ask for the lowest fare. If you're flexible with dates and times, tell the sales agent. Ask him or her to hunt a bit.

THE MAJOR AIRLINES

Air Canada (US tel. 800/776-3000; UK tel. 0990/247266)
Air France (US tel. 800/237-2747; UK tel. 0181/7426600)
Air India (US tel. 800/442-4455; UK tel. 0171/495-7950)
American Airlines (US tel. 800/433-7300; UK tel. 0181/572 5555)
Austrian Airlines (US tel. 800/843 0002; UK tel. 0171/434-7350)
British Airways (US tel. 800/247 9297; UK tel. 0345/222111)
Continental Airlines (US tel. 800/525-0280; UK tel. 0800/776464)
Delta Air Lines (US tel. 800/221-1212; UK tel. 0800/414767)
KLM (US tel. 800/777-5553; UK tel. 0990/074074)
Lufthansa (US tel. 800/645-3880; UK tel. 0345/737747)
Northwest Airlines (US tel. 800/225-2525; UK tel. 01293/543511)
Quantas (US tel. 800/227-4500; UK tel. 0345/747767)
SAS (US tel. 800/221-2350; UK tel. 0171/734-4020)
Southwest Airlines (US tel. 800/435-9792; UK tel. 01293/596677)
Swissair (US tel. 800/221-4750; UK tel. 0171/434-7300)
Trans World Airlines (US tel. 800/221-2000; UK tel. 0345/333333)
United Airlines (US tel. 800/241-6522; UK tel. 0845/8444777)
US Airways (US tel. 800/428-4322; UK tel. 0800/7835556)
Virgin Atlantic (US tel. 800/862-8621; UK tel. 01293/747747)

BUDGET AIRLINES & CONSOLIDATORS

Recently we have been buying airplane tickets almost exclusively from consolidators. Also known as "bucket shops," consolidators are travel agents that buy airline seats in bulk, in return for deep discounts. This business has become so sophisticated that most of them now buy their tickets from even larger wholesalers. To find the best fare at any given time, check the travel sections of The New York Times, the Los Angeles Times or any other big-city newspaper. Bucket shop ads are usually very small and list a lot of destinations. The US-based consolidators we use to get to London are **Cheap Tickets** (tel. 212/570-1179 or 800/377-1000); **Air Brokers** (tel. 800/883-3273); **Cheap Seats** (tel. 800/451-7200); **Travel Link** (tel. 213/441-3030); and **Travel Abroad** (tel. 212/564-8989).

PACKAGES VS. TOURS

When it comes to travel lingo, most people confuse packages and tours. In the industry, a tour usually refers to a group that travels together, follows a flag-toting leader and is herded on and off buses. Obviously we seldom recommend this kind of tourism.

A package, on the other hand, is a travel deal in which several components of a trip—transportation, accommodation, airport transfers and the like—are bundled together for sale to independent, unescorted travelers. Many independent travelers purchase complete vacations from travel agents without ever knowing that they're buying a package. That's O.K.—packages can offer great values. Package companies buy in bulk and are often able to sell complete vacations for less than you'd pay for buying each component individually.

Independent packages to London are offered by **British Airways** (tel. 800/247 9297) and most US airlines, including **American Airlines Fly AAway Vacations** (tel. 800/634-5555), **Delta Dream Vacations** (tel. 800/872-7786), **TWA Getaway Vacations** (tel. 800/438-2929), and **United Airlines' Vacation Planning Center** (tel. 800/328-6877).

CARS & DRIVING

You don't need a car in London and it's a hassle to have one. Traffic crawls along at a snail's pace and parking is difficult and expensive (at least $20/day); but public transport and taxis can get you everywhere. You might want to rent a car to explore the countryside, though trains are frequent and seem to go most everywhere.

AUTO RENTALS

As is usual, the big international car-rental firms are the most expensive. Rates vary, but expect to pay about £50 per day and £200 per week, including unlimited mileage, for a Vauxhall Corsa or similar two-door tin can. Competition is sometimes fierce, and we've seen deals as low as $150 per week. Compare **Alamo** (tel. 800/327-9633), **Avis** (US 800/331-1212; UK 0990/900-500), **Budget** (US 800/527-0700; UK 0541/565656), **Dollar** (tel. 800/800-4000), **Enterprise** (tel. 800/325-8007), **Hertz** (US 800/654-3131; UK 0990/996699) and **National/Europcar** (US 800/227-7368; UK 0345/222525).

Local rental firms are cheaper, but their cars are decidedly worse. Try **Holiday Autos** (UK tel. 0990-300-400) or **Practical Used Car Rental** (UK tel. 0171/284-0199).

At the other end of the spectrum there's **The Wonder Years** (UK tel. 0181/871-2777) offering chauffeur-driven Lincoln stretch limos for about £30 per hour.

MOTORCYCLES

Scootabout, 1-3 Leeke St., WC1 (tel. 0171/833-4607), is the best place in London to rent a bike. They've got everything from dinky mopeds to monster 1500s, the latter of which goes for about £37 per day, insurance included. Helmets are required, but they are illegal to rent in Britain, so you'll have to buy one or bring your own. Scootabout is open Mon-Sat 9am-6pm. Tube: King's Cross.

iN-SEASON: The bEST ANNUAL HAPPENiNGS

Weatherwise, the best time to visit London is in late spring and early fall. When it comes to crowds, summer is the cruelest season. Check www.avantguide.com before you go.

PUBLIC HOLIDAYS

Most businesses are closed January 1, Good Friday, Easter Monday, May 1 and December 25 and 26. In addition, many stores close on Bank Holidays, which are scattered throughout the year. There is no uniform policy for museums, restaurants and attractions with regard to holidays. To avoid disappointment, always phone before setting out.

January: Up to one million people show up for the **London Parade,** on the first day of the year. High-school bands and giant inflatables have the feel of New York's Thanksgiving Day Parade.

On the last Sunday of the month, hundreds of cavaliers march through London for the **King Charles I Commemoration.** A prayer service is held at Banqueting House in Whitehall, where, on January 30, 1649, the king was beheaded by the founders of Britain's first democratic Parliament.

February: **Chinese New Year** is celebrated in London's Chinatown on the Sunday nearest to the actual date. Dragon dancers snake through streets crammed with crowds, decorations and food stalls.

April: The **London Marathon** is run in the middle of the month. Registration information: Tel. 0171/620-4117.

May: The Chelsea Flower Show, usually held the third weekend of the month, is probably the world's most impressive flower extravaganza. Tickets: Tel. 0171/834-4333.

June: No matter that she was born in April, **Trooping the Colour,** the Queen's official birthday, is held on a Saturday in early June. The public is invited to watch the royals parade up and down The Mall from Buckingham Palace. Tickets: 0171/414-2279 or 414-2479.

You can get another glimpse of the monarch a few days later, at **Royal Ascot,** the highlight of the horseracing calendar. Tickets/Info: 01344/622211.

The **Wimbledon Lawn Tennis Championships** begin at the end of the month. Buy tickets at the gate for early rounds of play, or get an application form by sending a self-addressed envelope to: All England Lawn Tennis & Croquet Club, PO Box 98, Church Road, SW19 (tel. 0181/944-1066).

August: Begun as a small community event in the 1960s, the **Notting Hill Carnival,** held on a Sunday and Monday late in the month, has grown into Europe's largest annual street festival and attracts about a million partiers. Huge parades and several stages accommodate salsa bands and costumed revelers. Sunday is more family-oriented, while Monday is more manic. It runs from about noon to 7pm.

November: Yet another chance to see the royals during the **State Opening of Parliament** early in the month. The ceremony is private but crowds pack the parade route to see the procession, with the Queen waving her gloved hand from the comfort of her State Coach.

Bonfire Night, held on the weekend nearest to November 5th, commemorates the anniversary of the "Gunpowder Plot," an attempt to blow up King James I and his Parliament. Massive bonfires are lit in the city's parks and co-conspirator Guy Fawkes is burned in effigy.

On the second Saturday of the month, the **Lord Mayor's Show** brings pomp to The City when the Lord Mayor, followed by dozens of bewigged attendants, marches ceremoniously to the Law Courts for his swearing in. The 13th-century parade is followed by a huge fireworks display in the evening. Info: Tel. 0171/606-3030.

LONdONESE: A LOCAL 9LOSSARY

ENGLiSh ≠ AMERiCAN

Antenatal * Prenatal
Billion * Million million
Brixton Briefcase * Ghetto Blaster
Cheeky Monkey * Rude person
Chuffed * Pleased, Proud
Coffin Nail * A cigarette
Daft * Stupid
Dosh * Money
Extracting the Urine * See "Taking the Piss"
First Floor * Ground Floor
Mars Bar * Milky Way
Milky Way * Three Musketeers
Naff * Undesirable, Tasteless
Noughts and Crosses * Tic-Tac-Toe
Off-License * Liquor Store
Shite * Shit
Slag * Slut
Snog * Mash (kiss)
Stone * 14 Lbs.
Taking the Piss * Joking at your expense
Tosser * See "Wanker"

ENGLiSh ≠ AMERiCAN

Towels * Pads (sanitary)
Wanker * Masturbator
Meat and Two Veg * Male genitalia
Goolies * Testicles
Knackers * Testicles
Bollocks * Testicles
Tea Bagging * Testicle sucking

▷ And Some Jewels of Cockney Rhyming Slang

Plates And Dishes * The Misses
Zeig Heils * Piles (Hemorrhoids)
Merchant Banker * Wanker
Khyber Pass * Ass
Septic Tank * Yank (American)

FOR FOREIGN VISITORS ▶

DOCUMENT REGULATIONS

Americans, Canadians, Kiwis, Australians, Japanese and most Euros don't need a visa to enter Great Britain for up to six months; only a passport with an expiration date at least six months later than the scheduled end of your visit is required. Passport Control officials sometimes ask younger travelers to prove they have enough cash on hand before admitting them into the country. Our world-wise friends avoid this hassle by writing the name of an expensive hotel on their landing cards.

Citizens of most other countries, including South Africa, must obtain a tourist visa from a British embassy or consulate.

MEDICAL REQUIREMENTS

Innoculations are not usually required to enter Britain.

MONEY

See "Money" in Chapter 2.

CUSTOMS REQUIREMENTS

Each adult visitor may bring into Britain free of duty: one liter of spirits; 200 cigarettes or 50 cigars or 8.82 ounces (250 grams) of smoking tobacco; and £23 worth of gifts. It's verboten to bring foodstuffs (particularly cheese, fruit, cooked meats, and canned goods) and plants (including vegetables and seeds). There are no restrictions on the movement of currency.

US customs allows returning Americans a duty-free import of $400 worth of merchandise, 200 cigarettes or 100 cigars and one liter of spirits. .Above these amounts, travelers are assessed a flat 10% tax on the next $1,000 worth of goods. When you shop big in London, keep the receipts to show customs officials.

What's a British pound worth? For today's exchange rates, check-out the AvantGuide CyberSupplement™ at www.avantguide.com.

FOREIGN ESSENTIALS

• Business Hours

Most **offices** are open Monday through Friday from 9am to 5pm. **Stores** are usually open Monday to Saturday, and sometimes on Sunday. **Banks** are usually open Monday through Friday from 9am to 3 or 4pm; 24-hour automated-teller machines (ATMs) are installed at most banks and many other places as well.

• Climate

Average monthly temperatures are listed above. Check avantguide.com for this week's weather conditions.

• Computers/Internet

If you have trouble jacking-in, visit **Café Internet** (22-24 Buckingham Palace Rd., SW1. Tel. 0171/233-5786), a cyber spot with Web access that's the choice of London's digerati. Other top choices include **Cyberia** (39 Whitfield St., W1. Tel. 0171/681-4200); and **Webshack** (15 Dean St., W1. Tel. 0171/439-8000).

• Currency Exchange

See "Money" in Chapter 2.

• Drinking Laws

Britain's archaic licensing laws make it almost impossible to get a drink after 11pm (1030pm on Sundays) unless you are in a late-licensed restaurant or private club. Liquor stores and pubs are bound by the same hours.

- **Electricity**
220-230 volts (EU standard) and a large 3-prong outlet that differs from the US and continental Europe. American appliances must be plugged into converters; European appliances only need adapters.

- **Embassies/Consulates**
US Embassy, 24 Grosvenor Square, W1 (tel. 0171/499-9000);

Australian High Commission is at Australia House, Strand, WC2 (tel. 0171/379-4334); Canadian High Commission, 38 Grosvenor St., W1 (tel. 0171/258-6600);

New Zealand High Commission, 80 Haymarket, SW1 (tel. 0171/930-8422).

- **Emergencies**
999 is the number to call for the police, to report a fire or get an ambulance. From public telephones no coins are required for a 999 call.

- **Holidays**
Banks, government offices, post offices, and many stores, restaurants, and museums are closed on the following legal national holidays: January 1, Good Friday, Easter Monday, May 1 and December 25 and 26. In addition, many stores close on Bank Holidays, which are scattered throughout the year. There is no uniform policy for museums, restaurants, and attractions with regard to holidays. To avoid disappointment, always phone before setting out.

- **Information**
(see Chapter 2/Information).

- **Tax**
Unlike the United States where tax is tacked on at the register, in England a 15% Value-Added Tax (VAT) is already figured into the ticket price of most items. Restaurants usually include VAT in menu prices, but sometimes it is added to the bill, along with a service charge. The policy is usually written on the menu. There is no additional airport tax upon departure, and tax is included in all hotel rates.

- **Telephones**
To call London from the US, dial 011 (international code), 44 (Britain's country code), 71 or 81 (London's area code, without the '0' prefix), and the seven-digit local telephone number. For information on phones in London, see Chapter 2/Essential Services.

- **Time**
Located just 6 miles west of the Prime Meridian in Greenwich, London is at Greenwich Mean Time; 5 hours ahead of US Eastern Standard Time. British Summer Time, which moves the clock one hour ahead of standard time, is in effect from the last Sunday in April through the last Saturday in October.

- **Tipping**
Here are the rules of thumb: Restaurants, bars, nightclubs, taxis, hairdressers: 10%-15%; bartenders in pubs get nothing.

- **Video System**
NTSC

bRitish SYStEM Of MEASUREMEnts

LENGtH

1 inch (in.) = 2.54 cm
1 foot (ft.) = 12 in. = 30.48cm = .305m
1 yard = 3 ft. = .915m
1 mile (mi.) = 5,280 ft. = 1.609km

miles to kilometers
multiply the number of miles by 1.61
(100 miles x 1.61 = 161km).
kilometers to miles
multiply the number of kilometers by .62
(100km x .62 = 62 miles).

LIQUID VOLUME

1 fluid ounce (fl. oz.) = .03 liter
1 pint = 16 fl. oz. = .47 liter
1 quart = 2 pints = .94 liter
1 gallon (gal.) = 4 quarts = 3.79 liter = .83 Imperial gal.

US gallons to liters
multiply the number of gallons by 3.79 (10 gal. x 3.79 = 37.9 liters).
US gallons to Imperial gallons
multiply the number of US gallons by .83 (10 US gal. x .83 = 8.3 Imperial gal.).
liters to US gallons
multiply the number of liters by .26 (10 liters x .26 = 2.6 US gal.).
Imperial gallons to US gallons
multiply the number of Imperial gallons by 1.2 (10 Imperial gal. x 1.2 = 12 US gal.).

WEIGHT

1 ounce (oz.) = 28.35 grams
1 pound (lb.) = 16 oz. = 453.6 grams = .45 kilograms
1 ton = 2,000 lb. = 907 kilograms = .91 metric ton

pounds to kilograms
multiply the number of pounds by .45 (10 lb. x .45 = 4.5kg).
kilograms to pounds
multiply the number of kilograms by 2.2 (10kg x 2.2 = 22 lb.).

AREA

1 acre = .41 hectare
1 square mile (sq. mi.) = 640 acres = 2.59 hectares = 2.6km

acres to hectares
multiply the number of acres by .41 (10 acres x .41 = 4.1ha).
square miles to square kilometers
multiply the number of square miles by 2.6 (10 sq. mi. x 2.6 = 26km2)
hectares to acres
multiply the number of hectares by 2.47 (10ha x 2.47 = 24.7 acres).
square kilometers to square miles
multiply the number of square kilometers by .39 (100km2 x .39 = 39 sq. mi.).

TEMPERATURE

degrees Fahrenheit to degrees Celsius
subtract 32 from °F, multiply by 5, then divide by 9
(85°F – 32 x 5 ÷ 9 = 29.4°C).
degrees Celsius to degrees Fahrenheit
multiply °C by 9, divide by 5, and add 32
(20°C x 9 ÷ 5 + 32 = 68°F).

CLOTHING CONVERSION CHART

WOMEN'S SHOES
UK:	03	04	05	06	07	08	09
US:	05	06	07	08	09	10	11
Euro:	36	37	38	39	40	41	42

MEN'S SHOES
UK:	08	09	10	11	12
US:	09	10	11	12	13
Euro:	42	43	44	45	46

WOMEN'S CLOTHES
UK:	08	10	12	14	16
US:	06	08	10	12	14
Euro:	38	40	42	44	46

MEN'S CLOTHES
UK:	38	40	42	44	46
US:	38	40	42	44	46
Euro:	48	50/52	54	56	58/60

Serpentine Gallery